Seven Principles of Ministry
for the
Average, Radical Christian

Seven Principles of Ministry for the Average, Radical Christian

JAMES CUNNEEN

RESOURCE *Publications* • Eugene, Oregon

SEVEN PRINCIPLES OF MINISTRY FOR THE AVERAGE, RADICAL CHRISTIAN

Copyright © 2011 James Cunneen. All rights reserved. Except for brief quotations in critical publications or reviews, no part of this book may be reproduced in any manner without prior written permission from the publisher. Write: Permissions, Wipf and Stock Publishers, 199 W. 8th Ave., Suite 3, Eugene, OR 97401.

Unless otherwise noted, "Scripture quotations are taken from the New American Standard Bible ©, Copyright © 1960, 1962, 1963, 1968, 1971, 1972, 1973, 1975, 1977, 1995 by The Lockman Foundation. Used by permission" (www.lockman.org).

Some Scripture quotations noted by "NIV" are taken from The Holy Bible, New International Version©. Copyright © 1973, 1978, 1984 by International Bible Society. Used by permission of Zondervan Publishing House. All rights reserved.

The "NIV" and "New International Version" trademarks are registered in the United States Patent and Trademark Office by International Bible Society. Use of either trademark requires the permission of International Bible Society.

Resource Publications
An Imprint of Wipf and Stock Publishers
199 W. 8th Ave., Suite 3
Eugene, OR 97401

www.wipfandstock.com

ISBN 13: 978-1-61097-137-9

Manufactured in the U.S.A.

To my wife, Nancy

a woman of God

Contents

Introduction / ix

Section One

1 The Importance of Being Average / 3
2 The Need to Be Radical / 7
3 Principle # 1: Be What You Want Others to Be.
  Do What You Want Other to Do. / 13

Section Two

4 Principle # 2: Give Your Life to People,
  Not Just Your Knowledge. / 111
5 Principle # 3: Always Minister from the Clear Meaning
  of the Bible. / 140
6 Principle # 4: Never Stop Personally Doing Ministry . . . in Spite
  of the "Killer D's" of Distraction, Dissipation,
  Discouragement, Doubt. / 165
7 Principle # 5: Don't Hesitate to Lead, When Leadership is
  Needed. / 181
8 Principle # 6: Don't Use People to Build Your Ministry. Use Your
  Ministry to Build People. / 197
9 Principle # 7: Be Gracious, Yet Wise, in Your Relationship With
  Your Local Church as You Disciple. / 203
10 The Challenge—Will You Do It? / 212

Appendix / 215
Bibliography / 271

Introduction

I.

AVERAGE, RADICAL . . . ARE two words most people probably think of in a negative sense. The idea of being *average* usually implies "mediocrity" or "without distinction;" and *radical* seems to say unthinking fanaticism or extremism. They don't even seem to fit together in the same sentence; how can a person be average and radical at the same time?

But I want to use these terms in their positive sense.

average meaning . . . normal, mainstream-of-life person, of whom there are *many*

radical meaning . . . deeply committed to Christ

So the purpose of this writing is simple: to encourage the person who is a Christian, an average person, to be radically committed to his/her relationship with God, and radically committed to significant *personal* ministry.

This is for frustrated Christians, people who feel, "There *has* to be more to Christianity than this!" The normal Christian experience can be pretty bland. Some singing, listening to a sermon almost always geared to the spiritual lowest common denominator in the audience, non-applicable Sunday school lessons, a pot-luck dinner, the Christmas cantata, serving on a committee . . . it's familiar, comfortable, and even pleasant. But it's rarely exciting and rarely what the Bible seems to say we should be doing: telling the lost about salvation through Jesus Christ, and making disciples of all nations. For those who feel, "There has to be more to Christianity than this . . ."—there is.

For a person to do this kind of ministry will require, I believe, a radical commitment, for two reasons: first, I believe that God's opponents are vehemently opposed to normal, regular people being involved in significant personal ministry. God's enemy, I believe, would rather have relatively few Christians—i.e., clergy and "celebrities"—involved in ministry than millions of average people "striving according to God's power within them . . . to proclaim Him, and present every person complete and mature in Christ" (Colossians 1:28, 29) ; and secondly, it goes counter to our culture—*especially* our Christian culture. By that, I mean simply that most of the Christian environments I have experienced in the past ten to fifteen years have as their emphasis, the "community" of believers, rather than the worth and work of the individual. I would go so far as to say that in some instances the idea of individualism is seen as "lone-wolfism."

Certainly, a strong community spirit and working together of the different gifts and functions of the body of Christ, is a wonderful thing. But I believe that the primary relationship of the Christian faith is a person's individual relationship with God; that's why we call it a personal (person-al) relationship with God. Our relationship with other believers, community, is secondary. When a person has a good walk with God, not just a relationship with his local church, then real ministry is possible.

II.

Does God want Christians—normal, everyday-type people—to be active in ministry? I believe he does. Here are just a few of the well-known passages which call Christians to this work:

"Go, therefore and make disciples of all nations, baptizing them in the name of the Father, the Son, and the Holy Spirit, teaching them to observe all that I have commanded you . . ." (Matthew 28:19, 20).

". . . and you shall be My witnesses in Jerusalem, and in all Judea, and Samaria, and to the ends of the earth." (Acts 1:8 NIV).

Were these words spoken only to the actual listeners? Was it only the few Disciples (with a capital D) and immediate others for whom these instructions were given? There was at least one other person who took Christ's words personally to heart: the Apostle Paul.

". . . woe is me if I do not preach the Gospel, for I am under compulsion." (1 Corinthians 9:16).

"I solemnly charge you in the presence of God and of Christ Jesus, who is to judge the living and dead, and by His appearing and His kingdom: preach the word; be ready in season and out of season; reprove, rebuke, exhort, with great patience and instruction." (2 Timothy 4:1–2).

"... the things you have received from me, these entrust to faithful men who are able to teach others ..." (four generations of Christians here: Paul to Timothy, to faithful men, to others) (2 Timothy 2:2).

But there is a reality that persists today, the same reality Jesus addressed in the first century: scarcity of laborers in the harvest field of lost people (Matthew 9:36). He had observed the crowds of people in the towns and villages where he was teaching, healing, and proclaiming the gospel. Matthew records that he was moved to compassion for them because they were "... harassed and helpless, like sheep without a shepherd." Then the Lord summed up the situation like this: "The harvest is plentiful, but the workers are few. Ask the Lord of the harvest, therefore, to send out workers into His harvest."

Why are the workers for God so few?

As a young Christian, I heard a talk that deeply affected me. It was given, as I recall, by a man named Bob Byrd. This message was presented during a Christian conference at a Florida college where I was teaching. It was the ending of this message which most impressed me. The speaker referred to the very well known Matthew 28:19, 20 passage: "Go therefore and make disciples..."

He said, "Now, I don't pretend to be much of a theologian, but when Jesus said 'make disciples,' I think what he was saying is ... 'make disciples.'

"And I certainly can't claim to be an expert on the original languages of the Scriptures, but I believe that Jesus' phrase 'make disciples' probably translates into ... 'make disciples'!"

"Further, I am convinced that in saying, 'make disciples,' Jesus' intention was that people should ... 'make disciples'!"

On and on the speaker went. Then he stopped, looked straight at the audience, and quietly and simply said, "Are *you* making disciples?"

The answer was, for the most part, no.

In that audience were pastors and church workers, leaders of various campus ministries, college students and older adults, men and women ... all of whom were well familiar with the Matthew 28 "Great

Commission" passage. Yet few, if any, could honestly say that they were intentionally making disciples.

Why are the workers so few? Why do so few Christians make disciples today? Other than willful disobedience, what conditions exist today which seem to work against the average Christian having a significant personal ministry of soul-winning and discipling?

I believe part of the answer might lie in the Christian world's perception of what its part should be in proclaiming Christ and making disciples. And while there may be much discussion and disagreement about what Jesus really *did* with the first disciples (the twelve), there is no debate that he *had* them! He chose twelve to be with him. He chose twelve to whom he gave special attention. He chose twelve to teach, train, and send out into ministry. He chose twelve upon whom the reaching of the world with the gospel depended.

That I am a saved person today is a result of the fact that Jesus Christ chose twelve men to disciple. His imperative statement at the end of his ministry, in Matthew 28:19 "Go, and make disciples . . ." was meant to be literally understood, and it implied application for Christians down through the centuries and generations. Why then, does hardly anyone do it? Why is the making of disciples something we rarely see in out Christian communities today?

There is a *carry-over* from Judaism into Christianity that has, I feel, contributed to the fact that very few Christians do personal ministry. Part of the carry-over is that people think of the ordained clergy as Levitical priests; *they're* the ones who minister before the Lord. The laity, well, lays around and pays the salaries of the ministers. Another unhelpful carry-over from Judaism is the emphasis on the group with diminished focus on individual, personal relationship with God. These two things feed each other. A person with a weak personal relationship with God is not motivated to do the hard, and sometimes scary, work of evangelism and discipling. He or she is glad to blend into the group/congregation and let the pastors do the spiritual stuff. Ordained clergy may also be more comfortable with the group-nature of their congregations, as this fits into the traditional model of local church,

While I don't think that modern Christianity is characterized by submission to Jewish Law, I do think that modern Christianity tolerates, even embraces, holdovers from Judaism which hinder Christian ministry. Some of these holdovers are so common to Christian churches that

I believe most people don't even notice them or think about them. For example, "trivial" holdovers would include

Altars, or altar areas in churches . . . this is Judaic, not Christian.

Tithes and offerings . . . again, commanded and appropriate for Old Testament Jews, but superceded (tithes) and fulfilled (offerings) by Christ.

Emphasis on the building as "the house of God" . . . The Christian believer's body is now the "Temple," not any building made with human hands.

I refer to these as "trivial" because I don't think they are make or break issues for today's Christians. But there is one key element of Judaism that I believe does greatly hinder the involvement of many Christians in ministry: the emphasis on "ordained" clergy doing ministry—"ministry", that is, within the context of normal church activities, which rarely focuses on evangelism among the lost and bringing church members to maturity in the faith—and the "laity" not doing ministry.

III.

". . . new wine must be put into new wineskins. No one after drinking old wine wishes for new; for he says, 'The old is good enough.'"

—Luke 5:38, 39

Let me illustrate this with . . .

A Sad and Foolish Tale

Once upon a time . . . in the early 20th Century, when airplanes were in their infancy, a railroad king was captivated by the idea of flight. He wanted to be a part of this new means of transportation; and decided he'd build his own airplanes. So he called his chief manufacturing designer to discuss plans for building the new machines.

"The age of flight is here," he told his designer, "and it will change profoundly the way people travel. I want to shift over from building railroad equipment to building airplanes—the best airplanes in the world!"

"Bravo!" cried the designer. "At last a man with the vision and courage to commit to this exciting new technology. We'll begin the new design immediately."

"Good! Now, before you get going, there are a couple of things I want to make sure get included in the plan, things our loyal passengers have come to expect from our company." The railroad man stroked his chin thoughtfully. "First of all, the seats need to be much more comfortable. I've seen the seats on these planes, and they're made out of wicker. They're flimsy and poorly padded. Make them sturdy and well padded."

"But, sir," the designer protested, "the seats *have* to be very light. In fact, the whole structure of the airplane is light!"

"Not so. That's another thing I want changed. Let's make the whole affair solid and heavy. That'll give a smooth, comfortable ride."

"But . . . but, sir . . . If it's heavy, it'll never fly! The engines won't be able to get it off the ground," said the designer, with growing dismay.

"Nonsense," replied the railroad king. "Why, we build some of the most powerful locomotive engines in the world. Put a couple of those monsters in and we'll have plenty of power."

"Oh, sir! You're missing the point here of what an airplane is . . . How can something that heavy possibly fly!"

"Then we'll put rails under it. If we add wing-looking things on the sides of every car, it'll seem just like flying. The steam escaping from the drive wheels will look like clouds." Here the railroad king assumed a stern look. "And, to tell the truth, while flying is exciting, it is sort of frightening. I think our passengers would rather be comfortable, safe, and just *think* they're flying."

The designer sighed. "Then my job is easy. What you describe is what we already have."

The railroad king smiled. "Why, yes, it is, isn't it. How fortunate!" He patted the designer's shoulder. "We'll *call* it the Flyer."

A foolish story indeed. Ridiculous. The sad aspect of it is that it illustrates what the Scripture points out: when people are *comfortable with something old* (i.e., religion versus a relationship with God) it's difficult for them to make the transition to the new. For example, in the early days of aviation, people may be excited and intrigued by the concept of flight, but when it comes right down to it, they'll personally choose the old, safe, comfortable, and familiar. Similarly, Christians may speak enthusiastically about our freedom from the Judaic religion, but be more comfortable with the familiar rules and trappings of Old Testament religion.

There's an old joke about the town that was so resistant to change that when it finally admitted it needed a new jail, it still insisted upon these conditions:

- the new jail must be built with the materials from the old jail
- the new jail must be built on the same location of the old jail
- the old jail must be used until the new jail is built . . .

Modern day American Christianity can be like that manufacturer of railroad machinery, or the town that liked its old jail. It retains a lot of religious structure which is not only unnecessary but harmful, as it prevents biblical Christianity from operating as it should, with the power it should have: the power of the individual, average Christian doing ministry with commitment. It is a commitment to obedience to God, not commitment to the program of a local church. Commitment to Christ is a personal decision; it's simple and durable. Commitment to religious activities is usually vague and short-lived because group projects tend to emphasize the activity involved rather than the long-term goal. And because love of novelty is so normal in American Christendom today, few programs last very long before they're replaced with some other program.

What's the new, and what's the old?

The new is the "new covenant." The Messiah has come, and because of that, God allows a person to have an intimate relationship with him, as expressed in this Scripture:

"Since therefore, brethren, we have confidence to enter the holy place by the blood of Jesus . . . let us draw near with a sincere heart, in full assurance of faith . . ." (Hebrews 10:19–22).

The new is also a person having a significant Biblical ministry in the lives of others. Each man, each woman, who has drawn near to God can invest her or his life in precious, not worthless, things.

". . . a foundation . . . which is Jesus Christ. Now if any man builds upon the foundation with gold, silver, precious stones, wood, hay, straw, each man's work will become evident." (1 Corinthians 3:11–13).

The old is the "old covenant" of the Levitical priests, the one tribe who served before the Lord. The Levites "ministered in the house of God." The other 11 tribes simply went on with life, working and having families. The Levites performed the ceremonies in the house of God, interceding for the people and serving as a shadow and model of the perfect high priest and sacrifice to come. What the Levitical priests did was important, but the participation of the eleven non-Levitical tribes was not required or even allowed. This was right and proper for the old covenant. It could have been no other way.

The new is the ministry and maturity of individual believers. The old is an unhelpful extension of the Levitical priesthood into modern day Christianity.

IV.

Why is this the case? In the first two chapters of this book, I'd like to present two reasons why I believe biblical discipleship, done by normal believers, is so rarely seen in the American Christian community.

And I don't wish to focus on negatives. Navigator's staff trainer, Larry Whitehouse, once told a group of young ministers, "Any fathead can be on a wreaking crew. It doesn't take much to tear something down. Satan is the accuser of the brethren, and he doesn't need any help from you in criticizing other Christians. Be a builder, not a wreaker."

Good words. Good advice.

V.

Here are the goals of this book:

First, it is written to encourage those Christians who are thinking, "There *must* be more to the Christian life than this!" There is, and it's the obedience and fulfillment of doing personal Biblical ministry. I hope this writing will provide both encouragement and tools to serious Christians to help enable them to be effective Great Commission ministers.

Second, we'll discuss why two terms which normally have negative connotations: i.e., *average* and *radical*, are so important to the ministry of the "priesthood of the believer."

The third goal is to present some principles of ministry which I believe are clear guidelines for those who are committed to God to do personal ministry. These principles are as follows:

Be what you want others to be; do what you want others to do. "The things you have learned and heard and seen in me (says Paul), practice these things." (Philippians 4:9).

Give your life to people, not just your knowledge. "Having

thus a fond affection for you, we were well-pleased to impart to you not only the gospel of God but also our own lives . . ." (1 Thessalonians 2:8).

Base your ministry on a clear understanding of Scripture.

". . . learn not to exceed what is written . . ." (1 Corinthians 4:6) or

". . . distort the Scripture . . ."(2 Peter 3:16).

Never personally stop doing basic ministry. Do not allow yourself to be derailed by promotion, or the "killer D's" of Distraction, Dissipation, Discouragement, or Doubt. "And after Jesus had finished instructing His twelve disciples, He went on from there to teach and preach in the towns of Galilee." (Matthew 11:1).

Do not hesitate to lead . . . when leadership is needed (and it almost always is). "Be shepherds of God's flock that is under your care, serving as overseers—not because you must, but because you are willing, as God wants you to be . . ."(1 Peter 5:2).

Use your ministry to build people; never use people to build your ministry. This passage talks about good and bad shepherds. There are only do three things you can do with sheep: eat them, fleece them, or shepherd them. Be a shepherd. (Ezekiel 34).

Be gracious, yet wise, in your relationship with your local church. Your ministry goals may differ. "Be devoted to one another in brotherly love; give preference to one another in honor . . . (Romans 12:10) and ". . . those (in the Jerusalem church) who were reputed to be pillars, gave us the right hand of fellowship that we might go to the Gentiles, and they to the circumcised." (Galatians 2:6–10).

The fourth aim is provide some practical tools of ministry, and instructions on how to use them, so you can immediately begin to minister.

And last, is a call to action . . . to plant the seeds of a movement of persons doing life-to-life, disciple-making ministry.

Section One

1

The Importance of Being Average.

Let's face it . . . the idea of being an average person doesn't seem very exciting. We're not likely to ever see a bumper sticker on the back of a mini-van that says, "My child is an average student at Acme Middle School!"

So why is it good to be average? Here's the dictionary definition:

Average . . . "the usual, most often encountered thing, or person in considerable numbers." For our consideration, it's a person living a normal, mainstream life. What's the best thing about "average-ness"?—the sheer *numbers* of it! The very meaning of the word implies great numbers. As Paul said in I Corinthians 1:26, ". . . there are not many wise, not many mighty, not many noble . . ." but there *are* many average. And it is the greatness of numbers that represents the potential greatness of ministry power.

Simply put, a *lot* of average people doing something is better than a few superstars doing something, even if the superstars are "more gifted." Just think of the increase for the Kingdom of God if the average Christian, a real, "I've-personally-made-a-decision-to-ask-Jesus-to-forgive-my-sins" Christian, were committed to telling the non-Christians in her or his life sphere about Jesus, (with gentleness and respect: 1 Peter 3:15), leading some to Christ, and helping young believers on to maturity. Then, because most good ministry is more "caught than taught," these now-mature disciples can help others. That's real multiplication of believers, not just addition. It could transform the world. It would certainly transform the lives of the people doing it.

I also believe that average people are not as likely to be distracted from *essential* ministry as those who are well-known for talent, ability, or position. The great singer, dynamic preacher, gifted "author and speaker," do indeed contribute to the Christian community, but how much of what they do is *imitatable*?

Giftedness comes from God and is not reproducible into the lives of others. People's gifts and talents are given by the Holy Spirit ". . . distributing to each one individually just as He wills." (1 Corinthians 12:11) Yes, we might try to imitate other people's giftedness, but we really can't. Yet over and over again, the Apostle Paul exhorted Christians to imitate him, not his giftedness, but his godly disciplines, his walk with God, and his ministry.

In one ministry I remember a young man who started getting individual discipleship help from an older Christian. I met the older Christian for lunch, and he told me sadly that while the young man was teachable and faithful, he was not available.

Why? Because the young Christian had a wonderful talent for singing, and was constantly performing for many church services, conferences, and youth meetings. Was the young Christian serving and ministering with his "gift"? Yes, probably, but at the cost of his own discipleship and potential ministry in the years to come.

So why don't average Christians do ministry? Why aren't most Christians persevering in evangelism and disciple-making? There are perhaps many reasons, but let's consider these two:

- no models to follow . . . either among the laity or the clergy.

How many people, for example, in a normal local church congregation would view their pastor's job as a ministry model they could follow, indeed, would even think of doing so. More likely, they would view their pastor as a somewhat unusual person, ordained and called of God, to do things the average person would never dream of doing: preaching sermons, delivering the eloquent pastoral prayer, raising funds for the building program, e.g., In short, the pastor is probably viewed as a special person, a Levite, who serves before the Lord in the temple of the local church.

And let's be realistic: most pastors work amazingly hard, but except in the case of the very smallest churches, pastors rarely have time even for pastoring (the work "pastor' means shepherd). In churches of average size (200–400 attending services), the term *senior pastor* has come to mean a kind of small-business CEO responsible for budget, finance-raising, personnel matters, staffing, physical plant, sermon preparation and delivery, administration of the sacraments, and the "hatch, match, and dispatch" duties (christenings, marriages, funerals), hospital visitation, attending myriad social functions (to show "pastoral support"), marriage counseling, pre-marriage counseling, divorce-prevention counseling, and on and on.

Pastors themselves can barely do all that is required of them by their denominational supervisors, or church boards, much less the ministry of evangelism and disciple-making. So when the lay person looks at most pastors, or Christian leaders, in regards to evangelism or discipleship, there's often not much of a model. And it's not just the time factor; it's the overwhelming factor that often local church success is measured by size and numbers, not whether evangelism or discipling is happening. I would deduce that the vast majority of church growth today is by transfer—people shifting from one church to another—rather than being won to Christ by someone in the church.

And since the pastors and church staff—those the lay people look up to as spiritually mature—are not often doing this ministry, it is not logical that the lay people would feel any great need to do it, nor for the pastors to make any real effort to train anyone to do it. There is simply no compelling motive to do so, aside from the biblical injunction, and that, apparently, seems easily dismissed.

- the de-motivating factor of the carryover of Judaic religion into the modern day Christian church.

The Apostle Paul got pretty steamed at the Christians in one early church. In his letter to the church at Galatia, Paul said this,

> "You foolish Galatians, who has bewitched you, before whose eyes Jesus Christ was publicly portrayed as crucified? This is the only thing I want to find out from you: did you receive the Spirit by the works of the Law, or by hearing with faith? Are you so foolish? Having begun by the Spirit, are you now being perfected by the flesh?" (Galatians 3:1–3) "But now that you have come to know God, or rather to be known by God, how is it you turn back again to the weak and worthless elemental things, to which you desire to become enslaved all over again? You observe days and months and seasons and years. I fear for you, that perhaps I have labored over you in vain." (Galatians 4:9)

What's going on here? Very simply, these Christians in Galatia were turning back again to aspects of Judaism. It appears they were trying to combine their faith in Jesus Christ with the rules and rituals of Jewish Law. Let's be very clear about this. Christianity is not an *addition* to Judaism; it is the *fulfillment* of Judaism. Christianity is not an alternative to Judaism; it does away with Judaism. Hebrews 8:13 puts it this way:

"By calling this covenant (reconciliation through Jesus Christ, i.e., Christianity) 'new, ' He has made the first one (the Law and Judaism) obsolete, and what is obsolete and aging will soon disappear."

Did you get that? The old covenant is obsolete. It has fulfilled its role in providing the seedbed and ushering into human history the Savior of the world. Its rituals, its sacrificial system, its priesthood . . . all fulfilled, all now obsolete. And yet the believers in Galatia were turning back to it. This is why Paul rebuked them so severely. Galatians 5:1 says this,

"It is for freedom that Christ set us free. Stand firm then, and do not let yourselves be burdened again by a yoke of slavery."

For some reason, these Galatian Christians were going back to observing "months and seasons and years," integral elements of Judaism. Was the freedom Christ brought uncomfortable for them?

Was there a perverse attraction to again submitting to the Jewish rules and regulations, the very "yoke of slavery" from which Christ had set them free? Apparently so. And this is the great challenge for believers in churches today, to break free from the residual traditions of "religion" with its comfortable, but ineffective, practices, and enter into the "second reformation," putting not just the Bible but the ministry back into the hands of the people. This can often mean going against traditional practices in your own local church that have deep roots. And again, some Judaic traditions are far less troublesome for ministry than others. If the pastor of your church wants to focus on Malachi for the annual finance appeal, rather than the New Testament teaching on giving, it's not a big deal. But breaking free from the idea that lay people are not ministers *is* a big deal. That's a battle worth fighting.

2

The Need to Be Radical

Moderation in commitment is no virtue . . .

RADICAL . . . A PERSON dealing with central, essential principles or issues . . . one of the meanings of the word is "going to the root," that is, a person who goes to the root of their Christian faith, not the trivia of it. This is a person who is seriously committed to Christ and to ministry. In plain English, it is a person who is willing to labor in ministry out of love for and obedience to God . . . not for praise or recognition, and not needing the perks and pats of "support groups." It is a tough person, with inner motivation. It is not a spiritually fragile person, or a person who responds to the external motivations of prodding or rewards for doing what God commands them to do anyway.

"So you too, when you do all the things which are commanded you, say . . . we have only done what we ought to do . . ." (Luke 17:10)

I once attended what I thought was going to be a Christian seminar, but which turned out to be a kind of new-age "Let's just all be friends, because we're all going to heaven" get-together.

I should have known better; the title of the seminar was, *Where Then is the Judgment?* Supposedly based on John 3:17 "For God did not send the Son into the world to judge the world, but that the world should be saved through Him . . ." the conclusion of the teacher being, of course, that since everyone was automatically saved, no one should be concerned with "judging" people, i.e., discerning their spiritual condition, or preaching at them. I remember thinking that if anyone cared to read just one more verse of that passage in John, they'd have the answer to the seminar's question: "He who believes in Him is not judged; he who does not believe has been judged already." No Bibles, however, were in evidence at that seminar.

I quickly departed the seminar, but one distinct memory of it remains. The memory is of the speaker at one point ridiculing the old hymn, *Onward, Christian Soldiers*. The whole idea of warfare and soldiers fighting in war was both repugnant and laughable to this man. The reasoning was this: if there is no hell and no one is lost, if there is no judgment, no punishment for sins, no wrath of God, then the idea of fighting to save people was seen as barbaric. Surely the "sweet Lord" did not endorse fighting!

But does He? Winston Churchhill, supposedly, when told he was a genius, replied, "If so, it's the genius of recognizing the obvious."

I will state the obvious. There *is* a war going on. A great conflict is being waged, and hardly anyone seems to know it, non-believer and Christian alike. The Apostle Paul says this in 2 Corinthians 10:3, 4

". . . though we walk in the flesh, we do not war according to the flesh, for the weapons of our warfare are not of the flesh, but divinely powerful for the destruction of fortresses."

War? Warfare? We may have *heard* about this war, the Christian war. It's the war for the souls of people, and it's going on continually, every day. Why then do so few Christians enlist to fight? Perhaps one reason is that, as in Jeremiah's day, there is another voice heard in the Christian world, one of denial.

"And from the prophet even to the priest everyone deals falsely. And they have healed the brokenness of My people superficially, saying 'Peace, peace,' but there is no peace." (Jeremiah 6:13, 14)

This voice is not a call to battle, but a call to false comfort and deadening tranquility. We *are* asked to fight for the souls of people, as reconcilers, to end people's enmity with God. Paul said earlier,

"All this is from God, who reconciled us to Himself through Christ and gave us the ministry of reconciliation . . . he has committed to us the message of reconciliation. We are therefore Christ's ambassadors, as though God were making His appeal through us." (2 Corinthians 5: 18–20)

There is a real war going on and it's serious. War isn't pleasant; it's life-or-death frightening, exciting, ennobling, difficult, terrible, and its consequences are profound. Victory is both wonderful and joyful. The enlistment period for committed Christians is a lifetime. Above all, it is *serious* because people's eternities are involved.

And, no, it's not (primarily) the reconciliation among people, i.e., "Let's all be friends," but a reconciliation of people to God, resulting in eternal life, a salvation from eternal hell. We as Christians must recognize the nature of this warfare and do all that we can to present Christ's entreaty to the lost.

I once desperately said to a person I cared about, who seemed hardened to the gospel, "Please! When you're dying—and you know you're dying—cry out to Jesus and ask him to forgive you, to save you, even in the final moment!" This person may have thought I was a crazy man, but at least this person knew that I believed there was a real heaven and hell.

Have you ever felt desperate and anxious that someone you loved was turning away from Christ and salvation? That is a true feeling. It represents reality. The degenerate state of the world, the lost-ness of people, and the weak, pathetic response of the church (at least in the US), are real.

We have to be radical. We have to be committed to this. It's the heart of the reason, I believe, of why we're still on the earth. We can fellowship with Christ and each other better in heaven (Philippians 1: 23 and 1 Corinthians 13:12). We can praise and worship God and enjoy him more in heaven. We can do everything in heaven better, without the distractions of the sinful world, except win the souls of men and women and equip them to do the same. Our presence on earth, as the body of Christ, is to do what his body did—have a redemptive purpose for all we can win (1 Corinthians 9). It is not to take up space, breathe air, and enjoy the pleasures of the American middle-class lifestyle. Jesus even gave us His job description:

"As Thou didst send Me into the world, I also have sent them into the world . . . I ask this not only for them, but also for those who will believe in Me because of their words." (John 17:18, 20)

And yet I've heard even evangelical believers, both older and younger, express disdain for Paul's stated goal in 1 Corinthians 9: 19-22, of ". . . I have become all things to all men so that by all possible means I might save some."

"It's manipulative!" they say. "It's not genuine relationship. A ministry like that just turns people into projects. No good relationship can be built on an agenda like that!"

But Paul was right, and the modern views of relationships expressed above are wrong . . . at least when it concerns being saved or lost. Paul knew what was at stake and he said he'd do anything and "be" anything if it meant some got saved. The "genuineness' of the relationships was, in view of eternity, irrelevant to Paul. At the end of his life, Paul summarizes his ministry not as participating in warm fellowship, but this way: "I have fought the good fight . . . I have kept the faith." (2 Timothy 4: 7) It *is* a fight. It is war, and many soldiers are desired by the commander.

But as one of my friends, Rich Bates, put it, "Almost everyone *can* do it, but almost no one *does*."

Why? I see two reasons: (1) American Christendom has, I believe, increasingly moved away from the Word, and the convictions that develop in people as they know and obey the Word. Churches today ditch Sunday school classes and Bible studies in favor of multiple "worship" services, which are increasingly entertainment. "Seeker-friendly" sometimes means "Bible-scarcity," for churches may worry that the Word will offend potential members. A conviction means a belief strong enough to compel us to *do* something. The early followers of Christ said, "We cannot stop speaking of what we have seen and heard!" (Acts 4:20) I like that . . . they *can't not* act upon their conviction!

As Paul said, ". . . for I am compelled to preach. Woe is me if I do not preach the gospel!" (I Corinthians 9:16) Who compelled Paul? The early church leaders in Jerusalem? Paul said of them, "Those who were of reputation contributed nothing to me." (Galatians 2:6) I believe it was obedience to what Paul knew God wanted him to do. James puts it this way in James 1:22:

"But prove yourselves doers of the Word, not merely hearers who delude themselves."

A radical commitment to Christ and his commandments requires courage, and courage comes from convictions, strong convictions, and these come only from the powerful truth of Scripture. Where Scripture is missing or hard to find, convictions are also missing, and the courage to *do* anything for the Lord is weakened.

(2) I think the second, less indicting, reason people are not radically committed to Christ and the "great commission" is they simply

don't know *how* to do ministry. Seminars and workshops on evangelism and discipleship can be helpful up to a point, but what's really helpful is to do it with someone who already knows how. And there just aren't many of those folks. I think there are many Christians who would take that scary step of faith if only there was someone to come alongside and guide them. *You* could be that person who begins a whole generation of obedient Christians. Someone has to start, and the first step is simply to be willing to be committed. Use the tools and ideas in this book to begin. No, using a book is not as good, *at all*, as having a real live human with you to show the way. But if it gets you going, praise God! Then you can be the battle-seasoned warrior who helps the next generation of fighters.

It's exciting to begin these steps of obedience in ministry, and start to build relationships in which people can grow. And it's even more exciting when the one you're helping catches fire as she or he begins to minister to someone else.

A pastor friend of mine, Tom Warren, was meeting with a young man who had asked to be discipled. Or rather, Tom was *trying* to meet with him, since this young man had a hard time showing up. He was usually late when he did show up, and he rarely did his assigned Bible reading. My friend, Tom, was puzzling over how to help motivate this young man when an amazing thing happened. All of a sudden, the young man ignited. He actually came early to meet with my friend; he did his assignments; he was enthusiastic.

What happened to bring about this change? The answer: the young man's friend had asked him what the discipleship stuff was all about, and could the young man do it with him! The young man began to get with his friend. He then saw how good, how helpful the Christian disciplines were both for his friend and himself. By helping another, he had gotten out of himself and began to focus on eternal things.

If we give ourselves to others, we get over ourselves. It's not instantaneous, but it does happen, and when it does happen, there's joy and a sense of freedom that the self-absorbed never experience.

A challenging and encouraging Scripture that's relevant is this:

"Whoever has My commands and obeys them, he is the one who loves Me. He who loves Me will be loved by My Father, and I too will love him and show Myself to him." (John 14:21)

It's challenging because it demands obedience to commands. It's encouraging because the reward for obedience is so wonderful: Jesus says he will show himself to those who obey his commands. No, not visibly, but the *reality* of the person of Christ is on the other side of every act of obedience. It's what makes the Christian life exciting. Obedience to Christ's commands defines—in this context at least—love for the Lord. His promise in response to our obedience is that he "will reveal Myself to him . . . manifest Myself to him . . . show Myself to him."

What if we consider the reverse of that statement: Whoever has My commands and does *not* obey them, he is the one who does *not* love Me . . . I will *not* show Myself to him. Could this be the reason most people are bored with the Lord and their Christian lives? He simply is not real to them. If someone does not obey the Lord's commands, or selectively obeys, how is Christ real to that person? Yes, our relationship with Christ is a love relationship ("For Christ's love compels us . . ." 2 Corinthians 5: 14); his love is demonstrated by his sacrifice for our sins (Romans 5:8); but our love for him is demonstrated primarily by our obedience to his will.

"You are My friends if you do what I command." (John 15:14)

Again, in Matthew 7:24-26

"Therefore, whoever hears these words of Mine, and puts them into practice is like a wise man who built his house on the rock . . . but everyone who hears these words of Mine, and does not put them into practice is like a foolish man who build his house on sand."

What will it take to convince Christians to serve the Lord, not themselves? The first step is to strengthen our relationship with God; this is a matter of both heart and mind (or, logic, if you will). To walk with the Lord and serve him well must start in our hearts. Yet it's not just vague feelings or theoretical concepts. There are steps we can take to have a solid, personal relationship with God, and Biblical principles to guide us in ministry.

3

Principle # 1: Be What You Want Others to Be. Do What You Want Others to Do.

THIS SOUNDS SO OBVIOUS. But I think it is one of the most ignored principles of the Christian world. Hypocrisy was not just a problem in first century Judaism, when Jesus warned His followers,

"The scribes and the Pharisees have seated themselves in the chair of Moses; therefore all that they tell you, do and observe, but do not do according to their deeds; for they say things and do not do them." (Matthew 23:3)

Be what you want others to be . . .

- For the integrity of it; to say something is good, but not to personally live it, is hypocrisy. ". . . lest, after I have preached to others, I myself should be disqualified." (1 Corinthians 9:27)

The Apostle Paul could honestly say to young believers, "I exhort you therefore, be imitators of me." (1 Corinthians 4:16) Nine times Paul made statements similar to this, reflecting his personal obedience to Christ . . . "Be imitators of me, just as I am also of Christ." (1 Corinthians. 11:1), and his assurance to younger Christians that imitating him would benefit them. "The things you have received and heard and seen in me, practice these things, and the God of peace shall be with you." (Philippians 4:9).

Wouldn't it be wonderful if Christian leaders held to this model of holiness and godly practices? That they would say to their flock, "Be like me!" Then their admonition to others to be holy would have power.

- For the powerful leverage your life has in other peoples' lives. A "true life model," or as the engineers say "a proof-of-concept" model, is a strong motivation we can provide for others to take discipleship seriously. Conversely, if we preach biblical values and disciplines, and then not do them, it becomes a strong reason/excuse for others to dismiss an obedient walk with God.

Lives do reproduce. We used to have a saying in college ministry: *Children are hereditary; if your parents didn't have children, it's unlikely you will either.* The fact is, lives do reproduce. Whatever you *are*, is the most likely thing your spiritual children will be. We emulate our leaders.

- For the actual ministry it accomplishes. This seems so obvious, yet sometimes we overlook the sheer value of doing something, not just as a model or to validate a concept, but for the actual benefit of the act itself.

Let me explain. Not long ago, I was meeting with some collegiate ministry staff, and one of them asked me, "Why do you still do the door-to-door evangelism at student housing? I know you're allowed to, but what's the benefit?" I knew what he was saying. He was really asking, "Since you seldom see decisions for Christ, whom you could follow up . . . and not many people come to your Bible studies from that kind of evangelism, what's the value of it?" From a *ministry strategy* point of view, I appreciated his question, but it struck me that the very thing that seemed so unimpressive—just sharing the gospel with college students without any expectations of it "contributing" to our ministry—was the very thing that the ministry was all about, just on a small, unimpressive scale. It was good to go out and share the gospel, even if it didn't add numbers to our ministry team, because it was good for those students to hear the good news. From a pure seed-planting viewpoint, it was the best activity we could have been doing.

My point is simply that it can be easy to think "big picture" and forget the value of the actual doing of ministry itself, even on a small, seemingly "inefficient" scale.

Enough concepts; let's look at practical ways to be the persons of God we want to see others become. Paul's comment in the second letter to Timothy was this:

"You therefore, my son, be strong in the grace that is in Christ Jesus. And the things which you have heard from me in the presence of many witnesses, these entrust to faithful men, who will be able to teach others also." (2 Timothy 2:1, 2).

It's good to realize that along with the brilliant *concept* of this passage (the profound truth that lives can reproduce spiritually), there is a simple reality that there are "things" that we can pass along, or entrust, to others to help them walk with God and disciple others. So now we'll focus on some simple "things" to help us have a close relationship with God and know how to help others.

The "7 & 3"

First of all, you must know that there is nothing new in what I'm going to share next. The following material has to do with the disciplines of the Christian life, and with having Christ-like character. These aspects of our walk with God have been presented often, perhaps in slightly different forms, for hundreds of years.

The catch-phrase "7 & 3" simply refer to *seven disciplines* of the Christian life, that is, things that we can *do* to promote a good relationship with God . . . and *three character areas*, this is, what we can *be* in character to be pleasing to God.

The 7 are as follows:

1. Assurance of our salvation
2. Daily time with God
3. Fellowship
4. Prayer
5. Bible study
6. Scripture memory
7. Witnessing, or sharing our faith with non-believers

The 3 are as follows:

8. Purity of life
9. Having God's perspective on money and stuff
10. Humility

These three character areas are the *opposite* of the three areas of sinful behavior specified in 1 John 2:15, 16 ". . . lust of the flesh, lust of the eyes, and the boastful pride of life . . ."

Let's start. Here are seven practices of life that can help us have a solid relationship with God. They're good for us, and can be a helpful way for you to disciple someone else. The "teacher's guide" for all these discipleship topics are found in an appendix in the back of this book.

1. Assurance of salvation . . .

Can a person know *for sure* that she, or he, is a Christian? I believe the answer is "yes." If fact, I'd say that if a person is *unsure*, it certainly affects his relationship with God in a negative way. What if a woman wasn't sure if she were married? Assuming she was a moral person, it would sure affect her relationship with the man! And when we talk about being a Christian, we're really talking about whether a person has a *relationship* with God.

The statement of John 17:3 expresses a great truth: "This is eternal life, that they may know Thee, the only true God, and Jesus Christ whom Thou hast sent." (NASB) So our question now is, "How do you know for sure that you're a Christian?" It's not "Can I ever lose my salvation?" That's a different question altogether. What we want to be sure of is whether I have the right and privilege to *draw near* into the presence of God, and grow in my relationship with him.

There are at least three good statements from Scripture that can give us that assurance. I'll use an illustration I call the *"Tripod"* . . . no, not iPod! Tripod. A tripod is a very stable device that stands on three legs (the word itself means "3 feet"). The idea is that if we have three distinct ways from the Bible that assure us of our relationship with God, then the devil, or some wacko on TV, can't suggest to us that "you *can't* really be a Christian; no Christian could think or do what you just thought or did!" God's enemy loves to plant doubts in our minds about many truths, and this is one of them. If we have only one way we believe that we're Christians, for example, "I just know it in my heart!"—a kind of a monopod of assurance—then the enemy can suggest, "But that's only an emotion." Let's go for the tripod, and look at three good ways to know we're saved.

Picture a tripod in your mind. Here are the three legs:

Leg # 1 . . . *God says it!*

"And this is the testimony: God has given us eternal life, and this life is in his Son. He who has the Son has life; he who does not have the Son of God does not have life. I write these things to you who believe in the name of the Son of God so that you may know that you have eternal life." (1 John 5: 11–13)

I love the perfect logic in that statement. First point: God *has* given eternal life. Somebody's got it! Who's got it? Answer: the person who has the Son has the life. And just to make it very clear, it's stressed that the person who doesn't have the Son of God does not have eternal life. In logic, this is called the law of "mutual exclusion," that is, if one thing is true, it's opposite can't be true.

I have to admit with some guilt that I was amused by an episode of the TV show *The Simpsons*, in which Bart, in a stupor from watching too much TV, thinks it's Saturday. Sister Lisa tells Bart that it's really Wednesday and that he has to go to school. Homer, ineptly trying to be a peacemaking father, says, "Aw, kids, you're both right . . ."

Well, it can't be Wednesday and Saturday. It might be one or the other, or neither . . . but it can't be both.

When I do this "Tripod" with someone, I use the ribbon in my Bible to illustrate the truth of . . . *the life is in the Son.* The ribbon is in the Bible; if you have the Bible, you have the ribbon. The eternal life is in the Son; if you have the Son, you have the life.

Verse 13 of that passage says, ". . . that you may *know* that you have eternal life"

Not "wonder," or "hope" that you have eternal life, but *know* that you have eternal life. God, in his Word, tells us in black and white that if we have Christ, we have eternal life.

Leg # 2 . . . *Inner conviction!*

"The Spirit Himself testifies with our spirit that we are God's children." (Romans 8:16)

Let's just take the plain-sense meaning of this statement, without worrying about any profound theology. The Holy Spirit ("Spirit" with a capital "S") testifies (proclaims something to be true) with our spirit (a human's heart, mind, inner being . . . lower case "s") that we are indeed children of God.

Our understanding of this testimony, or statement of truth, is more than an emotional feeling. It's a spiritual appreciation, conviction, or recognition of the truth that God has accepted us as His children. (see John 1:12 ". . . as many as received Him (Christ), He gave power to become children of God.") Emotions go up and down every day, often based on the day's circumstances. The testimony of the Holy Spirit that we are in a Parent/child relationship with God is sure and unchanging.

Leg # 3 . . . *Outer Evidence!*

"But the fruit of the Spirit is love, joy, peace, patience, kindness, goodness, faithfulness, gentleness and self-control . . ." (Galatians 5:22, 23)

These are life qualities that become more and more evident as a person develops a close walk with God. The world has fake qualities that are counterfeits for these: for example, lust vs. love, fun vs. joy . . . but only God can build the real things into a life. The great thing here is that we can begin to notice these life qualities very soon after we begin our relationship with God. To be sure, we will continue to grow in these areas for our entire lives; there's no immediate perfection. But we can be encouraged by seeing the Holy Spirit giving us real results in our lives right away.

In the qualities mentioned above, love, joy, peace, patience, etc., what do you most want to see evident in *your* life? Ask God to help you grow in these areas as you work on your relationship with Him.

God says it!
Inner conviction!
Outer evidence!

2. Daily times with God . . .

Who was your *best friend* in high school? Can you remember? How did it come about that you became friends? For me, it was a guy named Jon. Jon was an unlikely person to become my best friend because he was so different from me; background, view of life, etc. were *very* different from mine.

But we both liked soccer and snow skiing, and were in a lot of the same classes, so it turned out that we spent a lot of time together. I remember one discussion we had about soccer formations that went on for two hours! Neither one of us was shy about sharing opinions, but we did listen to the other's ideas. As a result, we really did have a solid friendship.

While I doubt the reader is fascinated by my nostalgia about high school, the point of all this is that there are some real similarities in how we build relationships with people, and how we build our relationship with God. After all, He is Person, and I am a person . . . hence the phrase, a *person*al relationship.

One thing that's not similar is that I never really *planned* to make Jon a good friend; it just happened in a natural way. But I do deliberately plan to work on building a good relationship with God. The key point is this: I got to know my friend, Jon, because I saw him pretty much every day, either in classes or playing sports. And we talked a lot. If we'd only seen each other once a month or once a week, the friendship would simply not have happened. We can get to know God well in this same way, spend time with him daily, or as often as we can, and have a two-way conversation.

- We talk to the Lord in prayer
- We listen to the Lord, primarily, through his Word.

So what I'm urging us to do is read the Bible and pray every day. I don't mean in-depth intensive Bible study, or intercessory prayer for world missions. I mean relationship-building prayer, and reading the Bible in order to get to know God, to hear what he says to my heart as well as my mind.

"For the word of God is living and active . . . able to judge the thoughts and intentions of the heart." (Hebrews 4:12).

If all we ever do is pray, we miss out on hearing God's voice speak to us in Scripture. If all we ever do is read the Bible, we miss out on the relationship that comes from opening our hearts to God.

Just as it's true that parents know more about the needs of their baby than the baby itself, they are delighted when the little one starts talking, sharing his or her heart and mind with the parents . . . so too our Father in heaven is glad when we talk with him. It's part of our bonding, if you will, with God.

Have you ever had a friendship, or acquaintance, in which one talks most of the time and the other just listens? It's more like un-paid counseling than a friendship. If you're the listener, you may know a lot about the talker, but she or he may know little about you. One-sided relationships are not very satisfying.

A couple of *good examples* of what I'm talking about are David's thoughts in Psalm 5:3, and the Lord's example in Mark 1:35.

"In the morning, O Lord, you hear my voice; in the morning I lay my requests before you and wait in expectation." (Psalm 5:3 NIV)

David prays with expectation. He knows that God hears him and will respond. Do I wait in expectation when I pray?

"Very early in the morning, while it was still dark, Jesus got up, left the house and went off to a solitary place, where he prayed." (Mark 1:35 NIV)

Other passages in the Bible state that Jesus often did this sort of thing. Luke 5:15, 16 (NIV) says, . . . "crowds of people came to hear Him and to be healed of their sicknesses. But Jesus often withdrew to lonely places and prayed." Isn't it interesting that Jesus went off by himself to pray in the midst of a hectic ministry situation? Back in the Mark 1 passage, it goes on to say in verses 36 and 37, "Simon and his companions went to look for him, and when they found him, they exclaimed: 'Everyone is looking for You!'"

I think most of us can relate to that scene. As soon as our typical day begins, it seems that "everyone is looking for us!" The demands of the day are constant and arrive early. Yet how many of us excuse ourselves from having a consistent, daily time with God on the grounds that we are so busy, we just can't find the time. As the old expression goes, it's not a matter of finding time; we have to make it by trading something else for it. It may be a bit of sleep, or the morning newspaper, or the vegetative moments we take in the morning "waking up." Whatever we trade for our time with the Lord, it's worth it. Literally, to spend time with God each day in the Word and prayer is life-changing.

And while I hope I don't sound legalistic, notice that in the passages above, it was in the morning that David and Jesus prayed. No, there's nothing mystical about the morning; if your best time to get with God is the afternoon, evening, or late at night, do it! But for many of us, morning is good because we can prepare ourselves better for the day to come. Rather than lose my temper in traffic during the day, and ask God to forgive me later, I can ask God in the morning to help me not lose my temper. Then my time with God can be more "prepare" than "repair," or more "prevent" than "repent."

What are some *benefits* of spending time with God daily? There are many, but let me mention just two that are significant for me.

"I have told you these things, so that in Me you may have peace. In this world, you will have trouble. But take heart! I have overcome the world." (John 16:33).

Peace. Peace in the midst of a troubled world; it's the birth right of every Christian, yet few experience real peace of heart and mind. I once noticed that I was anxious about a lot of things, and then realized that I hadn't had a time with the Lord for four days. No wonder!

"When they saw the courage of Peter and John and realized that they were unschooled, ordinary men, they were astonished and they took note that these men had been with Jesus." (Acts 4:13).

The men who had been with Jesus, ordinary men, had courage. This is the verse I'd love to have on my tombstone! "He had courage because he'd been with Jesus!" What a giant benefit courage is. In this vague, wishy-washy world, in which few people seem to have confidence or courage about anything, we can. And while the early disciples may well have been brave men, I think the kind of courage noted here is an everyday kind of confidence.

What's the opposite this kind of courage? To be *dis*-couraged. Discouragement is the curse of the day in our modern stressful world. We need to be *en*-couraged, and time with the Lord each day can give us that.

How long a period of time should a good time with the Lord be? An hour? A half hour? I once met with a medical student at Duke, and he said that he tried to meet with the Lord for at least an hour a day. When I asked him how he was doing with that, he said, "Not so good." Then he said, "I think I owe him about 500 hours . . ." So I told him, "If you spend more that 10 minutes a day on your Quiet Time, you're in sin!" (Bad theology, but he got the point.) *Consistency* is the key to success here.

Daily times with the Lord can be very brief, and still be very good. There are 1440 minutes in a day; if we spent one percent (14 minutes), or even ½ of one percent (7 minutes) a day in the Word and prayer . . . and did it consistently . . . it would be victory. True, we have to spend 99% of the day on the demands of the day, but we can give part of 1% to time with God. Many short times in the Word and prayer build a better relationship than extended time once or twice a month.

Here's another thought: in your daily time with God, try talking to him about what you've just read in Scripture. If this seems too strange to you, forget it. But sometimes it's natural to ask the Lord questions about what you've read, or to thank him for showing you something meaningful or relevant to what's going on in your life.

My friend. Bob Lovvorn, used to do a funny skit with two guys having a conversation. The first would talk about his family, and the other would listen. When there was a pause, the second man would talk at length about problems he was having with his car. This went on and on. The point? There were two persons there, and they *were* talking to each other, but about two completely separate topics. Do we do this with the Lord, read something in the Bible, then close the Bible and pray something totally unrelated to what he just said to us? It's just a thought. I don't want to take this idea too far, but give it a try.

Take a look at *Psalm 1* as a good example of a daily quiet time. It's only six verses, but packed with wisdom and encouragement. Read it through and pray back thoughts and questions to God. Thank him for showing you some great truths in this short passage of Scripture, e.g.,

—that we shouldn't get counsel from the ungodly

—that we should be like trees planted near water, (i.e., spend time in the Word)

—that we can ask Him what it means to be "always green," and "fruitful in season."

Can you do it? Can you spend consistent time with God in the Word and prayer? Be prepared for a real battle, for the enemy hates to see Christians building a good relationship with God. It takes discipline and determination to do it. We used to call the Bible the "book with the 2000 pound book cover" because it was so hard to open it every day. But once you get it open, it's clear sailing, and it will change you life. There is joy and a sense of victory as we establish this daily practice. Spending daily time with God is life-changing.

3. Prayer...

The old joke goes, "A man found himself in desperate trouble and prayed this prayer, 'Lord, it's me: Bill. Fifteen years ago, I asked you to help me and you did. If you get me out of this mess, I promise I won't bother you again for another fifteen years.'"

This whole business of prayer is both profound and simple, both joyful and difficult. One of my friends said as a young Christian, he'd heard the old hymn, *Sweet Hour of Prayer*, and decided to give it a try. He set a clock on the table at his bed, knelt down, and began praying everything he could think of. When he could pray no more, he looked up and saw that eight minutes had passed! "And it wasn't so much *sweet* . . . as hard work!" my friend added.

I think Christian leaders sometimes assume that since prayer is so personal, that people automatically know how to do it, or at least feel comfortable with what they do know. Yet many believers I have talked with about prayer say they are quite perplexed by it. Aside from "grace" said at meals (and some of this is more nursery rhyme than prayer) and the often eloquent pastor's prayer at church, there's not much in the way of models of how to pray. Perhaps this is why Jesus' disciples asked Him, "Lord, teach us how to pray . . ." (Luke 11:1 ff).

Prayer is how we talk with God, sharing our hearts and minds, our hopes and fears, our joys and our worries. We pray, not so much to give information to God (Matthew 6:32 says he already knows), but to draw near into his presence, to know him better, to be open with him, to experience the privilege of freely requesting needs and wants to him. We know that he loves us, and will do what is best for us in response to our prayers. We can be sure that, unlike the man in the joke above who didn't want to bother the "big guy upstairs," that we know our heavenly Father, like all good parents, loves to hear us talk to him. Prayers from the heart never bother God.

Let me share with you some thoughts about prayer. From my own perspective, I see . . .

—three kinds of prayer,

—three big benefits of prayer,

—three conditions on prayer.

Three kinds of prayer:

—The first kind of prayer is the *chatting with God* we might do in the car on the way to work, or mowing the lawn. It might be prompted by some everyday stimulus that jogs our minds and reminds us to pray about something. Maybe I see a billboard advertising a job fair, and it reminds me of a church member who is looking for work. So I quickly bring that need before God. A bit later, I might think of another concern, or something that's good, so I quickly shoot up another few words of request or thanks.

I'm guessing that this kind of prayer comprises a big part of how people pray, and perhaps that's not bad. One person said of this sort of prayer, "Sometimes I'm not sure if I'm thinking or praying." I like that.

—The second kind of prayer is what I call *"pour out your heart"* prayer. This is more extended time in prayer, and usually concerns a worry, fear, or perhaps some good thing we want very much to happen.

I recall as a young Christian going to the beach at night, near Melbourne, Florida, and walking for hours, praying about big concerns. One night I remember looking up, and wondering where I was. I'd walked so far north on the beach, I didn't even recognize the location. I also used to go to an abandoned WWII military airport with three mile-long runways laid out as a triangle, and walk and pray. What good times those were, and how calm and refreshed I felt as I drove home. We see these kinds of prayers in Psalms 51 and 73. Psalm 51 is David's pouring out of his heart in confession and repentance concerning his sin with Bathsheba, and Uriah's murder. Unlike Saul, who was sorry he'd gotten caught, David was sorry he'd done it.

In this Psalm 51, David asks God's forgiveness.

" Create in me a clean heart. Wash me thoroughly from my iniquity, and cleanse me from my sin (vs.2) Against Thee, Thee only, have I sinned (vs 4—I'm not sure Uriah would agree with that statement!) Restore to me the joy of thy salvation!"(vs.12).

In Psalm 73, sometimes called the "fat cat" psalm, the psalmist bitterly expresses his resentment about the unfairness of life. He complains to God at length how the wicked and evil people have it easy while he, trying to be righteous, has nothing but problems and pain.

"For I was envious of the arrogant, as I saw the prosperity of the wicked . . . Surely in vain I have kept my heart pure, and washed my hands in innocence, for I have been stricken all day long . . ." (Psalm 73: 3, 13, 14).

But, having complained, then the psalmist sees life from God's perspective, and has a further insight . . .

"Until I came into the sanctuary of God; then I perceived their end. Surely thou dost set them in slippery places; Thou dost cast them down to destruction . . . (vss. 17, 18) When my heart was embittered, and I was pierced within, then I was senseless and ignorant; I was like a beast before Thee." (Psalm 73:21, 22)

And his conclusion to this prayer is this:

"Whom have I in heaven but Thee? And besides Thee, I desire nothing on earth. My flesh and my heart may fail, but God is the strength of my heart and my portion forever." (Psalm 73:25, 26)

In this Psalm, there seems to be a working through, and working out, of the issue of bitterness in the psalmist's heart. He feels free to "vent" to the Lord about his resentment, but in the end arrives at a place of having God's view of the situation and a wonderful peace of mind. We can do this too, but it may take some time to share our hearts and then come to see the Lord's point of view.

I believe this pour-out-your-heart prayer is valuable when we are facing a major decision in life, or have an overwhelming disappointment, fear, worry, hope, or even guilt about sin. Get away and get it out! Find a place where you can be undisturbed: a park, empty church on Saturday, where-ever. Think through on what the issue is, and don't be afraid to share your heart with God about the issue. We can be respectful and reverent and still be genuine about how we feel. Ask God to give you his perspective on the issue, and ask him to give you peace.

Is there something in your life right now that you know you need to deal with in prayer? Can you make the time available, maybe a half a day, to get away and pour out your heart to God about it?

—*Structured prayer* is the third kind of prayer. This is the "work of prayer." It usually involves praying through some kind of a prayer list. (I can hear the cries of protest already! "Prayer list! That's not spontaneous; that's not spiritual; that's just too mechanical!") This sort of structure and discipline may not mesh well with the spirit of the day—i.e spontaneity equals spirituality—but those who are the "prayer warriors" among us affirm its value. This is the kind of prayer that is hard to do for most of us because it *is* planned. The prophet Samuel told the people of Israel,

"As for me, far be it from me that I should sin against the Lord by failing to pray for you. (I Samuel 12:23)

At the end of this section, I'll have a suggestion for a starting point for structured prayer.

Three Benefits of prayer:

Again, to limit this to three benefits is to understate its value, but here are three benefits that stand out to me. Think of your own special blessings from prayer.

—*Freedom from fear* is a first great benefit. Getting God involved in our fears by praying is the best antidote to fearfulness.

"For you have not received a spirit of slavery leading to fear again, but you received a spirit of adoption as sons, by which we cry out, 'Abba! Father!'" (Romans 8:15).

"I sought the Lord and He answered me; He delivered me from all my fears." (Psalm 34:4).

—*Forgiveness* is another benefit. In one sense, this is what the Christian faith is all about: forgiveness for our sins. No other religion even addresses how sin is to be dealt with, except Judaism (but its way of atoning for sin, animal sacrifice, is no longer practiced, because atonement was fulfilled by the sacrifice of the perfect Lamb.) Other religions either ignore it or minimize its effect on a person's life. But for us Christians, forgiveness is a heartbeat away if we only come to God in prayer and confess.

"If we confess our sins, He is faithful and just and will forgive us our sins and purify us from all unrighteousness." (1 John 1:9).

—*Getting answers* is a third benefit . . . well, this certainly sounds obvious! Yes, we get answers.

"Until now you have not asked for anything in My name. Ask and you will receive, and your joy will be complete." (John 16:24).

Of course, anyone with any sense realizes that this promise does not mean that we can expect God to give us every foolish or selfish desire we can think up. A famous writer supposedly said something to the effect that when he was a child, he asked God for something, didn't get it, and from that point on, didn't believe in God. Nonsense! The flimsiness of that excuse is rather pathetic. God is no fool. There are *conditions* on prayer.

Three conditions of prayer:

Okay, this idea does take a little getting used to; we are so accustomed to thinking of God the Father as the "unconditional" God. That is, we don't think of God's love or promises as having "fine print" at the bottom of the contract, by which He weasels out of fulfilling His obligations (think phone companies!). As the Apostle Paul would say, "May it never be!" God never goes back on his word. Numbers 23:19 states this faithfulness clearly.

"God is not a man (or phone company) that he should lie, nor a son of man, that He should repent; has He said, and will He not do it? Or has He spoken, and will He not make it good?"

Sorry about that phone company crack; maybe I need to read Psalm 73 again . . .

So why then are there conditions on prayer? As we look at the Scriptures below, we can see that, again, this is just a matter of sensibility and that God is not foolish, so as to let his graciousness be abused, or that people's selfish whims would be honored.

—A first condition is to *be honest with God.*

"If I had cherished sin in my heart, the Lord would not have listened." (Psalm 66:18)

Picture in your mind a person praying something to God, yet clutching behind his/her back (figuratively) a secret, enjoyable sin that he just doesn't want to let go. What would God say? Would he say, as a permissive parent might, "Oh, well, it's no big deal," or pretend not to notice it? I don't think so. He is more likely to say, "What's that you're hiding behind your back?"

Can we really expect God to answer our prayers if we "cherish"—love and hold on to—some sin area that we know offends God, but that gives us the momentary, perverse pleasure that sin provides? The point here is that if we pray while hiding sin, we are not being honest with God. We could certainly ask him to help us conquer that area of sin; that would be a great prayer! But we can't play games with God, expecting to trick him, or expect him to overlook our dishonesty.

—Another condition is to *believe that God can and will answer.*

"But when he asks, he must believe and not doubt, because he who doubts is like a wave of the sea, blown and tossed by the wind. That man should not think he will receive anything from the Lord; he is a double-minded man, unstable in all his ways." (James 1: 6–8 NIV).

Now this takes a bit of thinking about! Our doubts so easily creep in, whether it's of a theological nature (is this in God's will?), of a self-deprecating feeling (I probably don't deserve this), or a feeling similar to the plea of the man crying out to Jesus, "I do believe; help me overcome my unbelief!" (Mark 9:24).

It may seem more likely to us that we'll *wonder* about the outcome of our prayers, than have confidence that God will give us just what we asked for. What are we to do with this warning in James?

I think this word of caution simply means that we shouldn't approach God with an attitude of skepticism about his ability or willingness to answer our prayers. In the Mark passage (9:22 ff) the man with an afflicted child says to Jesus, "*If* You can do anything, take pity on us and help us." Jesus' answer, to me, almost seems sarcastic: "If *You* can," said Jesus. "Everything is possible for him who believes." Meaning? It's certainly not about *if* Jesus can; it's about *our* faith that he can.

So if a person were to shrug his shoulders, so to speak, and think, "Oh, well, what've I got to lose? I doubt this will work, but I'll give it a try as a last resort. I don't think God really cares, or will do anything, but here goes," then prays "Lord, will You do such and such for me," then the statement above of the unbelieving man not receiving anything from the Lord certainly applies.

> —A third condition is to *pray with correct motives*. Of the three, this is perhaps the easiest to understand. If I regard God as a mere catalog to order stuff from for my own sinful pleasure, he won't respond.

"You ask and do not receive, because you ask with wrong motives, so that you may spend it on your pleasures." (James 4:3)

I think simplicity is a good starting place for building a good prayer life. We may sometimes feel that success in the Christian life is difficult and complex, but just as the daily times with God are achievable because they are brief, so too the beginning of a good pray life can be simple and brief. What follows in the years to come as you build on this righteous habit, is up to you.

I like the little acronym *TOM* for daily prayer:

T . . . thanks to God for something every day.

O . . . others—pray for the needs and concerns of others, at least one other.

M . . . me—pray for myself, at least one worry and one hope.

I know this may seem way too brief and basic, but, again, the key here is to do it every day. You can be driving, standing in line at the ATM, waiting for the boss to show up for the meeting, for your computer to boot up, and you can pray *TOM!* Once you get in the habit of this, it is almost inevitable that you'll add to it. You'll find yourself praying for more people, more concerns, giving God thanks for more answers. And the time may well come when you realize that it would be good to write down these prayer concerns. Then it's happened; you have a prayer list! Go for it.

4. Fellowship . . .

The first men's Bible study I ever went to, I lit a cigarette. It was a bit of a shock to the other men, but I didn't know any better. I wasn't a Christian yet; it was in the Canal Zone of Panama, and I was attending the US Army's "Jungle Survival Course." I had only moderately survived, having been hurt in the training, and the man who invited me to the Bible study was the American doctor who had treated me, the very first Christian I'd ever met. When I lit the cigarette, one of the men leaned over to me and whispered, "Maybe you could wait till the coffee break to smoke . . . " Ha!

It probably wasn't the best start of my long experience in Christian fellowship, but I loved that Bible study. I had no idea what they were talking about, but I was so impressed with the men. They were nice; they treated each other and me with respect, and they just seemed so *secure*. I had no idea why Dr. Herb Loizeaux invited me, an arrogant, somewhat obnoxious, professed atheist, to that Bible study with those men. But I'm pretty sure I know *now* why he did. It was to expose me to real Christian fellowship, and the acceptance, patience, and . . . teeth that were there. This really was "iron sharpens iron" fellowship (Proverbs 27:17), not "pillow fluffs pillow" socializing. Much of the reason I listened so carefully to Dr. Herb as he talked to me about the Lord was because of the indisputable evidence of his life and the lives of the men in that Bible study. Even then I remember thinking, "These guys are so much *better* than I am."

Fast forward lots of years. I was at a Christian conference, had gone to the bookstore and bought what I thought was an off-white T-shirt. The first time I wore that shirt, however, I got some funny looks from people, so I asked a friend if the T-shirt was off-white. "Well . . ." he said, hesitantly. A lady sitting nearby was more direct. "It's more like *off-red*," she laughed.

Yes, I had bought a pink shirt. And, yes, I'm color-blind. I need a *lot* of help when it comes to colors. I showed up for my first date with Nancy wearing a red paisley-swirl shirt and lime-green pants . . . really! Since then, Nancy and my daughters have helped me in this area.

Two experiences: the first was a serious thing, showing me that the lives of real believers is a great "proof" for the existence of God; the second just sort of laughable, but both point out the great privilege of Christian fellowship.

What makes for good fellowship? First of all, it's different from the parental role of discipleship: ". . . you know how we were among you, as a (caring) mother . . . and (imploring) father . . ." (1 Thessalonians 2:7, 11) It's more like the give-and-take of a brother and sister, sibling relationship. I think good, Biblical fellowship should have at least four things:

Encouragement . . .

Hebrews 10:24, 25 (NIV) says, "And let us consider how we may spur one another on to love and good deeds. Let us not give up meeting together, as some are in the habit of doing, but let us encourage one another . . ."

This encouragement can be both comforting for past pain or failure, and challenging to meet goals that lie ahead. Among the many ways Christians encourage one another is by honestly talking about their own struggles and how they trusted Christ to overcome them. This is so freeing and encouraging to young Christians, who are amazed that others face the same temptations. The secular world just doesn't share its weaknesses and defeats. Young believers need to know that everyone struggles with similar issues, and the God is able to not only help us with the struggles, but do it in a way that our faith actually grows (See 1 Corinthians 10:13 and James 1:2–4).

Learning from and sharing with each other . . .

"He gave some as apostles, and some as prophets, some as evangelists, pastors and teachers, for the equipping of the saints . . . until we all reach unity in the faith . . . and become mature . . ." (Ephesians 4: 11–13 NIV).

Let's face it, most of us just don't know all that much, compared to how much there is to be known. My pastor, jokingly, once gave the church a 3-question quiz to illustrate this point. The questions were something like this:

—What's the algebraic equation for the number that represents a 1/3 of 39?

—What's the chord progression for some obscure music key?

—What's "off-sides" in soccer mean?

Of the three questions, I only knew the third one. Many in the congregation missed all three. Agreed, we don't need to know chord progressions to enjoy music, and we may not use algebra on a daily basis, but isn't it amazing what a wealth of knowledge others have that we are clueless about.

Apply that principle to the amount of Bible knowledge, insight, and life applications we don't have! This is where small-group Bible study groups are especially valuable. Key point: fellowship should be primarily Word-focused; social activities are fine, but should be secondary to learning from each other how to apply the Bible to our lives. It's not just the leader of a Bible study that we learn from; it's everyone in the group sharing her or his personal experiences, and insights into the Scripture.

Protection . . .

"Two are better than one . . . for if either of them falls, the one will lift up his companion. But woe to the one who falls when there is not another to life him up." (Ecclesiastes 4: 9, 10)

This is not so much a matter of protecting someone from a sin problem (see *correction* below) as much of a matter of a young Christian being misled. People can be misled by false teachings, doctrinal stands which *exceed what is written*, Christian "fads," or lack of balance due to the young believer's own natural leanings.

The four classical "isms" of false teaching are these:

—liberalism = loosening Scripture

—legalism = out-"Bibling' the Bible

—mysticism = smoke, not fire or light

—universalism = compassion without truth (more on these later— see chapter 5)

Many believers have been tripped up in their growth to maturity by these and other tricks of the enemy, but being part of a solid Christian fellowship can make all the difference in avoiding these stumbling blocks. If you have a group of fellow believers who feel not only the right but the responsibility to challenge each other when wrong thinking slips in, it is a wonderful (though at some times, painful) protection.

Correction . . .

"But exhort one another daily . . . lest any of you be hardened through the deceitfulness of sin. (Hebrews 3:13 KJV)

While most translations use the word "encourage" in the first phrase, the last phrase implies that the nature of the encouragement is to help each other deal with, and get victory over, sin. We all need the accountability of our sisters and brothers in Christ to prompt us to live rightly by pointing out (in a loving way) areas of our lives which are not conformed to Christ. Even seemingly insignificant sins, if allowed to become habitual, have a hardening effect on our desire to live holy lives. The little sins "deceive" us into thinking, "It's no big deal." This is an ongoing battle because we live among a "perverse generation," and in his letter, James strongly emphasizes that . . . "friendship with the world is hatred toward God . . ." (James 4:4).

Just a quick word about this aspect of fellowship: correction . . . we do need to be willing to reprove one another, but there's a right and wrong way to do it. Here are five little guides for exhortation:

— *Ignore an incident; address a trend.* If a fellow Christian is just having a bad day, and sins uncharacteristically because of it, for goodness sakes, don't jump on it. But if you notice the behavior is becoming more frequent, or habitual, then graciously talk with him/her.

— *Never reprove someone primarily for the purpose of you feeling better.*

True, the area of sin may be distressing to you, but the main reason we correct someone is for her or his benefit, not ours. I remember a non-Christian girl in one of our college investigative Bible studies who rowed on the crew team for the college. Her "boathouse language" really bothered one of the other women, who took it upon herself to rebuke the girl for her bad language. We never saw the non-Christian girl again. The girl wasn't angry, just embarrassed. The woman who had rebuked her realized she had done it to ease her own discomfort about the bad language, not for the girl's sake. The Christian woman learned a good lesson from it, but the non-Christian girl was gone,

> —*Pray before you talk to the person.* Ask God to make you humble, not intimidating, so that the reproof is helpful, not hurtful.

> —*If you can, put your reproof in the form of a question.* When I was in training to go on staff with a Christian organization, we had lots of meetings about ministry strategy. One day, during a break, one of the other men brought me a cup of coffee, sat down with me and posed this question: "Jim, let me ask you something. I observed this morning that there were times when you interrupted others; did you feel the group wasn't headed where you felt it should go?" I answered, "No. That wasn't it. I was just impatient. It was wrong to interrupt. Thanks for sharing that with me." The man smiled and said, "Great! I'll pray for you on that one. I struggle with the same thing sometimes." The fact I can remember that interaction word-for-word after all these years is evidence of how gracious the man was, and how much I needed the correction.

> —*However the person responds, be at peace and pray for the person.* We don't know if a person will receive our admonition with understanding and appreciation, or reject it with bitterness. But getting a good response should not be our main concern. Share graciously with the person, then leave it to God. Who knows, years later they may well look back on that conversation with gratitude, even if they didn't at the time.

So how's your fellowship? Do you have Christian friends who encourage you?

Do you go regularly to a Bible study group where the Bible is discussed and there is a healthy accountability among the people? If not, work hard on finding a good Sunday school class, small group Bible study, or home group. It's better to get into a Bible study group that may or may not do social activities together, than a softball team that *may* decide to do some Bible study. Remember, the number one priority is that the fellowship be focussed on the Word.

5. Bible study...

There are two small, neighborhood churches close to our home. I drive past these churches several times a week, and always notice the messages on their signs. Here's one that appeared during the Easter season:

> Body piercing saved my life!

"Not bad..." I thought. That might make some people think. Jesus' suffering on the cross did indeed bring salvation to those who receive it. But that same week, the other church had this message on its sign:

> How to get to heaven... turn right and go straight!

Cute, but wrong. Titus 3:5 says, "He saved us, not because of deeds which we have done in righteousness, but in virtue of His own mercy..."

What's the point? Hopefully, no one will try to piece together accurate theology from signs, even church signs, along the road. Both signs were clever; only one was correct. But it does bring up a big challenge we face in ministry today: helping people base their life values on Scripture, not on the slogans, bumper stickers, or the little sound bites the world offers.

This means Bible study. And significant, personal Bible study is not a popular activity these days. Most Bible studies I'm aware of are "no-prep" studies which people attend without spending time in the Word beforehand. When a leader suggested an hour of preparation before the group met, one person commented, "Forget it! The last thing I need is more homework." When the study of God's Word is seen as an odious chore, rather than a privilege, something is wrong.

Is this just an inevitable part of our busy culture? Does it reflect, in this day of visual orientation (TV, video games, internet, movie special effects, on-line classes, *ad nauseum*), the discomfort many people feel with books? I'm not sure. But I strongly believe that consistent study of God's Word is essential for personal growth, conviction-building, and effective personal ministry. And given the fact that some popular Christian devotionals and "light reads" may contain doctrinal error, correct understanding of Scripture is crucial. So even if it's something of a battle to change people's thinking about Bible study, it's worth the fight.

Bible study is all about freedom. Understanding and applying scripture results in freedom from slavery to sin, and many of life's entanglements. When Jesus said to His followers, "... the truth shall set you free ..." (John 8:32), he meant it. Being a serious Christian who knows the Word and follows it doesn't make one into some kind of religious conformist, as the cynics would claim; it's just the opposite—it makes a person free!

The Bible is the key to getting free, and staying free, from sin.

... enslaved to sin (Titus 3:3).

"... the truth shall make you free ..." (John 8:32).

Look at these great Scriptures about freedom in Christ:

" It is for freedom that Christ has set us free. Stand firm, then, and do not let yourselves be burdened again by a yoke of slavery. (Galatians 5:1 NIV).

Isn't it interesting that Paul had to exhort the Christians in Galatia to "stand firm" in their freedom. These believers were not struggling to free themselves from the oppression of Judaic law; they were *wanting* to be enslaved again to it. Why? I believe that people can get so used to being in a system of rules and regulations that they're uncomfortable with freedom. First of all, freedom deprives them of the false sense of satisfaction of "working" for their own salvation. Secondly, people who like to run their own lives can be very uncomfortable in this new direct relationship with the living God. There's a comfort in having rules (and knowing how to bend them ...) rather than being in the presence of God, who knows their hearts.

"But now that you know God—or rather are known by God—how is it that you are turning back to those weak and miserable principles? Do you wish to be enslaved by them all over again?" (Galatians 4:9 NIV).

"For sin shall not be master over you, for you are not under law but under grace." (Romans 6:14).

Here's the big benefit of our freedom in Christ: we no longer *have* to sin. What the Judaic law did was show people clearly that they were slaves of sin. Romans 7:7, 17 point out that even when people want to do the right thing, they can't. That's slavery. At the end of that passage, Paul cries out, "Wretched man that I am! Who will set me free from the body of this death? Thanks be to God through Jesus Christ our Lord!" (Romans 7:24, 25).

Freedom from sin's mastery: that's grace. Sadly, a lot of Christians today ignore their freedom and choose to live just as they did before they became Christians.

Now here comes the practical application:

"If you abide in My word, then you are truly disciples of Mine; and you shall know the truth and the truth shall make you free." (John 8:31, 32).

What are some areas of enslavement we can be free from by abiding in (living according to) God's Word?

—To lust

—To greed, or anxiety about money

—To selfishness

—To insecurity and fear

—To bad relationships

—To . . . (what are some others?)

Let's look at how to do Bible study. The key points are these:

—What does the Bible actually *say* about an issue?

—What does it *mean*, both for the time it was written and for modern day?

—Is this something I can *do* in my own life?

These points may seem pretty obvious, but it's pretty amazing how often people are certain there is something in the Bible, that isn't . . . or they are amazed at what *is* in the Bible.

Examples: the person who is sure the Scripture says, "God helps those who help themselves," or that "Money is the root of all evil."

Neither is correct, nor stated as such in Scripture. It does say, "... the *love* of money is a root of all kinds of evil." (1 Timothy 6:10). That's a pretty big difference. As for God helping those who help themselves, it does say that God desires our obedience, but John 5:1ff. shows that God certainly helps those who *cannot* help themselves.

2 Peter 1:3, 4 says that we have been granted by God,

"... everything pertaining to life and godliness ... and by His precious and magnificent promises, we may become partakers of the divine nature and escape the corruption that is in the world."

My understanding of that statement is that Scripture, under the guidance of the Holy Spirit, has an answer or solution for every significant issue in our lives.

The meaning, or interpretation, of Scripture is far more clear-cut than most people think. Scripture almost always means just what plain, common-sense understanding tells us. This is the first and most important rule of how to interpret the Bible: it means what it says. Sure, there are times when the writing is obviously poetic or figurative, such as "Let the rivers clap their hands ..." (Psalm 98:8), but we easily understand these things. A Christian leader once said, "It's like eating fish; if you get a bone, just spit it out. Don't choke on it." If you find something that is difficult to understand, don't be disturbed. Get what you can for now, and trust that God may reveal more truth later.

Applying Scripture to our lives is the very reason the Bible is so important to us. It should not merely increase our knowledge, but change our lives. Application can be straightforward, e.g., "do not steal," or it may involve understanding the principle under consideration, then finding a good way to make it a part of our everyday life. For example, the Red Sea parted to allow the escape of Moses and the children of Israel. While we may not actually see a body of water parted, the principle is true that God will provide a way of escape, especially if we are being tempted to sin: "... but with the temptation, God will provide the way of escape also, that you may be able to endure it." (1 Corinthians 10:13).

Okay, knowing the truth means knowing the Bible. Knowing the Bible means making the effort to study it. Here's three little tools to help you study the Bible.

Tool # 1—*Doing a topical Bible study using the concordance*

You want to know what the Bible says about a certain subject, or topic. The simplest and most accurate way to determine God's teaching on any topic is to find as many verses or passages in the Bible as possible which relate to the topic. The best commentary on the Bible is the Bible itself, that is, other relevant verses.

For example, you'd like to find out more about this question, "What's a person's soul?" In the back of most Bibles is a section called the "concordance." Some are quite good and others are not so good. But a simple concordance is still the best starting point for a topical study. You can also buy an inexpensive concordance on-line, or at a Christian bookstore.

Look up the word, "soul," and the concordance will list several verses in the Bible that has the word, "soul."

The topic: "What is a person's soul?"

In my Bible's concordance, I found these verses in which the word, *soul*, appears:

a. Deuteronomy 4:29—. . . "search for (God) with all your heart and all your *soul*."

b. Psalm 16:10— ". . . Thou wilt not abandon my *soul* to Sheol . . ."

c. Psalm 23:3—"He restores my *soul*."

d. Psalm 24:4—". . . (he) who has not lifted up his *soul* to falsehood . . ."

e. Psalm 42:1—"As the deer pants for the water brooks, so my *soul* pants for Thee, O God."

f. Psalm 103:1—"Bless the Lord, O my *soul*; and all that is within me . . ."

g. Proverbs 24:12—". . . does He not know it Who keeps your *soul*?"

h. Ezekiel 18:4—"Behold, all *souls* are Mine; the *soul* of the father as well as the *soul* of the son is Mine. The *soul* who sins will die."

i. Matthew 10:28—"And do not fear those who kill the body, but are unable to kill the *soul*; but rather fear Him who is able to destroy both *soul* and body in hell."

j. Matthew 16:26—"For what will a man be profited if he gains the whole world, and forfeits his *soul*? Or what will a man give in exchange for his *soul*?"

k. Luke 1:46, 47—"And Mary said, 'My *soul* exalts the Lord, and my spirit has rejoiced in God my Savior.'"

l. Acts 4:32—". . . those who believed were of one heart and one *soul*."

m. 1 Thessalonians 5:23—"Now may the God of peace Himself sanctify you entirely; and may your spirit and *soul* and body be preserved complete without blame at the coming of our Lord Jesus Christ."

n. Hebrews 10:39—". . . those who have faith in the preserving of the *soul*."

o. James 1:21 & 5:20—". . . which is able to save your *souls* . . . save his *soul* from death . . ."

p. 1 Peter 2:11—". . . abstain from fleshly lusts, which wage war against the *soul*."

On this topic there are many different possible definitions for *soul*, so it is helpful to try to categorize the different meaning. These different category headings are just to help, not determine doctrine for the ages. It's an excellent exercise in self-discovery to begin thinking about Bible meaning in this way without worrying about "being wrong."

Possible categories for meaning of "soul":

Heart or passion, intense emotion	Inner person or "spirit"	The eternal part of a person that gets saved or condemned	Mind, intellect, personality, choice-maker
Deuteronomy 4:29 Psalm 42:1 Psalm 103:1 Acts 4:32 Luke 1:46, 47	Psalm 23:3 1 Peter 2:11 Proverbs 24:12 (?) 1 Peter 2:11	Psalm 16:10 Proverbs 24:12 (?) Ezekiel 18:4 (?) Matthew 10:28 Matthew 16:26 Hebrews 10:39	Psalm 24:4 Ezekiel 18:4 (?) 1 Thessalonians 5:23 1 Peter 2:11 (?)

Now, having looked up the verses, and having put them in simple categories, write a simple answer to the question: "What's a person's soul?" Go ahead, give it a try!

"It seems to me the most commonly implied definitions of *soul* in the Bible are . . . "

_____

_____

_____

_____

Again, let me stress this point: when we study the Bible, we shouldn't be afraid to ask questions and debate in our own minds the meaning of Scripture. We certainly want to be reverent about God's holy Word, but we should be confident, not fearful, about digging into the Bible, seeking truth. The key to being excited about Bible study is *finding out for ourselves* the great, freeing truths of Scripture.

Let me tell a little story to illustrate this. A few years ago, I helped a Christian youth worker put an addition on his home. He and his family had just moved to the city, and the home they bought was definitely too small for them. So, with both bravery and nervousness, he and I decided we could put the addition on ourselves.

This meant studying the architectural and engineering plans (blueprints), and trying to figure out how the new rooms would be built. It was a bit overwhelming at first glance. It all seemed very complicated, and I didn't even know what some of the terms meant . . . (what *is* a

Simpson LSSU "hip-to-truss connector," anyway?) And, I'll admit, we were also a bit afraid of making some kind of big mistake.

But as we spent time poring over the plans, and thinking about how things fit together, bit by bit, it started to make sense. And the biggest help came as my friend and I got up on the existing roof, with the plans in our hands, and could visualize how the new rafters would run and connect. All of a sudden, we went from being intimidated to excited by the project.

It occurred to me that this is a pretty good analogy to people approaching serious Bible study for the first time. It does seem like an intimidating task. Words and concepts are unfamiliar, and a person might understandably think, "I just don't get it!"

As people spend time in the Word, however, thinking hard about what it means, understanding does come, bit by bit. And when people *apply* what they're learning to their lives, it gets really exciting. Just as understanding the blueprints is meant to lead to actual construction, so too understanding of the Bible is meant to lead to applying those truths to our lives.

The book of Joshua says this: know the Scriptures, think about them, and *do* them.

"This book of the law shall not depart from your mouth, but you shall meditate on it day and night, so that you may be careful to do according to all that is written in it; for then you will make your way prosperous and then you will have success." (Joshua 1:8).

Tool # 2—*Doing a topical Bible study using cross-referencing*

Topic question: "What's the benefit of studying Scripture?"

This is going to seem complicated and difficult, but it really isn't. First, do a quick check of your Bible's concordance to get a handful of relevant verses on the topic. Or call a pastor or other Christian leader and ask, "What's the best Bible verse you know about . . . (your topic)?" Then pick what seems to be the best or most significant verse from the concordance list, or the pastor's verse, and use it as a starting point for cross-referencing.

Note: The term "cross-referencing" meaning finding other verses or passages in the Bible which give information about the topic you're studying. We can find these other verses using people's suggestions, our own memory as we know the Word more and more, special Bible study "helps," or the cross-reference tool (the fine print) found in the margins of many Bibles. Does your Bible have tiny print at the sides of the text, or in the middle margin? It's a great help! If your Bible doesn't, you can buy one that does in your Christian bookstore. Just make sure you tell the person at the store, "I want a Bible with cross-references."

Okay, pick a good verse on your topic. For the above topic, I'm picking 2Timothy 3:16, 17. I got this verse looking in my Bible's concordance under the word "Scripture." There were lots of verses listed, but I like 2 Timothy 3:16, 17 for a starting point.

Now look your Bible at 2 Timothy 3:16, 17. Write it down.

"All Scripture is inspired by God and profitable for teaching, for reproof, for correction, for training in righteousness; that the man of God may be adequate, equipped for every good work."

Now look in the margin at the fine print (have your magnifying glass handy!) and find the number of those verses . . . 16, 17. Got them? The Scriptures listed in fine print are the cross references for 2 Timothy 3:16, 17. Be aware that some cross-reference tools take it a step further, and the different clauses and phrases in a verse are lettered (with lower case letters) with the cross-reference verses corresponding to those letters.

For example: John 3:16 might be lettered, "For God so (a) loved the world that (b) He gave his (c) only begotten Son . . ." The cross references shown in the margin after (a) will pertain only to the phrase, ". . . loved the world . . ." The cross references shown for (b) will pertain to the phrase, ". . . He gave his . . ." and so on. See how it works?

Okay, now for the fun! Well . . . "fun" might be a bit of a stretch, but it does have the satisfaction of a treasure hunt.

Do three "Rounds" of cross-referencing. That is, for the first "round," write down all the fine-print Bible references shown in the margin for 2 Timothy 3: 16, 17. Find the verses in the Bible, read them to see if they are meaningful for your question of "What are the benefits of studying Scripture?" Put OK next to those you think are relevant, and NO next to the ones which are not.

What do I mean by relevant or not relevant? Let's say you're trying to find out from the Bible about the nature of angels, and you start with a verse which has the phrase ". . . a multitude of angels . . ." You may find a cross-reference verse that contains the phrase ". . . a multitude of sheep were there." Obviously, the concept being cross-referenced is

Principle # 1: Be What You Want Others to Be. . . . 43

"multitude," and that verse doesn't help your study on angels. That would be an irrelevant cross-reference, against which you put down a NO.

Jot down a brief note on each verse you think is helpful. Now find the cross-references for each of the "new' verses you got in the first round. In other words, locate each relevant verse in your Bible and look at the cross references listed in the margin for each of these verses. This is Round two.

Do the same a third time. By this third round of cross-referencing, you'll notice the verses are either mostly irrelevant or the same ones you've already got.

Here's my cross-reference Bible study on the question: "What's the benefits of studying Scripture?"

Round one of cross-referencing, using 2 Timothy 3: 16, 17 as a starting point:

—Romans 4:23, 24 (jotted note) = not only for Abraham's sake was the Bible written, but for ours, in regards to salvation through faith. OK

—Romans 15:4 = what was written in earlier times was written for our instruction, that through "perseverance and the encouragement of Scripture" we might have hope. OK

—2 Peter 1:20 and following verses = refers to the Bible inspiration (doesn't apply to the specific question, even though it's a great verse!) NO

—1 Timothy 6:11 = talks about fleeing from unrighteousness. NO, not really.

—2 Timothy 2: 21 = ". . . if a man cleanses himself from these things . . . prepared for every good work . . ." = refers to one's preparation for ministry. OK

—Hebrews 13:21 = equip you in every good thing to do His will . . . OK (we saw from 2 Tim. 3:17 that Bible study will equip the person of God for good works, so this is relevant as it pertains to good works)

Round two of cross-referencing, using the OK verses from Round one:

Verses in the margin for Romans 4:23, 24

—Romans 15:4 = NO—already have this one

—2 Corinthians 9:9 = NO

—1 Corinthians 10: 1 = "these things" refers to verses 1 through 10, things that happened to them as an example, and they were written for our instruction. OK (great passage!)

—2 Timothy 3:16 = NO—already have this one verses for Romans 15:4

—Romans 4:23 = NO already have

—2 Timothy 3:16 = NO already have verses for 2 Timothy 2:21

—1 Timothy 6:11 = NO

—2 Timothy 2:15 = "... workmen not ashamed, rightly handling the Word of truth ... OK

—2 Corinthians 9:8 = God provides all we need for good works ...OK?

—Ephesians 2:10 = good works which God prepared us to walk in ... NO, not really

—2 Timothy 3:17 = NO already have verses for Hebrews 13:21 (first part of the verse only)

—1 Peter 5:10 = refers to the fact that those who minister will suffer ... NO

Round three of cross-referencing, using OK verses from Round two:

Verses for I Corinthians 10:11

—1 Corinthians 10:6 = NO same as 10: 11

—Romans 4:23 = NO already have this one verses for 1 Timothy 6:11

—2 Timothy 2: 22 = NO already have this one

—2 Timothy 3:17 = NO already have this one verses for 2 Timothy 2:15

—Romans 6:13 = don't present your bodies as instruments of sin = NO

—James 1:2 = after suffering comes crown of glory = NO

—Ephesians 1:13 = after listening to the gospel, the message of truth, you were saved and sealed into the Holy Spirit = OK

—James 1:18 = He chose to give us birth through the word of truth, that we might be a kind of firstfruits of all he created. = OK

What do we have? Even though it took some effort, we've gotten some good information about the rewards of knowing the Bible. Here's a quick summary:

- 2 Timothy 3:16, 17 = Bible study is profitable for teaching us truth, it "reproves us" if our thinking is wrong in some way, it corrects us, and then it trains us to live in a right way.

- Romans 15:4 = study the Bible for encouragement and to give us hope.

- 1 Corinthians 10:11 = (referring to verses 1 through 10) for our instruction, to avoid the disqualifying sins of people in the past ... this passage is a gold mine!

- 2 Corinthians 9:8 = to know that God will give us what we need to serve him in doing good works.

- Ephesians 1:13 = knowledge of the Word brings people to salvation and "seals" them into the safety and protection of the Holy Spirit. Good in two ways: we're "sealed and safe" in the Holy Spirit, and we can use the word to lead people to salvation.

- 2 Timothy 2: 21 = this is a bit of a stretch, but it has to do with a person fleeing from things which would prevent him from being prepared and doing good works ... we know what these contaminates are and how to flee from them by study of the Word (John 8: 31, 32 "... know the truth and it shall make you free.")

- 2 Timothy 2:15 = Great verse on doing Bible study! Knowing the Bible allows us to "... rightly handle the word of truth." that is, to be able to use the Scripture to help other people with their life issues.

And this is just a start; once we're in the Scripture and get our brains thinking about benefits of Bible study, we'll pick up on lots of others as we read Scripture, for example, during our quiet times.

Tool # 3—*Passage analysis Bible study*

Passage analysis Bible study simply means tackling a passage of Scripture, perhaps a chapter or short Bible book, and going through it verse by verse.

The procedure is simple.

First, read the whole passage (for example: John, chapter 4) to get an overall idea. Write what you think the main idea of the passage is in one sentence.

Secondly, read each verse slowly and determine if it has interest or poses any questions or puzzles. (your *observation*) Jot down any thoughts or questions. You do not need to try to find something for every verse. Hold off on trying to interpret at this time.

Thirdly, do some quick cross-referencing on the verse, using the cross reference aid in the margin of your Bible or any other helpful aid in the back of your Bible, such as an Index of Topics, maps, etc. In a very real sense, passage analysis Bible study is doing a series of mini-topical studies. Each question, or interesting point about which you'd like to know more, becomes a little topical study. The same tools and techniques apply that we used for doing a topical study: i.e., the concordance and marginal cross-reference aid.

Fourth, answer your questions. Go ahead and interpret the verses. (your *interpretation*) Again, don't be afraid say what you think the passage means. Your goal is to find out what the writer of Scripture, "carried along" by the Holy Spirit (2 Peter 1:21), meant when he wrote the passage. It is true that there is only one meaning intended by God in Scripture, and our job is to find that meaning, but there can be numerous applications.

Fifth, see if there is any practical application to your own life, either immediate or long-term. (your *application*) Be realistic... you can't find applications for every verse in the Bible. Determine if there is any larger application you can derive from the entire passage, e.g., "Is the application something I should act upon? Is it something I should learn? It is a reaffirmation of a truth I already knew? Is it one part of a greater understanding or action?

Example: a study of Chapter 4 of the Gospel of John
PASSAGE: JOHN 4:1 and following
"Jesus and the woman at the well"

Verse:	Observation / Questions:	Interpretations:	Applications:
4.	Question: "Where is Samaria?"	look at map: area between Jerusalem and Galilee	none
6.	Observastion: Jesus gets tired!	He really is human!	do a quick study on Jesus' human / God nature
9.	Question: "Why does the woman say Jews have nothing to do with Samaritans?"	see Ezra 4:1–6 (from the marginal cross-reference aid)	be aware of cultural and religious differences when talking with people
10–13	Observation: Jesus makes a transition from H2O to "living water."	Jesus ties real life issues to eternal life; He's evangelizing.	How can I do this when I am sharing?
etc., etc.			

Just a quick word on interpreting the Bible: this is what theologians call "hermeneutics." I'm not sure where this word comes from; is it from "Hermes," the Greek messenger of the gods, the guy with winged feet and hat? I don't know, but for our purposes, it just means guidelines for correctly getting at the meaning of Scripture. For scholars, this is a massive topic, but let's consider some guidelines that will hopefully help. How to feel confident in interpreting Scripture

The goal in Bible study is, essentially, to figure out the *plain-sense meaning* of the portion of the Bible being studied. A key aspect of this is to discern what meaning the author intended to communicate.

For example, in the ministry of Jesus: The Apostle John concludes his Gospel by saying,

"There are also many other things which Jesus did, which if they were written in detail, I suppose that even the world itself would not contain the books which were written." (John 21:25)

What was the intent here? Are we to take this literally, or figuratively? It's obvious that it's a figure of speech. Jesus' three and a half years of ministry could not comprise enough actions, even in detail, to actually fill the world with books. This is an easy one. The writer's intent was to impress upon the reader that Jesus' ministry was extensive, and John uses a hyperbole (literary exaggeration) to express this.

How about when Jesus calms the storm at sea?

". . . there arose a great storm in the sea . . . Then He arose and rebuked the winds and the sea, and it became perfectly calm." (Matthew 8: 24–27)

What is the writer's intent here? Liberal theologians may say that when Jesus spoke, it calmed the fears of the men in the boat to such an extent that it *seemed* the storm itself became calm. This could lead to the thought that probably the storm was not as severe as the excited travelers reported. But what is the writer's intent? Does Matthew intend the reader to take the calming of the storm literally, or does Matthew intend to impress us with Jesus' psychological prowess? This is easy too. It is intended to be understood literally.

Let me mention here that some people may not *agree* with the literal interpretation of this miracle, but there is a huge difference in someone saying, "I don't agree with what the Bible says." and someone who says, "That's not what the Bible means." Do you see the difference? The first person is at least honest and admits that he or she knows what the Bible is saying clearly, but that she or he doesn't like it. The second person is denying the plain-sense meaning of the Bible and twisting it to agree with his/her existing mindset, i.e., that Jesus didn't actually do a miracle, because of its implication, i.e., that Jesus is God.

How about these? Jesus feeds the 5000 . . . Jesus raises Lazarus from the dead . . . Jesus turns water into wine . . . In each of these cases, the writer intends to describe an actual event brought about by supernatural

Principle # 1: Be What You Want Others to Be. . . . 49

power (which is what a miracle is). In each of these instances, those who deny the deity of Christ can find a figurative interpretation (the 5000 had all been hiding their lunches . . . Lazarus wasn't really dead . . . and so on.) But the intent of the writer is that these occurrences are to be understood literally.

Here's a second guide: consider the *context* and *culture*.

What do I mean by *context*? Quick story . . . I was sitting in a church near the back of the room (no judging—the place was full!). On the stage up front was a drum set, and the big (bass?) drum had a picture and words on it. I was too far away to read the words, but I could see that the picture was an American flag. The Sunday was just before Independence Day, and I could see that there were three words, in the configuration of "*I Pledge Allegiance.*" I assumed that those were the words even though I really couldn't read them. After the service, I got close enough to see that, indeed, the drum did say *I Pledge Allegiance*. The flag in the background and the Fourth of July date provided the *context* for me to make an accurate guess.

In terms of Bible study, when I say we should look the *context*, I simply mean that we take into account all of the passage we're considering. The old joke is the girl who thinks her dating life is not what it should be, so she claims only the first part of Luke 9:23 ". . . if any man would come after me, let him . . ." (Luke 9:23 says, "If any man would come after me, let him deny himself, take up his cross daily, and follow Me.").

Taking a verse out of context is one of the surest ways to get a wrong reading of Scripture. For example, consider James' statement, ". . . faith, if it has no works, is dead, being by itself." (James 2:17) contrasted with the apparent "faith alone saves" message of Romans 5:1, "Therefore, having been justified by faith, we have peace with God through our Lord Jesus Christ."

This is one of the seeming "contradictions" in the Bible, but the context of the James passage helps us understand that this is written to exhort Christians to show their faith by evidence, in the manner of Jesus' testimony that "you know a tree by its fruit."

Culture is what the people in that place and time understood to be normal and usual in terms of behavior or customs. Here's an example: Acts 15 and the Council of Jerusalem's decision that people did not have to become Jews in order for them to be Christians (Acts 15:5 and 10), but only that people should . . .

"... abstain from things contaminated by idols and from fornication and from what is strangled and from blood." (Acts 15:20).

This instruction had cultural concessions to the Jews: regarding contaminated items and the food restrictions of strangled or bloody meat. These are aspects of the Jewish law that no longer apply to Christians, but the presence of so many Jewish Christians in the early church made it a wise decision to advise Gentile Christians not to be munching a juicy pork sandwich while in fellowship with the Jewish believers. This counsel by the church leaders should be understood from its cultural moorings, not as a basis for Christians today to follow Jewish dietary laws.

Here's the third guide: don't let gray areas of Scripture cast doubt on areas that are clear. This just means that we should be aware that some Bible verses seem to imply a doctrinal truth that seem different than the majority of other Scriptures. It's important to carefully consider all of the biblical passages to have clarity on the issue. Let the passages whose meaning is clear stand, and consider the "different" verses as requiring more study and understanding.

An example of this would be the question concerning the effect of water baptism in regard to salvation. One scriptural passage that seems to imply that water baptism is a necessary part of salvation is Mark 16:16.

"He who has believed and been baptized shall be saved..."

Yet other scriptural passages, in more definitive language, indicate that while water baptism is a beneficial testimony, it is not required for salvation.

"For I am not ashamed of the gospel (Paul says), for it is the power of God for salvation to everyone who believes..." (Romans 1:16) "For Christ did not send me to baptize (Paul says), but to preach the gospel ..." (1 Corinthians 1:17).

"Sirs, what must I do to be saved?" (the Philippian jailer asked.) "And they said, 'Believe in the Lord Jesus, and you shall be saved' ... and immediately he was baptized, he and all his household." (Acts 16:30 and 33).

Conclusion: There is a lot of information available in the world today. Much of it is wrong, either deliberately or ignorantly. The plain-sense meaning of the Bible is truth and should be our clear and final authority on everything! Be a woman or man of the Word! A big part of being committed to God is to be committed to his Word.

6. Witnessing . . .

". . . you shall be My witnesses . . ." (Acts 1:8)

"Evangelism" . . . "witnessing" . . . "telling non-Christians about Jesus" . . . "sharing the Gospel" . . . There are lots of different terms for this topic, but they all have this in common: they create nervousness or downright fear in most Christians!

Once I was taking a young man with me to some college dorms to talk with students about Christ. It was the first time the young man had done this, and he was somewhere between nervous and scared. As we got to the entrance of the dorm he said, "Tell me again why we're doing this?" I laughed. I knew just what he meant. I said, "Ask me that in about an hour."

An hour later, as we walked back to the car, the young man asked, "Can I retract my question?" The reason he said this: we'd just had a good time talking with students about their lives and sharing a simple gospel illustration with them. A couple of the students said they'd never heard this stuff before. They all had listened carefully and respectfully. Whatever the young man had feared, it hadn't happened. But what *had* happened was that he got to see the convicting power of the Word as the students read for themselves the gospel verses.

Just out of curiosity, I asked him later, "If you hadn't been with me in the dorms, what would you've been doing?" He looked at his watch, and was a little embarrassed when he answered, "Probably watching old episodes of Gilligan's Island on the retro. channel."

So now, if we have a less-than-encouraging time talking with someone about Christ, we'll sometimes say, "At least it's better than watching Gilligan's Island."

(Note: In the unlikely case that the producers of Gilligan's Island are reading this book, the above story is not a put-down of Gilligan's Island . . . it was a cute little show.)

Here's another story. The first time *I* ever "went out on evangelism" was at a small university in Florida where I was teaching. The fellow that took me out to the dorms was Max Weighmink, a Navigator campus minister (*The Navigators* is a non-denominational ministry). We had been getting together, one-to-one, to do Bible study, and this week he surprised me by saying, "Hey, let's go talk to students at the dorms." So off we went. I was pretty nervous, and I'll have to admit the thought came into my mind, "What if we come across some of my own students . . . there goes my cool professor image!"

Max told me I didn't have to do anything, just be with him and pray while he was talking with guys. (It was a men-only dorm . . . there used to be such things) Max did ask me, "You can pray with your eyes open, can't you?" I told him I could.

I was amazed at his courage! We knocked on one dorm room door, and a voice yelled, "Yeah!" So we went in, and there was a student looking at a pornographic magazine. When Max told him we were interested in talking with him about spiritual issues, he looked sarcastically amused. Here's how the conversation went, the best I can remember it:

Student: "No thanks." (When we'd asked if he'd like to talk with us.).

Max: "Oh, I'm sorry to hear that, because it's really interesting. "

Student: "No, I'm definitely not interested."

Max: "Well, if you were, the first thing I was going to say was just how much God loves us . . . you too."

Student: "Hey, listen, no offense, but I don't buy the religious thing at all."

Max: "I know what you're saying. I think part of why God seems so meaningless is because we're separated from him." Max pulls a New Testament out of his back pocket, find Romans 3:23, and hands it to the student. "See? Right there."

Student: who, amazingly, takes the Bible and looks at Romans 3:23. "So what? Who cares . . ."

Max: "Great question! Perfect question! You're absolutely right. Why should anyone care? The answer is about 50 pages back, in a chapter called John . . ."

I stood there astonished. As the conversation went on—for about fifteen minutes—the student read five more verses of Scripture focused on the Gospel. It was a strange sight to me, this guy with the New Testament in one hand, and a pornographic magazine in the other. After the third verse, the magazine slipped to the floor. I remember thinking, "Man, is *that* symbolic!"

As we left, the student actually thanked us for coming. He looked kind of stunned. I sure *felt* stunned. Here was a young man, not hostile perhaps, but certainly not interested in talking with us, who never-the-less was exposed to a clear presentation of Christ's offer of salvation. I was sure impressed with Max's boldness.

Here's the even more amazing thing: when Max and I left the student's room and went out on the landing, Max smiled and said, "I'm always scared to death when I do this; my knees are shaking."

And I had assumed he was totally calm and unafraid. Wow, was that encouraging to me! The lesson to me was that it's not just fearless people who share Christ with others (there are a few such people, I think), but average people who take seriously Christ's admonition to be His witnesses . . . like Max, me . . . and you. How do we get motivated and conquer our nervousness about witnessing for Christ, that scariest of all Christian endeavors? Let's consider some Scriptures.

Point # 1—Here are three facts & one conclusion

Fact one: people without Christ will spend an eternity in torment.

". . . the lake of burning sulfur, where the beast and the false prophet had been thrown. They will be tormented day and night forever and ever . . . If anyone's name was not found written in the book of life, he was thrown into the lake of fire." (Revelation 20:10, 15 NIV).

Fact two: people cannot believe in Christ unless they hear about him.

"How, then, can they call on the one they have not believed in? And how can they believe in the one of whom they have not heard?" (Romans 10:14 NIV).

Fact three: people will not hear about Christ unless a human being tells them.

"And how can they hear without someone preaching to them?" (Romans 10:14 NIV).

Conclusion: *You* are a human being who can, and should, tell people about Christ.

Point # 2—Here is a "Logic Loop" about witnessing for Christ. That is, it's a kind of circular logical process in which the conclusion leads us back to the start.

To begin with, the disciples said this, ". . . we cannot stop speaking what we have seen and heard." (Acts 4:20) The early disciples, though they had been ordered by the religious authorities to not witness for Christ, made the statement that they could *not not* speak about Christ. I like that.

Think about the idea of a "zone of discomfort," a circumstance or situation which makes one definitely uncomfortable. For many Christians, the "discomfort zone" *is* speaking about Christ; for these early followers, the discomfort zone was in *not* speaking about the Lord!

This verse was a great challenge to me personally as a young Christian. I told God that I wanted to be such a disciple, a man incapable of *not* telling others about Christ.

How did the early disciples come to this point?

"But Peter and the apostles answered and said, 'We must obey God rather than men.'" (Acts 5:29).

This gives us an insight into the hearts of the disciples—their basic motivation was one of obedience. What were they obeying? Just before his return to the Father in heaven, Jesus told his disciples, "You will be My witnesses in Jerusalem, and in all Judea, and Samaria, and even to the ends of the earth." (Acts 1:8) Has God commanded other believers, us, to tell people about Christ?

"I solemnly charge you in the presence of God and Christ Jesus, who is to judge the living and the dead, and by His appearing and His kingdom: preach the word; be ready in season and out of season . . . be sober in all things, endure hardship, do the work of an evangelist, fulfill your ministry" (2 Timothy 4:1, 2, 5)

That's a pretty powerful command the Apostle Paul gives in verse 1. We're charged . . . in the presence of God and Christ Jesus who will judge the living and dead . . . preach the word. Wow, this Scripture states very strongly that we are to be bold in proclaiming God's Word whether is seems "convenient" or not ("in season and out of season"). Verse 5 implies that even if we might feel "I'm just not an evangelist!" we are never-the-less told to . . . *do the work of an evangelist*. To those who might quibble and say that that command was for Timothy only, I would say that since it's now in the Scripture, it applies to us. Otherwise, we're guilty of reading Timothy's mail.

What's the result for *us* when we obey God in this regard? Let's look at John 14:21 again.

"He who has My commandments and keeps them, he it is who loves Me; and he who loves Me shall be loved by My Father, and I will love him, and will disclose Myself to him." (John 14:21)

This verse says that Christ loves those who obey his commandments and that he will "disclose (show) Myself to him." This is a great truth—Jesus reveals himself in a real, exciting way to those who obey him. The early disciples in Acts 4:20 said they couldn't stop speaking of what they had *seen and heard*; today we can be excited and motivated just as they were, by Christ revealing himself to us in his Word and through the Holy Spirit as we obey him.

This Scripture leads us right back to Acts 4:20. We "can't not" speak of what we have seen . . . and when we obey his commands, he shows himself to us. The spiritual reality of Christ is just on the other side of every act of obedience.

Point # 3—What hinders Christians from boldly sharing their faith in Christ? Consider these Scriptures:

"I am not ashamed of the gospel . . ." (Romans 1:16).

". . . rejoiced because they had been considered worthy to suffer shame for his Name." (Acts 5:41).

"And so Jesus also suffered outside the city gate to make the people holy through His own blood. Let us, then, go to outside the camp, bearing the shame He bore." (Hebrews 13:12, 13).

(Note: don't even look at Luke 9:26!).

Today, I believe, the issue is the same as it was in the first century: *shame*, or embarrassment. Christians may feel boldly about Christ inside their church communities, but embarrassed about him out in the world. But Jesus did not die in the Temple or any religious place; he died in public, either naked or mostly disrobed, and (supposedly) in disgrace. We as Christians today are also to "go outside the camp"—take the gospel outside of the walls of the church—being willing to be embarrassed about identifying with Jesus Christ and boldly telling the lost about salvation through Christ. As we do so, we have the assurance of this wonderful promise:

"So is My word that goes out from My mouth, it will not return to me empty, but will accomplish what I desire and achieve the purpose for which I sent it." (Isaiah 55:11)

God's word will not go out into the world and return empty; it will accomplish what He wants it to do in peoples' lives. Our job in witnessing is to simply tell people about Christ; it's up to the Holy Spirit and the power of the Word to do the persuading. This takes the burden off us to "convert" people, and puts it on God where it belongs.

Point # 4—Three stages in the growth of a witness for Christ:

Ability . . . simply knowing how to share the gospel, using the Scripture in an illustration or testimony.

Availability . . . the attitude that "God, I'll tell someone about Christ if you bring him or her to me." This is the stage which defines most Christian leaders, pastors, full-time workers.

Accountability . . . the conviction that God wants us to take the responsibility to go out and try to reach people, not merely wait for them to come to us . . . and the commitment to do it.

Point # 5—How to share the Gospel:

This is a simplified *Bridge to Life* illustration, originally designed by the *Navigators* ©. Used by permission. The "SDSD, all 3" acronym is my own version.

The SDSD refers to the first letters of the four points of the illustration; the "all 3" refers to each verse being from chapter 3 of the different Bible books.

- S = Peoples' **Situation**—Romans 3:23 ". . . for all have sinned and fall short of the glory of God."

- D = God's **Desire**—John 3:16 "For God so loved the world that He sent His one and only Son that whoever believes in Him shall not perish but have eternal life."

- S = God's **Solution**—1 Peter 3:18 "For Christ also died for sins once for all, the righteous for the unrighteous, to bring us to God, being put to death in the flesh, but made alive by the Spirit."

- D = Peoples' **Decision**—Revelation 3:20 "Behold, I stand at the door and knock. If anyone hears My voice and opens the door, I will come in and be with him and he with Me."

This is a pretty simple illustration to remember. Each of the four verses is from a chapter three, and once you get past the first one, Romans 3:23, the verse numbers go 16, 18, 20.

Let's go through how to share this with someone. We present this little illustration as simply as possible, drawing it out by hand on whatever paper is lying around. It may seem odd, but the less "professional" this gospel illustration is, the better.

Start by asking if you could draw out a little sketch that illustrates what the basic idea of Christianity is. I often say something like, "I'd like to show this to you, and see what you think." This lets the person know that I respect his or her opinions and input. It communicates that I'm not going to preach at them, or "guilt-trip" them.

Look at the little illustrations below. For the sake of clarity, I've shown this in two sketches, but when you do this with someone, you'd draw just one picture, adding to it as you go along.

Start by having the person you're sharing with read Romans 3:23, using his or her own Bible if possible (if she/he has one). For some psychological reason, people will trust their own Bible more than yours because it's been in their apartment, even if it's only propping up the DVD player.

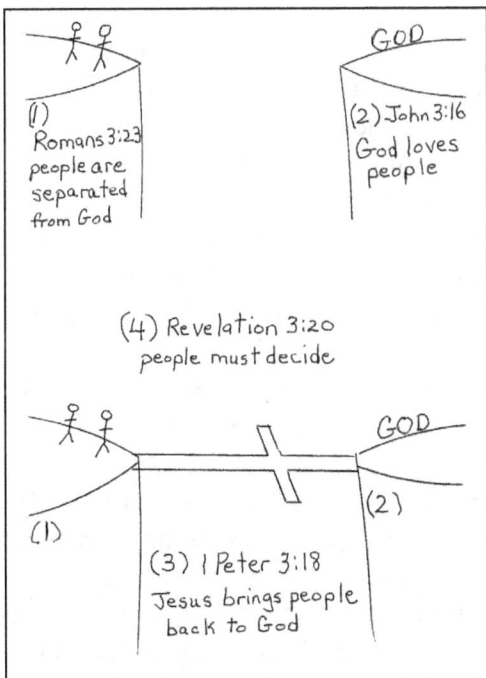

When the person reads the verse aloud, he sees the verse, and hears the words in his own voice in his own ears. This seems to give added credence to what he is reading.

Then draw in the two cliffs (yes, those are cliffs) with "people" on one side and God on the other side. If you want to, you can draw in little stick figures on the people's side. I have a good time making fun of my artistic ability, or lack thereof, when I do this sketch.

Then ask "What do you think that statement means?" (By the way, we call Bible verses "statements" because it sounds less religious. So, it's a *chapter* called Romans, *section* 3, and *statement* 23.) You can ask if she or he believes it's true that all people do wrong things, what the Bible calls "sin." The key thing for the person to understand is that we can't do wrong, selfish things and expect to be able to go into the presence of God, who is holy. We'd pollute God's presence, and God won't let that happen, even though he loves us.

Let most of the statements about what the verses mean come from the person to whom you are witnessing. Your part is asking questions. *SDSD, all 3* is mostly presented by asking questions and listening carefully to the answers. This helps the person hearing the gospel to not dismiss the concepts of the gospel as *your* opinion.

Then ask the person to read John 3:16. Ask "What do you think this statement means?" The idea of a loving God is the most difficult truth about God for modern people to believe or trust, because of all the pain and evil in the world, i.e., "If God is so loving and powerful, why does he allow that stuff to happen?" You can say that the Bible has a really good answer to that question, but ask if you could get into that later, or at another time. (Hint: it has to do with Romans 1:20–32).

The key point here is that God loves people, and sends his own Son, Jesus, to be the solution to the separation between God and people. If people believe in Jesus, they have eternal life.

Have the person read 1 Peter 3:18. Ask "What do you think that statement means?" Get the idea? Jesus dies for sins (people's sins) to bring us back to God. His death is a substitute payment for wrongs that people have done. Go into as much discussion as the person wants, but try to get through the illustration itself as quickly as possible. If too many side issues come in, it can muddy up the simplicity of the gospel.

Have the person read Revelation 3:20. Ask . . . you know what! "What do you think that means?" This just describes the decision each person must make about whether he or she *wants* a relationship with God. The door of a person's life that Christ is knocking on has only two functions: it opens to let Christ in, or it stays closed to keep Christ out.

That's it. Sometimes I'll ask in a friendly way, "Where do you think you are on this illustration? With God? On people's side? Somewhere in the middle?" There really isn't a middle position theologically, i.e., you can't be "sort of with God," but that viewpoint does express a degree of interest in moving toward God. Remember, don't preach at people. Be on their side and share good news with them. As my shop teacher used to say when we were using a power saw, "Don't force it. Let the tool do the work." In this case, let God's Word and the conviction of the Holy Spirit do the work of persuading. You simply, graciously and kindly, present the truths to the person.

The basic Biblical concepts are quite clear:

—Romans 3:23 . . . people do wrong things and it separates them from a holy God.

—John 3:16 . . . God loves people, but they can't get back to him on their own, so he sends an "agent", his Son, Jesus, to be the bridge. If people believe in him, the Son, they have eternal life. The next verse explains what it is a person must believe about the Son.

—1 Peter 3:18 . . . (best verse in the Bible about what Jesus did specifically!) Jesus dies for all sin, for all people, for all time to bring us back to God. His death is a substitute payment for sins on our behalf. This verse also mentions the resurrection, God's proof of his power over death.

—Revelation 3:20 . . . each person must make a personal decision whether to open the door of his or her life and ask Jesus to forgive his sin and come into his life. While some theologians may insist this Scripture is not really descriptive of a salvation decision, it is a clear illustration of a decision about opening the door between a person and Christ, whether it is a decision to be saved or to be more in obedience.

That's it! Can you use the little "SDSD, all 3" illustration to present the gospel to another? It's fine to practice this on your fellow believers, but even more exciting and profitable is to "practice" on non-believers! I recall one lady in North Carolina who was very nervous about sharing this illustration in front of the Bible study group, so she practiced on several of her non-Christian neighbors . . . great!

Remember what SDSD stands for, Situation, Desire, Solution, Decision . . . and what "statements" go with each step.

(People's) Situation = Romans 3:23

(God's)   Desire = John 3: 16

(God's)   Solution = 1 Peter 3: 18

(People's) Decision = Revelation 3:20

Then, just have the person you're talking to read those statements from a Bible, and you ask them, "What do you think that means?" for each statement. Give the person positive feedback, even praise, for their responses. Like the man who said, "I can live a month on a good compliment!" everyone likes to be praised. When I share the gospel, I realize that the lost are not opponents. I work to find good things to say to them about their insight into the verses, and the way they're approaching this profound issue.

Application!

Let's talk about two approaches to witnessing.

The first is going out to where people live or get together and initiate the conversation. In the old days, we called this "cold turkey" evangelism, and of course, it was the last thing anyone wanted to do.

The second is relationship evangelism. This means sharing the Gospel relationally with people you already know: family members, friends, co-workers, or neighbors.

Now here's the big surprise: the so-called "cold turkey" evangelism, which most Christians dread, is really pretty easy. In fact, to those of us who have worked to make Acts 4:20 (. . . can't *not* speak of Christ . . .) part of our lives, the "going out" style of evangelism is *much* easier than the relational kind.

Why is this so? First of all, there's no relationship at risk. If you talk with someone, for example, at some collegiate apartments, and a person says, "Not interested." (which, by the way, is about as harsh a rejection as we ever get), you haven't lost a friend or offended a relative. You just say, "Thanks, anyway." And move on.

Secondly, believe it or not, strangers have no hesitation at all in opening up to someone *they* don't know, for the same reason; there's nothing at risk. In fact, college students will often ask questions or share thoughts they would probably never share or ask with family or friends.

Thirdly, because you don't have to build up to sharing the gospel, or worry about making a smooth transition, you get to share the gospel pretty much anytime you go out.

You simply ask, "Want to see this?" They say, "Sure." And you do it. If they don't, you just say, "Thanks anyway," and move on.

And really all witnessing for Christ is simply two things: meeting people and telling them about Jesus.

How do we do this "going out" kind of evangelism?

The easiest situation is to go to student apartments near a college or university. If you live in a city or town with a university, there's sure to be lots of student apartments. Or, you can go to neighborhoods near your church. There's a "neighborhood survey" in this section.

Fast funny story: Once in a neighborhood, a friend and I began talking with a lady with a pretty ferocious dog on a leash, a boxer, I think. As we tried to talk with this lady about the Lord, the dog never quit barking and snapping at us. Finally we said goodbye, and walked away.

My friend, who was from the rural South, drawled "I wish I owned half that dog."

I said, "What do you mean?"

He said, "I'd shoot my half."

(by the way, my friend and I like dogs a lot . . . it was just funny).

We use a brief, five-question survey to break the ice with people and to jump right into a discussion about spiritual things. We do this survey in a fun, light-hearted manner, to put the persons at ease.

People's responses to the survey questions are very helpful. For example, if a person says her or his background is such-and-such a denomination, you recognize that he or she may have a real reverence for God, but little Bible knowledge. If a person with no church experience tells you she has a 10 interest (on a scale of 1—10), you can draw her out on why this is so, or what kind of spiritual issues she finds interesting. Listen carefully to what they share with you; don't be thinking about what *you're* going to say next. As the saying goes, "it's not about you." The survey gets the ball rolling, and most people love to talk about themselves and to share their opinions.

The last question of the survey has to do with defining what a Christian is . . . we then ask them if they'd like to take a few more minutes to see the "answer" to the last question. If they say "yes," we show them the SDSD, all 3 illustration. Pretty simple.

The nice thing about this kind of sharing is that you can gain a great deal of confidence in presenting the gospel, because you can share almost every time.

Here's our little survey:

FIVE QUESTION SURVEY

1. Do you have any religious affiliation or background?
2. On a scale from 1 to 10, what number would you give to your own personal interest in spiritual issues? (1 being very little & 10 being very high interest)
3. Would you say that interest has increased, decreased, or stayed the same during the past two or three years?
4. What one thing would you change about organized religion if you could? (something that bothers you about religion)
5. If someone from another culture (Hindu, etc.) were to ask you, "What is a Christian?" what would you say?

"If you'd like to, we have a real fast answer to that last question . . . it's a little illustration. If you'd like to see it, we could come back, or show it to you right now."

Further thoughts:

Dress casually (jeans- yes; ties- no). Be friendly and low-key. "Hi, we're with a Christian group and doing a little survey . . . 5 questions . . . takes 3 minutes. You get a million dollars if you get them all right!" No long pauses, solemn looks, etc. Don't introduce yourselves; they don't care and it's awkward. Jot down their first name later if they say you can come back. Don't write their phone number . . . that'll make them nervous. You already know where they live.

Don't be defensive, or judgmental of them, no matter what they say about God or religion. The lost are not the enemy; they're the victims of the enemy. Give some praise to the people you're talking to, even if they are negative about their experiences/opinions about religion. For example, you can say to someone who has shared a strong opinion, even if it's wrong or harsh, "I appreciate your saying that. It shows you've really done some thinking about these things." We want this to be a good "encounter" with a Christian for them, even if they're not convinced about the truth of the gospel. It could be a first positive step toward Christ.

Some people will be agreeable to seeing the gospel illustration then and there, but even more will agree if you ask if you can come back another time. This way they don't feel trapped, and it lets you keep your word about how much of their time you said you'd take.

Remember, our job is to present truth to people, not to try to persuade them to become Christians. (". . . not by the will of man . . ." John 1:13) If you get intense in a way they perceive as pressuring them, they will quite understandably become defensive. The goal of surveying is to share the gospel with those who might not have heard. It's between them and God, under the conviction of the Holy Spirit, whether they make a decision for Christ. And that decision may well come at a later time which means we may not ever know about it. That's okay. Some sow; some water; some reap. But it's all valuable for the kingdom.

Here's a little story I like to remember in reference to evangelism with college students. I was with a friend, Fred Robbins, one night at some student apartments, and we knocked on a door of an apartment. Inside were four or five guys. As I recall, there was some beer drinking going on. We said our little thing, "Hi, we're with a Christian group . . . etc" and one of them looked disgusted and said, "You guys are sure in the wrong place!" Fred and I said "Thanks," and went our way.

We were finishing a chat with a young woman on the floor below the beer-drinking guys, when one of them came looking for us and said, "The guys say you can come back up and do your survey, but I gotta tell you, they're just going to give you a hard time." Fred Robbins is pretty unflappable, and he just looked at me and shrugged. So up we went, into the lion's den. We talked with those guys for nearly a half hour, and at the end of it, one of them was almost in tears as we talked about God's love for them. Was it because Fred and I were brave or cool? No. We went into that apartment with humility, took the teasing graciously, then shared the Word of God. It's the power of the Word that softens the heart and gives light to the mind. What a privilege it is that we can still do this kind of witnessing to young people.

If you live near a college or university, and have some student apartments near the school, give this kind of evangelism a try. Get your bravest Christian friend to go with you. We've found that two people going to student apartments, or neighborhood homes, is ideal. Three is weird, and going alone is too scary.

Get some experience and practice in sharing the gospel illustration, so when you have opportunities to share *relationally*, you'll be able to do it confidently.

And here's a brief survey you can use in neighborhoods:

NEIGHBORHOOD SURVEY

1. Do you have any church or religious background?

2. On a scale of 1–10, how interested would you say you are in spiritual issues? 1 would mean very little interest, and 10 would mean a lot.

3. What kinds of things do you think a church could do to help people the most?

4. What do you think are the most important issues people face today... for example:

    How to raise kids

    How to be at peace & not worry

    Money issues

    Anything else?

5. Is there anything we could pray about for you... any worry, or something you'd like to have happen?

6. Do you think you've come to the point in your own spiritual journey where you know you'd like to connect with God? (if yes, share "SDSD, all 3")

Thanks very much for doing our survey. We want our church to be meaningful, and your answers are very helpful. Thanks!

Relationship witnessing... here's a simple 5-step illustration to help you think about how share with family, co-workers, and friends.

How to Share the Gospel Relationally—Five Steps to Get There...

1. Friendly talk—"I have become all things to all men..." (1 Corinthians 9: 22)

2. Identify with Christ—"I'm not ashamed . . ." (Romans 1:16)
3. Serious talk—". . . I observe that you are very religious . . ." (Acts 17:22ff.)
4. Share *your* story—Paul tells his story of how he became a Christian. (Acts 26: 4–23)
5. Share the gospel—"There is salvation in no one else . . ." (Acts 4:12)

Let me talk about this a bit. The idea of these five steps is that it allows us to think about where we are in our relationships with people, and how we could get to share Christ with them in a clear, inoffensive way. Just for the sake of illustration, let's say that a new family has moved into your neighborhood, or you have a new co-worker at your job.

Look at the *first step*, which is labeled "friendly talk." No hardship here; this is simply talking with the new neighbor or co-worker about all the usual stuff: sports, kid's softball, lawn mowers, etc. Draw this person out on what she/he is interested in. In 1 Corinthians 9, Paul says he is, ". . . all things to all people so that by all means I might win them." He goes on to say that to Jews who were under the Law, he, Paul, seemed to be just like them; to those who were without the Law, he seemed to be like *them*. To the weak, he seemed weak. He was simply "going where they were," in order to bring them to Christ.

I'd love to give a seminar sometime called "How To Be a Godly Phony Like Paul," the idea being that we accommodate ourselves to unbelievers, not to participate in their sin, or hide who we really are from them, but to get to know them, win their trust, and share Christ with them. So even if you despise NASCAR racing, but your new neighbor loves it, take an interest, for his sake and the sake of the gospel.

Now for *step two* . . . identifying with Christ. Pray that you can let this person know that you're a Christian, or at least a "religious" person (which is how they'll think of it). This is really pretty easy to do; we just have to get over any negative ideas that it's a bad thing to be thought of by non-Christians as "religious." This is where Paul's comment to the Romans (1:16) that he was . . . "not ashamed of the Gospel . . ." comes in.

This can be as simple a thing as saying to the new neighbor, "I hope having all the cars in front of our house on Tuesday nights doesn't bother you. That's our men's Bible study group." Or, just have a Bible on your desk at work. Obviously, don't identify with Christ in "church-talk" language, e.g., "By the way, just so you know, I'm a washed-in-the-blood-believer, and Jesus Christ is my Lord and Savior." That's all true, but not a good way to express your position to non-Christians.

Why is it important to let them know? For one thing, the longer we go in a friendship without letting the other person know we're Christian, the harder it becomes to share with him or her. Then when we try to bring up spiritual issues, they feel surprised or, even worse, tricked. Any hesitation that if we "show our hand" too quickly, we'll alienate them, is understandable but is really not a factor. People normally don't care if you're religious or not; they only care if you are a pushy or obnoxious religious person.

Secondly, believe it or not, many people will respect you for being religious, even in today's culture. They might feel it's a bit weird, but they'll still respect it. You may even find you'll get questions from non-Christians about religion, usually prefaced by a statement like, "Hey, you're religious . . . what'd you think about such-and-such?" These kinds of questions quite naturally open up more opportunities to move toward the gospel.

It may also be that when your non-Christian friends or relatives face serious illness, or other kinds of crises in their lives, they may come to you for comfort and counsel. They probably have no one else. This is when it's good that you're known as the "religious one" in the neighbor. Maybe it's not cool, but it's good for the Kingdom.

Thirdly, and even more amazingly, if they know you're "religious," you can tell them you'll pray for them about the things in their lives. For some reason that I can't quite fathom, even people who claim to be agnostic don't seem to mind being prayed for! Perhaps they feel good that you care about them and their concerns, or maybe they just think, "Why not? I'll take all the help I can get."

Step three . . . shifting from talk about superficial things to more serious topics of conversation takes a little more effort. In Acts 17, Paul speaks to the citizens of Athens, a city filled with idols of all kinds, in this way (my paraphrase):

People of Athens, I've been walking around in your city and I've noticed you have lots of idols, even one to an "unknown god." I guess that one's there to cover any you don't know about. My conclusion is that you are very religious people, and that's good, but I don't think you're really sure who you're worshipping. Let me tell you my thoughts on this.

Principle # 1: Be What You Want Others to Be. . . . 67

Then Paul goes on to share about the true God, not an idol made by human hands. He did a great job of making a transition from man-made idols to the living God. We may not be in a situation like Paul's in Athens, but we can work at making a shift from talking about everyday things to topics that can lead us to the gospel.

Try to think through on what serious topics might be hot-button issues for your neighbor or co-worker. Does she or he have teenagers to raise? Is he disappointed about getting passed over for the promotion? Has she expressed some fears or worries about money? The point here is to be a good listener. Very few people in this culture have a friend who will draw them out about important concerns and then listen sympathetically. It's okay to share some of your own thoughts or experiences about the issue, but it's always safe just to listen and tell her you'll pray for her about the concern. It's often the case that when a person does open up and share a concern with another person, that the other person listens briefly, then offers lots of advice, relevant or not. So it's good for you just to listen and say, "Wow, that really is important. The minute I get home, I'm going to pray for you about that."

Once we've built the foundation of a friendship, we can gently ask about their children, their job, their worry about health, or whatever the serious issue of their lives may be.

Step four . . . telling your own story about how you came into a relationship with God. This is your personal testimony. Again, Paul, in Acts 26, tells his story to King Agrippa of how he became a follower of Christ. It's basically a story of what he, Paul, was like before he met Christ, how it happened that he encountered Christ, and what it had meant to him since. When I first learned how to share my testimony, or story of salvation, it was common to try to get the whole gospel into the testimony. But my experience with this was it ended up sounding like a sermon rather than a step to *getting to* the gospel. So I prefer now to go gradually, and use the story of my coming to Christ as a way of relating to the other person, introducing God into the issue, and being a transition to asking if I could show him the gospel illustration.

How would this work with you and, let's say, your neighbor? Suppose your single-parent neighbor is having a tough time with her 15 year-old daughter. You might say something like the following:

"I know what you mean. I was really afraid of what would happen when my kids got to be teenagers. In fact, I had a lot of fear about relationships in general when I was younger. I was so afraid people wouldn't like me, that I'd do anything for them, and I never stood up for myself. So I got used and dropped a lot. I was afraid my kids would see this and realize that they could get away with anything, and that I wouldn't stop them or stand up to them, even when it was good for them.

"But by the time they got to be teens, I'd discovered an amazing thing. I was insecure about my relationships with people because I didn't have a relationship with God. Once I got that, it made all the difference in my other relationships. It really kind of freed me up to be myself, because I didn't worry about what other people thought of me. Well, I cared, but it didn't control me. It was my one good friend in high school who told me about God and how Jesus fits into the whole thing.

"I'd love to tell you about how I got to know God sometime. I think you're the kind of person who would really understand this stuff."

Did you notice something in this little story? It connected the Christian to the non-Christian with the common ground of *good relationships*, but it didn't really present the gospel. But if you can get to talk in this vein with a friend or neighbor, it's a pretty small step to showing them the little gospel illustration. ("Hey, let me show you this little deal about God. I'd love to hear what you think about it!) Then show them "SDSD, all 3."

Keep your story simple and genuine. If your personal story doesn't relate to what the other person is wrestling with, you can always say, "Wow, I never had *that* struggle, but I sure struggled with self-esteem and insecurity" (or whatever it may have been). You can still tell your story, and make the connection that we all struggle with *something*, even if they're not exactly the same struggles, and that God helped you with the struggle. The nice thing about sharing your personal story is that it's just that: your story. The other person can listen and see what you're saying, but without feeling preached at.

Step five . . . sharing the gospel with your neighbor or friend. So, you're gotten to know the person through friendly, superficial talk. You've let them know you're a Christian, or at least a religious person. You've made the transition and connected with them on at least one serious issue that concerns them. And you've told them, conversationally, about your own coming to consider a relationship with God as being the answer to what you were struggling with.

Now, simply ask her or him if you could show them a little illustration that shows how people get into a relationship with God. Tell them it just has four statements from the Bible, and you'd like to see what they think of it. Because you draw it out yourself, rather than a published tract, I think it seems less "religious" or canned. It's also less intimidating or awkward because you're both looking at the sketch, not at each other.

Draw out the "SDSD, all 3" illustration, asking questions of them about the Bible statements, and at the end thank them for their comments about it. You've now shared God's "living and active" Word (Hebrews 4:12), and given a person an opportunity to consider and receive Christ. Praise God!

Here's how I'd recommend you use this stair-step illustration:

1. Think of two non-Christian friends, neighbors, relatives, or co-workers: for example, Kyle and Drew, or Britney and Stacey.

2. Pray for each of those two people every day for just a few seconds, something like this, "God, please let me be able to let Kyle know I'm a Christian," or "Let me get a chance to talk about some more serious issues with Kyle," or whichever step you want to see happen. That's all. Just pray for that step.

3. When what you're praying for happens, pray that God would allow you to get to the next step. If you've just met them, pray you'd have a good, friendly chat with them. If you've already gotten to know them a bit, pray you'd be able to identify with Christ. If you've done that, pray that you'd be able to get to talk with them about some more serious topic. When you've done that, pray you could share your "story." Get the idea?

4. Don't stop praying for that step until you do it! *Then* pray for the next step. One thing this will do is make you aware every day that you have two people on your heart, with whom you desire to share the gospel. It will motivate you to take action. If you've prayed every day for a month, "God, please let me identify with Christ to Kyle and Drew," and you still haven't done it, you may feel pretty motivated to figure out a way to do it, even if it's just so you can pray something different, that is, for the next step. Seriously, if you'll do this, you will be amazed at the change in your own heart and motivation to share Christ with people.

Okay, now you've shared the gospel. You've gotten to go through the gospel illustration with one of the people you've been praying for. The fact is, you've done something very few Christians ever do their whole lives, been a clear witness for Christ!

Now what? Basically, it means talking with them about their questions, concerns, and puzzles about being a Christian. In Acts 17:32, it says,

"Now when they heard of the resurrection of the dead, some began to sneer, but others said, 'We want to hear more from you about this.'"

It's the ever-present truth: when people hear the gospel, some laugh at it and others want to learn more. So after you've share the gospel with someone, engage them in learning more. If they're mockers, you'll soon know it. Start by asking, "Remember that illustration I showed you? Have you had any more thoughts about it, or any questions?" If they bring up any questions, great! If they say, "No, I don't really have any questions, but I am thinking about it," that's still good. You can bring up some of these questions yourself to discuss with them. All of this will move them toward the point where you know they understand enough to make a decision for Christ.

After a while, you'll become aware of one of two situations: either they're losing interest, or . . . they're understanding what it means and taking it seriously. In this case, you could say, "You know, I really feel like you understand about Christ. Is that a decision you want to make?" If they hesitate, you can ask, "Is there anything that would keep you from making that decision?"

There can be things which make people hesitant to ask Christ in:
. . . fear of the unknown
. . . not wanting to give up sin
. . . other gods—self, $, etc
. . . still don't know enough
. . . have lost interest

In the Gospel of Mark, Jesus tells a parable about a farmer who sows seeds on the ground.

"Night and day, whether he sleeps or gets up, the seed sprouts and grows, though the farmer doesn't know how . . . but . . . as soon as the grain is ripe, he puts the sickle to it, because the harvest has come." (Mark 4:26—29).

The farmer's part is to sow the seed, then harvest the mature grain. He doesn't even understand how the seed germinates, sprouts, grows, and matures. That's God's part. But he does know when it's ready to harvest.

Our part in evangelism is like that. We are asked by the Lord to sow the imperishable seed of the gospel. How God turns people's hearts, minds, and wills to him, only he really knows. But we can tell when it's happened. We can recognize when a person has responded to the truth of God's Word, and we can quietly say, "Won't you ask Christ into your life now?"

A friend once sent me this encouragement from Psalm 126:

"Those who sow in tears shall reap with joyful shouting. He who goes to and fro weeping, carrying his bag of seed, shall come again with a shout of joy, bring his sheaves with him." (Psalm 126:5, 6).

Isn't that great! Being courageous to tell others about Christ may seem hard and scary, but the result is joy for us and for them.

7. Scripture Memory . . .

What comes to mind when you hear the phrase "Scripture memory"? I'd guess many Christians would think of children's programs like Awana's, or the "sword drills" kids used to do at church camp. Perhaps a result of this connection is that people might think of Bible memorization as something kids do, not adults.

But committing portions of the Bible to memory is a fantastic benefit for anybody, young or old(er). To "know it by heart," as we used to call memorization, is one of the most useful and encouraging ways to connect with Scripture. As with evangelism, there can be some nervous anxiety about memorizing Scripture, not fearfulness as a rule, but a "I just can't do it!" concern that some adults may have.

Actually, I think that most people are quite good at memorizing. Maybe the reason they feel they're not is simply that there aren't many circumstances in modern life that require careful, precise memorization. Most data that we use frequently is electronically stored and available with speed-dial ease. It was a long time before I even knew my own cell phone number by heart.

It may be that people worry about the *discipline* that's required to memorize a Bible verse, but that's the very thing that makes Scripture memory so valuable. It's the careful focus and *work* that it takes to commit a verse to memory that slows us down, makes us dwell on the words, and imparts understanding and conviction.

I think there are two major benefits of Scripture Memory:

First, it's a uniquely powerful input on the Word of God in *my* life, especially in helping me combat sin.

"How can a young man keep his way pure? By guarding it according to Thy Word . . . Thy Word I have laid up in my heart that I might not sin against you." (Psalm 119:9, 11).

A college student at Iowa State said he'd identified four big "red flag" areas of sin that tempted him, and he'd memorized a verse of Scripture for each red flag. Then when he was tempted, he'd just quote the appropriate verse to himself as a guard against the temptation. What a great idea! I don't know what his red flags were (I can probably make a guess at a couple), but here are four good ones:

—When we're tempted to say something stupid, hurtful, or boastful.

"For we all stumble in many ways. If anyone does not stumble in what he says, he is a perfect man, able to bridle the whole body as well." (James 3:2).

—When we're wrestling with lustful thoughts.

"But I tell you that anyone who looks at a woman lustfully has already committed adultery with her in his heart." (Matthew 5:28).

—When we're struggling to overcome worry.

"Do not be anxious about anything, but in everything by prayer and petition, with thanksgiving, present your requests to God. And the peace of God, which transcends all understanding, will guard your hearts and your minds in Christ Jesus." (Philippians 4:6, 7).

—When we are angry.

". . . for the anger of man does not achieve the righteousness of God." (James 1:20).

Even the Lord, to combat the temptations of the devil, as related in Matthew 4:1 ff, answered each temptation by saying "It is written . . ." then quoted an appropriate Scripture. If we have the truths of Scripture "laid up" in our hearts, we have an instant response to the temptations in our lives too.

We also benefit from Scripture memory by gaining a more profound understanding of the Bible passages we're "laying up in our hearts."

"This book of the law shall not depart out of your mouth, but you shall *meditate* on it day and night that you may be careful to do according to all that is written in it. Then you shall make your way prosperous and then you shall have good success." (Joshua 1:8).

Our culture and fast-paced lives do not often promote deep thinking, mentally dwelling on issues or ideas for an extended period of time in order to get beneath the surface level of understanding, i.e., the obvious. I think that's what meditating is. Reflecting at length on a passage of Scripture is greatly helped by memorization, for it allows the person to think deeply about the verses in a slow, careful way.

When I was a young Christian, I was part of a group that encouraged Scripture memory, but I really struggled with it. My attempts were pretty half-hearted and I didn't do well. But one day as I started out on a long car trip alone, I decided I'd memorize a whole chapter of the Bible, just to prove to myself that I could do it. I memorized Colossians, chapter 3, that day.

All these years later, I still have it committed to memory, but more importantly, I have gotten *so much* encouragement and understanding from that one passage. For me, the parts of the Bible I've memorized become especially powerful and useful.

Here's another great benefit: we can use the memorized Word to *help others*.

"Be diligent to present yourself approved to God as a workman who does not need to be ashamed, handling accurately the word of truth." (2 Timothy 2:15) . . . "For the Word of God is living and active. Sharper than any double-edged sword, it penetrates even to dividing soul and spirit, joints and marrow; it judges the thoughts and attitudes of the heart." (Hebrews 4:12 NIV)

Simply having an appropriate verse of Scripture to share with another person in a time of need is often the best help we can give. It is the nature of the Word of God, as Hebrews 4:12 points out, to clarify an issue and even reveal if a person has a wrong heart attitude about the issue.

As 2 Timothy 2:15 implies, accurately handling God's Word is an essential part of doing Christian ministry. And my experience is that in the vast majority of ministry situations—in which people need counsel, advice, or problem-solving—the issues fall into only five or six types. That means in a relatively short time, you can have a good solid foundation of memorized "answers" from Scripture to address many people's life situations.

When my wife and I were in collegiate ministry in the Midwest, I visited some of the ministry team guys in their dorm room. It was evident that there had been a intense discussion going on when I arrived. So I asked, "What's the hot topic, guys?"

No big surprise here . . . it was about girls, and the dating practice of one of the Christian guys in the group. To put it mildly, what the young Christian thought was acceptable in dating was pretty worldly. The students said they'd been arguing about this for days. That the young Christian's friends were concerned for him was very good; that they weren't basing their objections on Scripture was not. Without the authority of Scripture, arguments become just a war of opinions.

I said, "How about I Timothy 5 . . . the first couple of verses. Does that help, as a general rule?" One of the guys got a Bible out and read the verses aloud. In this passage, Paul is talking to Timothy about relationships in the Christian community. He urges Timothy, and other young men, to relate to ". . . younger women as sisters, with absolute purity."

I asked the guys if any of them had sisters. A couple of them did. "Have you ever gone to a movie, or something with your sister, I mean, just for fun?" Yes, of course. "Did you make out with your sister?" Cries of outrage . . . "That's gross!"

"Yes, it would be . . . and wrong. Like it or not, guys, the Bible says you're supposed to treat young women like you would your sister."

The discussion went on from there, but it was different. It was now no longer *opinions* about what was right or wrong, but how they felt about what the Bible said about sexual purity. The guys in that dorm room understood what the Bible was saying, whether they agreed wholeheartedly with it or not. But they had not known that verse, and that made all the difference. Having memorized that Scripture verse, and the topic it addressed, I believe I was able to help get some Biblical insight into that dorm room discussion.

How to get going on Scripture memory

For some, the best start is to just write down all those great Scriptures you've kind of known for years. You know, the ones you can roughly paraphrase, but don't know the references. Jot them down on cards (small index cards cut in half are great), with the references, and go at it.

There are also several good published Scripture memory guides that I know of, but I think one of the best is one that's been around for many years, the Navigators' *Topical Memory System*. You can buy the "TMS" at most Christian bookstores, or order it from NavPress.

As the name indicates, the TMS has Bible verses that are topically selected and arranged. I won't describe the TMS in detail; I'll just mention that there are five big categories, with six sub-categories in each big category, and with two verses for each sub-category. That is, there are 60 verses, or brief passages, in this memory system, and the Scriptures selected are keyed to topics geared to Christian growth, sharing the gospel, and victory in the Christian life.

One important aspect of beginning to memorize Scripture: don't over-challenge yourself. One verse per week, with review, is probably about right for most people. Scripture memory can be one of the areas of great encouragement and success if the expectations are realistic. Remember, it's the long haul that's important, not just a burst of achievement at the beginning.

Here's a story I love; I doubt that it's true, but it's funny. Supposedly, at a campus in the Northeast, a Navigator staff person gave a TMS with its 60 verses to a student, and said, "I'll see you next week." The following week the student met with the Navigator staff, having memorized all 60 verses, and said, "I've gotta tell you . . . I don't think I can keep up this pace."

When you memorize a verse of Scripture, regardless of which version of the Bible you're using, memorize it "word perfect." The point here is that you can't *review* a verse if it's paraphrased or quoted slightly different every time.

As with so many things in the Christian life, a great key to success is having someone else do it with you. Recruit a couple of friends to join you in this excellent input of the Word. Then when you see these friends, check each other on your verses. My experience is that most Christians really like checking verses with others. It gives them a sense of progress in their Christian lives, something that many believers seldom feel. In fact, I think Scripture memorization (along with evangelism) is one of the practices most believers think is something "really mature" Christians do.

Is there a trick to memorizing? It may seem unusual to discuss the "mechanics" of memorizing, but in today's culture, many folks are unaccustomed to the process. Here are some thoughts:

If you've purchased a Scripture memory guide, like the *Topical Memory System*, the booklet included is quite good in presenting ways to memorize and review verses. Different people memorize in different ways.

—some actually visualize the verse card itself.

—some learn by rote . . . saying the verse over and over again, phrase by phrase, until it *sounds right* when they quote it.

—some memorize by first grasping the concept of what the verse means, then "hanging" the actual words on the framework of the meaning.

—some join the reference to the verse by use of a mental picture . . . this is helpful for verses which seem unusually difficult to remember. I did this for Hebrews 10:31, a verse that just seemed to elude me. I pictured a tent pitched near a cliff; a "biblical-looking" Hebrew (robes, etc.) walks out of the tent to get a drink of water because he is a "thirsty one." He falls over the cliff into a giant hand. Get the picture? Hebrew-tent-thirsty one (Hebrews ten, thirty-one) . . . "It is a fearful thing to fall into the hands of the living God." (Okay, laugh! But I bet you remember this verse!)

Maybe the toughest part of succeeding at Scripture memory is reviewing the verses you've already memorized. When I'd gotten about 10 or 11 verses pretty well nailed down, I realized that if I learned two new ones, I forgot a couple of the old ones. My mental picture of this was like a person walking across a big patch of muddy ground using two wide boards to get across. He'd stand on one, pick up the one behind and place it in front, then move to that board, pick up the one behind, and do this over and over.

That's how I felt I was doing Bible memory; when I gained one in front, I'd lose one behind. The key is to have a little system of review, so even if we do get rusty on some, we're still making progress. A simple way is to just keep all your index cards with verses in one place. Once every few months or so, go through them from the very beginning and review them.

Some verses seem to imbed themselves in our brains the very first time we see them, and review is easy. Others are difficult to remember no matter how many times we review them. Just be patient with Scripture memory, have a friend check you on a regular basis, and you'll have a powerful grip on the sword of the Word. It's a discipline that produces a reward beyond your greatest expectation.

These are the seven disciplines. Please remember that becoming consistent in such things as Quiet Times, prayer, Bible study, witnessing, Scripture memory . . . does not come quickly. Don't get discouraged if you fail and fail again. The goal is to grow in your relationship with God, to draw nearer to him and learn to trust him. That we do this through such disciplines may not seem particularly spiritual, but this simply reflects the reality that we're still living in fleshly bodies on earth, and God is Spirit. As Paul says in Philippians 1, he desired to ". . . depart and be with Christ, which is better by far . . . " that is, in heaven we'll be face to face with the Lord. But until then, we work on our relationship with the living God by time in the Word, prayer, and obedience.

The 3 of the "7 and the 3 . . . "

The 3 refers to the three *character areas* of holiness, humility, and having God's perspective on money and material goods. These are the three "opposite" attributes of the sin areas stated in 1 John 2: 15, 16 ". . . lust of the flesh, lust of the eyes, and pride of life."

The opposite of lust of the flesh is holiness.

The opposite of lust of the eyes is contentment, and having God's perspective on money and stuff.

The opposite of pride and self-esteem issues is humility.

The first thing to realize about growth in character is that it is a life-long work-in-progess. In regard to holiness, humility, and seeing stuff and money as God does, it would be unwise to think, "Okay, I've got that area mastered." The prideful thought, moment of lust, or coveting something can and will raise its ugly head from time to time. The question is this: am I growing—making good progress—in these areas of Christ-like character, or am I in a continual state of defeat?

My friend, Bob Lovvorn, on staff with The Navigators, had a good illustration of this battle between the world's values and Christ-like character. (Giving credit where credit is due, I don't know if this illustration originated with Bob Lovvorn; I only know that I heard it from him.) He called the illustration the "Chain and Rubber Band" illustration; it's based on Romans 12:2

"And do not be conformed to this world, but rather be transformed by the renewing of your mind, that you may prove what the will of God is, that which is good and acceptable and perfect."

"Conform" means to *take on* the shape or form of the world, like putty pressed into a mold. "Transform" means to *change* the shape or form of something, based on a design or pattern that the thing or person desires to be, in this case, the good and perfect and acceptable will of God. The idea was to picture a person standing between two items: a Bible on one side, and a world globe, representing the world and the world's values, on the other side. The values of the world are clearly defined by 1 John 2:15, 16:

"For all that is in the world, the lust of the flesh, and the lust of the eyes, and the boastful pride of life; is not of the Father but of the world."

The unchangeable truth of the Bible is also clear: "The totality of the Word is truth, and every one of thy righteous ordinances endures forever." (Psalm 119:160).

The person in the middle, between these two irreconcilable value systems, is attached to both items by either a chain or a rubber band. If the chain, strong and inflexible, is attached to the world, and the rubber band is attached to the Bible, then the person will be pulled along behind the world and its values. He or she will feel a tension from the stretching rubber band attached to the Bible as she or he moves away from the values of Scripture. This person will probably feel guilt or shame, but the drag of the world pulls anyway. He or she may not be *as bad* as most in the world, but is none-the-less trailing along behind in the world's direction, which is usually toward increasing depravity.

There may come a point at which the rubber band is stretched beyond its strength and it breaks. Then there is no feeling of guilt, shame, or conviction at all, and the person—even if a saved Christian—may seem little different than the non-Christians who love and pursue the values of the world. (see I Corinthians 5:1–5 for an example).

If, however, the chain is attached to the Bible, with the rubber band attached to the world, the person will not be dragged along behind the world. The person will certainly feel the strain on the rubber band as the world's values become increasingly perverse, but he or she will be held against the pull of immorality, greed, and arrogance. In fact, as the person is increasingly transformed by the Word's renewal of their minds, it pulls them closer and closer—chain link by chain link—to the truth which sets them free.

Holiness

Not too long ago, a young person involved in a college ministry said to friends during a Bible study, "Do you think we'll be done by 8:30? I don't want to miss _____. My roommate and I always get together to watch that show." The TV show mentioned was a weekly serial noted mostly for obscene language and a light-hearted portrayal of on-going sexual immorality between the main characters.

Saddened as I was that this young Christian watched that particular TV show, I was even more discouraged by the fact that the person apparently lacked any discernment that the show might be bad, since it was mentioned so openly during the Bible study.

Is this a big deal? Those of us involved in ministry with young people these days notice some real conflict between biblical holiness, and the language and behavior which seem to be the cultural "norm." Some Christian college students commonly use words that used to be considered questionable at best, and do not seem troubled by music downloads or music sharing without payment. Part of this is due, I believe, to changes in our culture. The common use of some obscenities, for example, results in part, I think, from young people not knowing the origins of the words they use, most of which have sexual or human-body-function etymologies. Plus, many Christians seem to have a high felt need for secular entertainment, and the use of these words and behaviors in movies and TV is very common. To some people, even believers, whatever is common is seen as normal, and whatever is normal is seen as acceptable. Discernment is lacking here.

Whatever the reason, there is often a casual attitude toward personal holiness. My own impression is that holiness is not seen as desirable or attractive to some Christians today. Perhaps they have an idea that holiness is boring, depressing, or restrictive.

One thing I am convinced of, holiness of life must be based upon a deep personal conviction and desire. It does not come from a group agreeing to "emphasize holiness this semester;" it does not come from electronic "safeguards" or "software covenants" to keep on-line users from pornography; it does not come from a youth pastor patrolling social networking pages; it does not come from sermon admonitions. It comes only from an individual person declaring in his or her heart before God, "Please, Lord, help me to live a holy life!" It takes a deliberate commitment to walk with the Lord in purity, and a willingness to be different, not just from the world but also from the prevailing lax Christian culture. Holiness is, at heart, personal, not communal (thought it certainly affects the Christian community; again, see 1 Corinthians 5:1–13).

The willingness to be holy means a willingness to be different, and that takes courage; the courage comes from convictions, and those convictions come only from knowledge and obedience to Scripture.

It's a challenge to bring holiness into focus in the midst of a secular culture which either ridicules or redefines it. Holiness today concerns *at least* these issues:

—sexual purity . . . if single, chaste; if married, faithful.

—thought life . . . are we holy in heart and mind as well as actions?

—integrity . . . being honest, and doing what you say you will do.

Let's establish some basic assumptions about holiness:

The Bible is our ultimate guide, not the news media or TV shows or what our friends say. "All Scripture is inspired by God and profitable for teaching, for reproof, for correction, and for training in righteousness." (2 Timothy 3:16).

The Bible does speak to the issue of personal holiness in a practical way ". . . all things pertaining to life and godliness." (2 Peter 1: 3, 4).

What God commands is for our good. ". . . keep the Lord's commands and statutes . . . for your own good." (Deuteronomy 10: 12, 13).

I think a good starting point for discussing holiness is to look at a familiar verse:

"No temptation has seized you except what is common to man. And God is faithful; He will not let you be tempted beyond what you can bear. But when you are tempted, He will also provide a way out so that you can stand up under it." (1 Corinthians 10:13 NIV).

It may not sound like such good news that our most common excuse for sinning—"I just couldn't resist!"—is taken away here, but it *is* good news. It says straight out that we're all basically tempted in the same ways, that God won't let us be tempted more than our level of faith can bear, and that he'll always give us a good way out, so we don't have to give in. In a way, it's kind of flattering if we feel we are faced with strong temptations. It implies that God must know that we're strong enough to resist these temptations since he won't let us be tempted beyond our strength. This promise of God lets us know we have more than a fighting chance of being holy if we really want to be.

"As obedient children, do not conform to the evil desires you had when you lived in ignorance. But just as He who called you is holy, so you be holy in all your behavior, for it is written, 'Be holy, because I am holy...'" (1 Peter 1:14, 15).

When Peter exhorts people to be holy, it's not just some pretty fluff n' stuff Bible jargon. It's meant seriously and literally. And we can actually do it. We can live holy lives.

Sexual purity:

How would you describe the way the world thinks about sex? What is the world's "recommendation" to people concerning how they consider their sexuality?

There's certainly no big surprise here. As a "proof of statement," I could simply refer you to any given evening of TV, or the vast majority of current films. The world's view of human sexuality is, at best, that people are simply biological beings with reproductive instincts, and that as long as disease or pregnancy controls are taken, those instincts should be given free rein. To do otherwise, the world implies, is to go against nature.

It's a sad irony that the *perversion* of God-given sexuality is seen as normal and good, and that those who desire to be godly in this regard are portrayed as perverse and abnormal. That's the world's view in a nutshell. "...who call evil good, and good evil..." (Isaiah 5:20).

What effect do you believe the worldly philosophy about sex has on Christians' thinking about sex?

   a. No effect at all

   b. A damaging effect

   c. A helpful effect... it "balances" out the Bible

The answer is b. The influence of the world's value system inflicts devastating damage to people, non-Christians and believers alike, who allow themselves to be drawn into a sexually immoral life. The damage is physical (37 STD's today, the viral ones incurable); emotional (promiscuity and infidelity result in guilt, shame, and a diminished self-worth); relational (sense of betrayal, broken trust, anger) . . . and the damage is usually permanent, if the Lord's forgiveness and healing is not sought.

What is the Bible's general teaching about our bodies and sex? Here are some helpful verses of Scripture:

> "Therefore, do not let sin reign in your mortal bodies so that you obey its evil desires. Do not offer the parts of your body to sin, as instruments of wickedness, but rather offer yourselves to God, as those who have been brought from death to life; and offer the parts of your body to him as instruments of righteousness . . . Therefore, I urge you, brothers, in view of God's mercy, to offer your bodies as living sacrifices, holy and pleasing to God . . ." (Romans 6:12–14 & 12:1 NIV)

The impressive thing to me about this passage is that it so directly confronts our choice-making as regards holiness. Remember your old 7th grade English class, when the poor teacher tried to explain "implied pronouns"? Boring then perhaps, but serious stuff now, because the implied pronoun in the passage above is "You."(You) "therefore, no not let sin reign . . ." (You) "do not offer the parts of your body to sin . . ." (You) "offer yourselves to God . . ."

Why is this significant? Because it puts the responsibility for holiness on us. We either take it seriously or we don't. The word "holiness" may evoke a feeling of mysticism, but the striving after personal holiness is anything but mystical. It is very practical, a matter of daily determination. Look at 1 Thessalonians 4:3–7 for a good statement of our responsibility in holiness, especially as it relates to our sexuality.

"For it is God's will . . . that you should avoid sexual immorality; that each of you should learn to control his own body in a way that is holy and honorable, not in passionate lust like the heathen, who do not know God . . . The Lord will punish men for all such sins, as we have already told you and warned you. For God did not call us to be impure, but to live a holy life." (1 Thessalonians 4:3–7 NIV).

It is important that we "control" our sexuality rather than be controlled by it. In truth, it is a clear defining of a major difference between

Christians and those "... who do not know God ..." or it certainly should be! When Christians—especially those who identify themselves as Christian leaders—fail in this matter of sexual purity or fidelity, not only is it personal defeat, but it's one of the most terrible indictments against the truth and power of the Christian faith, at least in the eyes of non-believers. Paul told the church at Rome that their conduct was seen and judged by the world: "... through your breaking the Law, do you dishonor God? FOR THE NAME OF GOD IS BLASPHEMED AMONG THE GENTILES BECAUSE OF YOU." (Romans 2; 23, 24)

Paul writes to the church at Corinth, folks that struggled in this area, this clear and practical theology:

"Flee from sexual immorality. All other sins a man (person) commits are outside his body, but the one who sins sexually sins against his own body. Do you not know that your body is a temple of the Holy Spirit, who is in you, whom you have received from God? You are not your own; you were bought with a price. Therefore honor God with your body." (1 Corinthians 6:18-20 NIV).

Can there be any greater motivation for sexual purity than the realization that the Holy Spirit of God dwells within us? If our bodies are the dwelling place of God, and the sexually immoral person uses his or her body to commit sexual sin, it defiles the very place the Holy Spirit dwells. Remember the anger of the Lord about the Temple in Jerusalem being used as a place of fraudulent business (Mark 11); how much greater a shame is the use of the temple of God now for purposes of immorality.

Quick thoughts on dating: The Bible doesn't say much specifically about the relatively modern practice of dating, but there are some valuable principles on mutual respect, trusting God for a mate, and holiness in relationships.

Probably the *worst* example of dating in the Bible is found in Judges 14:1-3; Samson says to his father, "Get her for me, for she looks good to me!" What a classic adolescent-minded standard for selection: "She looks good!" Samson's relationships with women are definitely not an example to follow.

Here are three guidelines for dating:

1. I Timothy 5:2 "... treat younger women as sisters, in all purity."

This is a good foundational principle, because it is a safeguard. Christians may date today as a social function, as much as a prelude to courtship, so the brother-sister admonition is especially helpful. Christian group activities are often the best bet for social dating, rather than being alone one-to-one, as there's less chance that hormones or romantic solitude will cause problems for even well-intentioned believers.

   2. II Corinthians 6:14, 15 "... do not be yoked together with unbelievers... What does a believer have in common with unbelievers?"

There's no such thing as "dating evangelism," and certainly not "marriage evangelism," so don't even entertain the idea of dating a non-Christian because that's the first step toward marriage. I might take this one step further, and suggest if you are a serious Christian, don't date a merely nominal Christian. As many have discovered, to try to do serious ministry when the spouse is not interested, is like driving with one foot on the gas and the other pressed hard on the brake.

   3. Jeremiah 29:11 "'I know the plans I have for you,' declares the Lord, 'plans to prosper you and not to harm you, plans to give you a hope and a future.'"

Trust God for choosing a person to be your husband or wife. This is God's promise to believers who trust him, that he will not hurt them but give them a hope and future, including a good mate. This is a promise he will keep. Abraham was a person who believed and trusted.

"He did not waver through unbelief regarding the promise of God, but was strengthened in his faith and gave glory to God, being fully persuaded that God had power to do what he had promised." (Romans 4: 20, 21 NIV).

Keeping our thought life pure:

Read James 1:13–15. What's the process that begins with temptation (which is not sin in itself) and ends with an "accomplished sin"?

"... but each one is tempted when, by his own evil desire, he is dragged away and enticed. Then, after desire has conceived, it gives birth to sin; and sin, when it is full grown, gives birth to death." (NIV)

Remember, the temptation is not sin. Even the Lord was tempted, but did not sin. (Hebrews 4:15 "... tempted in every way, just as we are, yet without sin.") It's what we do when we're tempted that counts. In the description above in James, *giving in* to temptation seems to go like this:

—here's a temptation . . . for example, a temptation to sexual lust.

—if a person's desire is wrong (evil), he or she will be dragged away.

—the sin is conceived, comes alive . . . now it's sin, not just temptation.

—the sin grows naturally to its full size, or potential to harm.

Where does one break this cycle, so that even when tempted, the sin is not conceived?

In the mind. The battleground is our mind, our thought life. We all know this is so; it's *thinking* about the sinful pleasure (evil desire) that the temptation provokes which brings defeat. We don't unknowingly find ourselves in sin, wondering "How in the world did *that* happen!?" We know how it happened because we thought about it and chose the sin and the defeat for its moment of perverse pleasure. Romans 8:6 says,

"For the mind set on the flesh is death, but the mind set on the Spirit is life and peace."

Colossians 3:1, 2 puts it this way:

"If then you have been raised up with Christ, keep seeking the things above, where Christ is, seated at the right hand of God. Set you mind on the things above, not on the things that are on earth."

Here are some other verses on having a pure thought life.

". . . whatever is true, whatever is noble, whatever is right, whatever is pure, whatever is lovely, whatever is admirable if anything is excellent or praiseworthy, think about such things." (Philippians 4:8)

Someone has suggested that this verse would make a good criterion for selecting TV shows or movies. That is, ask; "Is this true, pure, worthy of praise?" Wow, would that change some entertainment habits.

". . . we take captive every thought to make it obedient to Christ." (2 Corinthians 10:5).

Want to try something pretty radical? Mark a day on your calendar and literally apply this verse, to take every thought "captive to Christ." What do you think will happen? Do you think you can do it? I realized that sometimes when I had read Bible verses like that one, I tended to view them as lofty, unrealistic statements of piety, and not really applicable. Well, one day I decided to actually see how long I could last, in attempting to take every thought captive to Christ. I imagined I'd last about five minutes, but I was amazed at how achievable it was. Much of that day was victorious in terms of having a pure thought life.

The very discipline of keeping my mind focussed on a sort of "What would Jesus think about this?" (WWJT?) mentality, allowed me to experience far more victory in my thought life than I had imagined possible. Dear friends, this is an area of our lives where great progress can be made. I think it's important because our thoughts are so private and we're so good at shielding our thoughts from others, we can become easily defeated.

Honesty and integrity:

I'll admit it; there's a part of my sense of humor that loves exaggeration. I like the silliness of stories like the Florida citrus grower that said his oranges were so big it only took four to make a dozen. Or the time a tourist asked that same grower if he'd squeeze him some orange juice. The grower asked how much he wanted. The tourist said he wanted about twenty quarts. The grower snorted and said he wasn't going to waste a whole orange for just twenty quarts!

But there's another kind of reality-twisting that erodes the foundation of Christian character: lying. Paul said to the Colossian church,

"Do not lie to each other since you have taken off your old self with its practices, and have out on the new self, which is being renewed in knowledge in the image of its Creator." (Colossians 3:9, 10 NIV).

James also says to tell it like it is: ". . . let your yes be yes, and your no, no, so that you may not fall under judgement." (James 5:12).

So why do we lie, exaggerate, or imply things which we know are not true? There are probably several reasons. I'll speak from my own experience in struggling with lying and exaggeration.

—A person might exaggerate in the belief that others will be more impressed with him, or find him more interesting, than if he told them the truth. The sad implication of this, of course, is that that person's self-esteem is based upon what other people think of him or her, and that's about as pathetic a plight as a person can experience, for we can never find peace and satisfaction in trying to impress everyone.

—A person might lie to get out of some tough situation. For example, if someone asks a person to baby-sit for them, that person might not want to say "I'm sorry, but I'm exhausted and just want to rest up this weekend." The easier thing to do is make an excuse that sounds less selfish. "Oh, I'm sorry, I'd love to baby-sit, but I've already told so-and-so that I'd help them with their algebra." Of course, as Mark Twain said, "No one has a good enough memory to be a successful liar." And sure enough, the person who needed the baby-sitter will probably ask you weeks later, "How's so-and-so's algebra coming?" Your look of total incomprehension about the fictitious algebra student will reveal your lie.

—A person might lie in a group simply to top a story someone else has related. If someone has told of a cousin who hiked the Appalachian Trail, there's sure to be someone whose grandfather did it *twice*, before it was even marked as a trail! This kind of thing happens in both non-Christian and Christian group settings.

—There's another form of dishonesty that I found myself guilty of more than once, even as a Christian: it's saying I'd do something and then not doing it. I once told our campus ministry leader that I'd line the goal areas of the soccer field before our game on Saturday. Saturday came and the field was not lined. The leader asked me why, and I gave some kind of lame excuse. He looked me right in the eye and said quietly, "Cunneen, you're an unfaithful man."

I know that sounds harsh and politically incorrect, i.e., you're supposed to reprove the behavior, not the person, and so on. But it was exactly what I needed to hear. Faithfulness *is* doing what you say you're going to do. It defines God's faithfulness. "Has He said, and will He not do it? Has He spoken, and will He not fulfill it? (Numbers 23: 19)

I was meeting with a young man about a year ago, and I told him the story of the unlined soccer field, and he said, "Are you telling me this because I said I'd do the Bible study for today, and I didn't?" I said, "Yes." If you asked that young man today, "What's the most valuable thing Cunneen ever shared with you?" he'd probably say it was the soccer field story.

I think that the best encouragement for us to work hard on strengthening our IQ, Integrity Quality, is to appreciate some key truths:

—I am how God made me, which is good; I don't need to impress anyone by exaggerating.

—If I tell a lie to get out of a tough situation, I'll probably still have the situation facing me in the near future, and people often see through the lies anyway. The only difference is that now others have a lower opinion of me.

—If I lie just to please someone, or say what I think they want to hear, I either have to live it out or show them that I didn't mean it.

—Good relationships are always based on truthful communication. If I lie to people, I'm going to hurt my relationships because people won't know if they can trust me.

—It hurts the heart of God when I lie.

—If I say I will do something and I do it, it reflects faithfulness. (When we tell someone "I'll pray for you about that," do we do it?)

Here are some suggested ideas for building a life of purity: Of first importance . . . there is always God's forgiveness for when we fail. "If we confess our sins, God is faithful and just to forgive us our sins and cleanse us from all unrighteousness." (1 John 1:9)

Don't take the long look! (2 Samuel 11:2-4) David was tempted when he saw Bathsheba, but he could have had victory over the temptation. Instead, he sent for the woman he saw taking a bath, and adultery and murder followed. Determine in your heart that you really want to be a pure man or woman of God. Can a person really love and follow the Lord and be "friends with the world" as well? There's no middle ground here.

". . . don't you know that friendship with the world is hatred toward God? Anyone who chooses to be a friend of the world becomes an enemy of God." (James 4:4).

Often the best and simplest way to victory is to flee, that is, get away from the temptation. We each know very well the things and situations which tempt us to sin.

Suggestive pictures in magazines . . .

Romance novels—as distorted an image of true love as pornography is of true sex . . .

Certain TV and movies . . . don't be deceived; they do have an effect . . .

The internet . . .

Be aware of your most vulnerable areas, and stay away from them. Don't buy the enemy's false logic that if you're a real Christian, you can play around with sinful temptation and not be harmed.

"Flee the evil desires of youth, and pursue righteousness, faith, love and peace along with those who call on the Lord out of a pure heart." (II Timothy 2: 22 NIV)

Begin where you are, and be faithful in the little things. Starting right now, what are two key issues of purity in our lives we want to have victory in . . . and I mean, *right now*? Please, God, help us to be men and women of holiness and purity.

"He who is faithful in a very little thing will also be faithful in much . . ." (Luke 16:10).

God's perspective on money and stuff.

This is a somewhat difficult topic. I won't suggest any applications for this one; that'll be up to each person to decide, because though the principles don't change, people's circumstances do. What might be a good practice for one situation might not be in another. Let me give you an illustration.

Quite a few years ago, while I was visiting a missionary couple in rural Kenya, there was a discussion about one of the local pastors receiving a motor bike. Money had been given for that purpose, and since this pastor served several widely separated churches, the motor bike seemed like a good idea. But it was decided, in part by the pastor himself, that having the bike would hurt his relationship with his church people because it would put him in a different social/financial status from them. So the pastor turned down the motor bike for something more valuable, his relationship with his people.

In another situation, it might be appropriate and good for ministry to dress well and drive a nice car. Paul's comment in 1 Corinthians 9:22 that he has become "all things to all men, that he might win them" may have relevance here. The helpful thing to do is try to see this issue of money and material goods from God's perspective, and steer clear of the extremes of either greed or self-abasement in this matter.

In Philippians 4:11–13 (NIV), Paul says,

". . . I have learned to be content whatever the circumstances. I know what it is to be in need, and I know what it is to have plenty. I have learned the secret of being content in any and every situation, whether well fed or hungry, whether living in plenty or want."

There are two points in Paul's statement that I think are important. The first is that Paul seems to have *risen above* the whole issue of prosperity or lack of it. He didn't embrace poverty as a virtue, nor did he seek the supposed security and comfort of having plenty. I wouldn't go so far as to say that it was irrelevant to Paul, but it certainly wasn't the biggest concern in his life, probably not even in the top ten. He said he was content about his situation no matter what his circumstances.

The other thing I find interesting in Paul's statement is that he said he has *learned* to be content. This is very encouraging. Most of us could not say that victory in this area of our lives is natural to us. In fact, being content in "any and every situation" seems quite unnatural. So it's good that Paul himself says he "learned the secret of being content." It means that since contentedness is a learned, not natural, response, each of us can make good progress in this area by learning to trust God's provision.

Here's another good passage:

". . . give me neither poverty nor riches, but give me only my daily bread. Otherwise, I may have too much and disown you and say, 'Who is the Lord?' Or I may become poor and steal, and so dishonor the name of my God." (Proverbs 30:7, 8).

We can call this passage in Proverbs the practical, objective view of how people are about money. The writer is saying, "Look, we understand how most people are. If they have too much wealth, they'll just forget about God. (see Matthew 19:24) That happens a lot. On the other hand, if they have too little money, they'll get bitter, certainly with other people and maybe even God, and some may even think, 'I'll just steal some money from other people who probably don't deserve it anyway! Who cares!'"

So, this issue of money is both practical and spiritual: the practical is a common-sense objective way of thinking about money and how it works; the spiritual is our learning to trust God about our provision and safety in this matter.

For many Christians, having material goods usually means the pleasure or fun of it, rather than the boasting rights of it. In fact, it's far more likely that Christians will be somewhat apologetic about owning material goods, rather than flaunting them. We might even do a bit of rationalization about our stuff, e.g., "If I had that _____, I could use it for ministry!"

The greater temptation is money, for money is two things: the power to buy all the stuff that's fun and pleasurable, and the sense of security that goes with it. I've known very few Christians I would say had problems with *greed*, but I've known quite a few I'd say struggle with *anxiety*, to which they believe money is the solution.

The Bible's view on money and stuff.

"Then He (Jesus) said to them, "Watch out! Be on your guard against all kinds of greed; a man's life does not consist in the abundance of his possessions." (Luke 12:15 NIV)

He went on to tell the parable of the rich man who believed that his wealth would assure his happiness and ease.

". . . I'll say to myself, 'You have plenty of good things laid up for many years. Take life easy: eat, drink and be merry.' But God said to him, 'You fool! This very night your life will be demanded from you. Then who will get what you have prepared for yourself?'" (Luke 12:19, 20 NIV).

What's the foundational truth Jesus was teaching here? No, I'm not going to quote from the old sermon that the only man in the Bible with a retirement plan was called a fool by God. But this story rings true with many people, Christians included.

There was a TV ad that shows people walking around with a dollar sign and huge numbers tucked under their arms, as though they were carrying a three-foot-long loaf of French bread. The numbers represent what that person thinks he or she needs to retire comfortably. The numbers usually range from one to two million dollars. The message is this: if *you* don't make plans to take care of yourself in the future, no one else will. The other message is this: a person's life *does* consist of her or his possessions/wealth. With it, you have happiness and ease. Without it, you're toast.

Of course, it's obviously not a Christian ad, but how many of us who *are* Christians take such advice with great seriousness? Do we ask ourselves, "Do I have enough? What *is* my retirement plan? Will my spouse and I be okay?" If we answer "No" to those questions, there can be real fear. I think part of the problem in this issue for Christians is that we *are* familiar with God's promises, such as Matthew 6:33: "But seek first His kingdom and His righteousness, and all of these things (needs for life) will be given to you as well." That familiarity may not breed contempt, but it may breed indifference. Such Scriptures have become cliches' in the believer's mind, acknowledged with a shrug of the shoulders before he or she continues agonizing over how to provide for ones-self. It's a kind of "Yeah, I know it says that, but let's get real."

So I think a part of gaining freedom from anxiety about money is learning to take seriously the simple statements of God's love, power and wisdom concerning our lives. Then, rather than bored apathy, we have real excitement when we find a Bible statement in which God promises to take care of us. What about Matthew 6:33? What's God's promise concerning our physical needs? What are the conditions on the promise?

It says to "seek first His kingdom" . . . what would this mean for you?

And (seek first) "His righteousness" . . . what does *this* mean?

My own personal application of Matthew 6:33 is that seeking his kingdom means being involved in ministry. By sharing my faith, and helping others to grow, I would be participating in the growth of God's Kingdom. Seeking his righteousness implies to me an effort to live a righteous life myself. "Righteous" simply means" being right with God."

However you earnestly apply this challenge to "seek first His kingdom and righteousness," the promise is that "all these things will be yours as well." I believe the *as well* indicates that the "things/needs" are an additional benefit, the first being the freedom from fear and worry about not having the "things."

There's another interesting statement by the Apostle Paul, in Colossians 3: 5

In a list of sinful practices which Paul admonishes believers to "put to death," Paul says greed actually *amounts to idolatry.* Why would Paul call greed idolatry?

Take a look at Isaiah 44:16–19. This absolutely wonderful passage of Scripture describes a man who has cut a tree down. It says . . .

> "Half of the wood he burns in the fire; over it he prepares his meal, he roasts his meat and eats his fill. He also warms himself and says, 'Ah, I am warm; I see the fire.' From the rest of the wood he makes a god, his idol; he bows down to it and worships. He prays

to it and says, 'Save me; you are my god.' They know nothing, they understand nothing; their eyes are plastered over so they cannot see, and their minds closed so they cannot understand. No one stops to think, no one has the knowledge or understanding to say, 'Half of it I used for fuel; I even baked bread over its coals, I roasted meat and I ate. Shall I make a detestable thing from what is left? Shall I bow down to a block of wood?'" (NIV)

But isn't this exactly what people do today! They worship what they make. If someone asks another person, "What do you make?" it's obvious the question refers to money, i.e., "what's you salary?" Idols are made. An idol is anything that a person worships, and worship (or "worth-ship") is given to whatever has great *worth* in the mind of a person. The man in Isaiah 44 seems such a primitive fool, to carve some crude figure from a piece of wood and then fall down before it and say to it, "Save me! You are my god." But we who are not crude and primitive do essentially the same thing if we trust in money, which we made, to save us. Then it is an idol, and our "worth-ship" of it is idolatry.

As Paul says in Romans 7:15, we do the very thing we know is wrong to do. We trust that which is not *trustworthy*. It's not even alive. It has no compassion and cannot save. What do the following Scriptures say about the effect of love of money, or worrying about money, on Christians?

"The one who received the seed that fell among the thorns is the man who hears the word (of God), but the worries of this life and the deceitfulness of wealth choke it, making it unfruitful." (Matthew 13:22 NIV).

In this parable of the "sower," or the "four soils," the word of God has been sown on ground which receives it, but because of the "thorns" of worry about life's problems, and money's deceitful promise of being the solution to the problems, the Christian is not fruitful for the Kingdom.

"People who want to get rich fall into temptation and a trap and many foolish and harmful desires that plunge men into ruin and destruction. For the love of money is the root of all kinds of evil. Some people, eager for money, have wandered from the faith and pierced themselves with many griefs." (1 Timothy 6:9, 10 NIV).

Here, it's people's love of money, and eagerness to have money, which have caused them to move away from their faith, and actually brought them many griefs. How ironic that people look to money to avoid the grief of life, only to "pierce themselves" with lots of grief because of it.

"Do not be anxious about anything, but in everything, by prayer and petition, with thanksgiving, present your requests to God. And the peace of God, which transcends all understanding, will guard your hearts and your minds in Christ Jesus." (Philippians 4: 6, 7 NIV).

What do you think is the difference between the "love of money," mentioned in 1 Timothy 6, and the "anxiety" that Philippians 4 talks about? It's a good distinction, and as I said earlier, I know very few greedy believers, but quite a few anxious believers. Prayer involves bringing the Lord into this issue, and telling him that we do want the peace that "transcends understanding;' that's the kind of peace where we might feel, "I should be worried about this, but I have peace . . . it's amazing!"

We do want to trust him on this, but how? Have you ever heard the saying: "There are two ways to be happier: figure out a way to make more money, or figure out a way to be content with what you already have." Wow, I really like that! And here's the answer to how to "figure out how to be content."—one of the best verses in the Bible on God's provision says this:

"Keep your lives free from the love of money, and be content with what you have, because God Himself has said, 'Never will I leave you; never will I forsake you.'" (Hebrews 13:5).

Do we believe that promise? God himself says, "I will never leave you; I will never forsake you." That's the reason a Christian can be content, because God has stated he will never leave or forsake us. But as one college student put it, "The problem is that my need for money is *so* visible, and God is so invisible! It's hard to believe in what I can't see." That was "doubting Thomas's" issue, wasn't it?

Yet this promise by God, in *writing*, is the foundation of our ability to trust God for our provision and care. My wife, Nancy, and I have this Scripture as our sole retirement plan (well, other than Social Security, which is looking iffy). Am I trying to guilt-trip you, or suggest you do the same? No. Remember the first few sentences of this section; I'm not going to make any suggested applications for anyone. I just want to let you know that I'm not preaching something that I'm not practicing. Nancy and I believe and trust this Hebrews 13:5 statement by God.

The decision whether to trust God in this area, or follow the world's value system concerning money and stuff is ours. How could a person know if he or she had a love of money, or unrighteous concern about material things? What would be the signs?

—thinking very often about cars, clothes, electronics (e.g., huge TV's), etc.

—worrying often about money, even if you have enough for your family's needs

—impulse buying, especially with credit cards, of items that have little to do with

—necessities

Can you think of others?

Here's an important question: can a person be rich and still godly? I believe the answer is "yes." Remember, it's the *love* of money that's the problem. In 1 Timothy 6:17, 18, Paul says to command those who are rich to be generous and willing to share, and to not put their trust in riches. But Paul doesn't say that those who are rich are weak spiritually because of it. My wife and I are good friends with a couple whom the world would call well-to-do, yet they are among the most generous and sharing people I know. They serve the Lord in ministry, often in quite humble service, and use the money with which they have been entrusted for the support of a lot of other ministries. I suspect they wish at times to live a simpler life, not having the stewardship of finances, but they administer their role in this way with a good heart.

Well, how are we all doing in this area? Is there an issue here? What's the first step in getting victory in this important matter? What's a real something you could trust God for in your life, right now? Is it staying away from malls? Is it training yourself to think, "The car I've got works fine. I don't need the new one." Is it disciplining yourself to pray every day about your family's needs, asking God to be at peace about his provision?

Take that first little step. Remember Luke 16:10 . . . "He who is faithful in a very little thing will (learn to be) be faithful in greater things."

Concerning—giving money to the Lord:

The following thoughts focus mainly on two passages of Scripture: 2 Corinthians 8:1–15 and 2 Corinthians 9:6–15. I won't write them out completely, but you might enjoy reading through these verses to get a general grasp of the New Testament principles on giving. Here are the key verses for the sake of our discussion:

"And now, brothers, we want you to know about the grace that God has given the Macedonian churches. Out of the most severe trial, their overflowing joy and their extreme poverty welled up in rich generosity. For I testify that they gave as much as they were able, and even beyond their ability. Entirely on their own, they urgently pleaded with us for the privilege of sharing with us in this service to the saints." (2 Corinthians 8:1–4 NIV).

Is giving money to God's work something only those with lots of money can do effectively? Apparently the churches in Macedonian didn't think so. Did those churches consider it a burden to give? What was their attitude about it?

The point here is that these Macedonian church people viewed supporting "the saints" in Judea as a privilege, not a burden. These churches were certainly not wealthy, and probably quite poor. Yet they pleaded with Paul not to be left out of the joy and privilege of giving! Isn't that amazing? It's as though they were saying, "Hey, just because we're poor, and you know it, please don't overlook us when it comes to giving!"

I'm not sure how many points of comparison we can make between the Macedonian churches in the first century and today, but one thing is clear: those church people didn't feel badgered or into giving; they wanted to.

Paul then goes on to explain to the church at Corinth, which was apparently less enthusiastic about giving, that giving was not a one-way process, i.e., to deprive them and make life easy for others.

"Our desire is not that others might be relieved while you are hard pressed, but that there might be equality. At the present time your plenty will supply what they need, so that in turn their plenty will supply what you need. Then there will be equality, as it is written: 'He who gathered much did not have too much, and he who gathered little did not have too little.'" (2 Corinthians 8:13–15 NIV).

We don't hear much about this today, do we? What Paul was saying is pretty simple: when some people have more than they need, they can give to those less fortunate for their needs. Then when *those* people who had received help were better off, they could help others, or even the ones who had helped them before. Paul said it would work this way "that there might be equality" or a leveling-out of believers aiding each other.

It's difficult to see how this principle operates today. One implication would be that when people have sufficient income, they give to their local church; then when the people have need, the local church would provide for the people. I have indeed observed this to some degree, but not often and not to any great extent. One cultural factor might be that what we consider a need today would not have been seen as a critical need in Paul's day.

Local church leaders may also have a different view on this situation. Their perspective may well be that the church has thousands of members, and lots of people have problems, and the church can't take care of everyone's problems. The accepted norm seems to have become that church members are supposed to give; churches are supposed to receive, and it's normally a one-way deal. The idea that the local church would consider itself responsible for—or even aware of—the hardships of the members seems remote at best. I really don't know what the answer to this issue is . . . most local churches I am aware of are struggling to meet their own financial needs, much less the needs of members of their congregations. Perhaps the best application for us as *individual* believers is to be aware the needs of fellow Christians and help in an appropriate manner. It's a matter of the heart and intellect; our hearts must be to help, and our minds must determine if the need is genuine or if our help would only worsen a person's addictive lifestyle. Whatever our perspective on this principle of "material equality" is, we do want to respond to the spirit of this Scripture:

"If anyone has material possessions and sees his brother in need but has no pity on him, how can the love of God be in him? Dear children, let us not love with words or tongue but with actions and in truth." (1 John 3:17, 18).

Okay, let's consider another passage about giving.

"Remember this, whoever sows sparingly will also reap sparingly, and whoever sows generously will also reap generously. Each man should give what he has decided in his heart to give. Not reluctantly or under compulsion, for God loves a cheerful giver. And God is able to make all grace abound to you (like the Macedonian churches), so that in all things at all times, having all that you need, you will abound in every good work." (2 Corinthians 9: 6-8 NIV).

What's the effect on the giver of generous giving as opposed to meager giving, according to 2 Corinthians 9:6? It's the "law of the harvest"—what you sow, you reap—and the amount you sow, that's the amount you reap. (See also Luke 6:38 for another way of putting it. "For with the measure you use, it will be measured to you.")

Do you think this concept would cause someone to give generously for the wrong reason? In other words, might some unscrupulous person try to "hack" the system, and give generously purely in order to reap generously? Ha! The answer to that one is 'no.'

This is a system that simply cannot be hacked, because a person has to trust God and his word enough to believe the promise will work, and a person with that kind of trust of God is not going to try to cheat the Lord. "God is not fooled; a man reaps what he sows . . ." (Galatians 6:7 NIV).

In the 2 Corinthians 9:6–8 passage above, what's the Bible say about the *attitude* a person should have when she or he gives? What's pleasing to God and what isn't?

The attitude is cheerfulness. And this attitude comes from the person deciding for herself, or himself, what he or she will do regarding giving. Giving is *not* to be done from a sense of obligation or reluctantly. Did you hear that? It is *not* to be done reluctantly or under obligation. How different this is from the obligatory Jewish tithe! Do you think the Jewish people ever felt reluctant to give? Of course they did; much of the book of Malachi addresses that very issue. (See Malachi 1 and 3).

But we are Christians, freed from the Law, and invited to make up our own minds about our part in giving, not reluctantly or under a sense of compulsion, but cheerfully.

And in the last statement in 2 Corinthians 9, God says what he will provide for those who give cheerfully ". . . all grace . . . in all things, at all times . . . having all that you need, you will abound in every good work." There are a lot of "all's" in that statement.

That's New Testament, Christian giving!

What are your thoughts on giving? Do you feel that financial giving is a reluctant obligation, or a privilege? As one old saint put it, "Of all the blessings of the Christian life, I'd sure hate to lose the blessing of giving."

Humility

"Seeing ourselves as God sees us . . . "

Pride

"All of you, clothe yourselves with humility toward one another, because "GOD OPPOSES THE PROUD, BUT GIVES GRACE TO THE HUMBLE." (1 Peter 5:5 NIV)

This verse tells us clearly about God's attitude toward pride. He opposes the proud. That statement taken seriously, as it should be, presents the biggest boxing mis-match imaginable, having God as one's opponent. Think about it.

"In this corner, weighing 150 pounds, clothed in arrogance, is the prideful human being. In the other corner, with infinite weight and power, clothed in glory, is the Creator and maintainer of the universe, the Lord God." That's not a contest in which the human is likely to do well.

What can cause a person to become prideful? Can you think of an event or occurrence that caused you to have an inflated view of yourself or your abilities?

For me, a big one came in my first year in a teaching position at a small college. The school's re-accreditation examination was in process, and I had been asked to present my department's programs and plans. I don't remember doing a particularly great job of it, but for some inexplicable reason, the accreditation examiners raved about it. Honestly, to this day I can't imagine why the program got such a good critique. Perhaps the examiners were just having a really good day, and they felt generous (or merciful).

But my boss, the dean of the college, was thrilled. I heard "Great job!" for a week every time I saw him.

What do you think that did to my 28 year-old ego? I was flying high. At the time, I had a pretty exalted opinion of myself! Looking back, I think I did a mediocre-to-fair job of the presentation, but just happened to hit the examiners on a good day and got far more praise than I deserved.

Here's a true funny story about getting recognition. My friends, Andy and Nancy Pearson were praying about a mission's assignment in one of the former Soviet Union countries in the Baltics. Andy had gone to the country to evaluate it for ministry possibilities and his family's needs. As he returned to Orlando, a crowd of photographers and news reporters waited at the gate. As Andy came down the ramp to the terminal, he must have been puzzled. But the crowd of news people weren't there because Andy was returning with a decision to serve the Lord in the Baltics; they were there to welcome an Orlando Magic basketball player joining the team at a salary of about a million dollars a month. Ha! The world's recognition seldom (if ever) goes to those whose sights are set on eternal things.

I'm not saying that getting a word of praise or recognition is always bad; sometimes it's a wonderful encouragement. (Remember the man who said," I can live a month on a good compliment!") But we always want to have a realistic self-opinion, and that's why I define "humility' as *seeing ourselves as God sees us*: neither super-beings, nor worms. Let's look at a few Scriptures about this issue:

> "To some who were confident of their own righteousness and looked down on everybody else, Jesus told this parable: 'Two men went up the Temple to pray, one a Pharisee and the other a tax collector. The Pharisee stood up and prayed about himself: 'God, I thank you that I am not like other men—robbers, evildoers, adulterers—or even like this tax collector. I fast twice a week and give a tenth of all I get.' But the tax collector stood at a distance. He would not even look up to heaven, but beat his breast and said, 'God, have mercy on me, a sinner.' I tell you that this man, rather than the other, went home justified before God. For everyone who exalts himself will be humbled, but he who humbles himself will be exalted.'" (Luke 18:9-14 NIV).

Unlike some of the Lord's other parables, this one is blatantly obvious. The Pharisee was confident of his own self-righteousness. Jesus says in the parable that the Pharisee even prayed about *himself*! His thanks to God was really not so much an expression of gratitude as self-praise. "I'm glad I'm better than other people," is the heart of his prayer, and this pride was based on his life situation and his observance of religious rules. The "boastful pride of life" cited in 1 John 2:16 applies in this illustration of Jesus'.

Are Christians susceptible to this kind of pride, or confidence about our own righteousness? Sure we are. Could it even be that the longer we've been Christians, the more we might be tempted to compare ourselves favorably to others, including other believers. I doubt we would ever actually say aloud, "I'm thank God I'm not like those others," but we might think it.

In contrast, a pastor friend of mine once said, "I love the Lord and have the Holy Spirit in me . . . so why aren't I a *better* man!" It wasn't self pity, just a humble yearning to be more like Christ.

Here's a more subtle one.

"Now listen, you who say, 'Today or tomorrow we will go into this or that city, spend a year there and carry on business and make money.' Why, you do not even know what will happen tomorrow. What is your life? You are a mist that appears for a little while and then vanishes. Instead, you ought to say, 'If it is the Lord's will, we will live and do this or that.' As it is, you boast and brag. All such boasting is evil." (James 4:13–16 NIV).

Why is this kind of thinking wrong? From one perspective, it seems like a person who'd say that is just planning ahead. What is the presumption that's criticized here? I think what James is saying is wrong is the attitude that we're in control of our own lives. James seems to be saying, in effect, "It's not really up to *you* to make plans about the future; it's up to God to determine what will happen next year, or even tomorrow."

I recall an "animated" (i.e., heated) discussion in a Sunday school class one time in which the two sides had to do with how much of our lives we really control. One person argued that we make lots of choices that determine our lives. The other person argued that we have very little control over our lives, and the choices we make are limited to what God puts before us. The "control guy" said, "Well, I certainly chose the person I married!" To which the other person said, "Not really . . . you were able to choose to marry her only because God allowed you to *meet* her! It was mostly God's choice because you can't choose to marry somebody you've never met!"

Well, the discussion kind of went downhill from there, but it was an interesting consideration: that we may take for granted our choice-making and control of the events in our lives. Have you ever heard Christians say something like, "I'll see you next week, God willing . . ." or, "Let's play golf tomorrow, the Lord willing . . ." It may have become a cliché, but it does reflect the humility James was saying is realistic and appropriate.

Another aspect of pride is un-teachableness, or resistance to the authority God gives to our spiritual leaders. Look at Hebrews 13:17. What problem can result if a person is too prideful to submit himself or herself to spiritual leadership?

"Obey your leaders, and submit to them, for they keep watch over your souls, as those who will give an account. Let them do this with joy and not with grief, for this would be unprofitable for you."(Hebrews 13:17).

I don't know if you've ever tried to teach a person who had "the attitude," that is, the un-teachable attitude. It's definitely no fun or joy to deal with these folks, because they fight you every step of the way. And as grief-filled as it is for the teacher, it's also unprofitable for the one who needs to learn. I was this way with one of my Christian leaders, until God convicted me of being un-teachable, and just in time too, because my leader told me later he was on the point of not meeting with me anymore. He told me that getting with me exhausted and drained him. I thank the Holy Spirit for his conviction, because I had a lot of profit from learning from that man.

What can a person do to be more humble if he feels he struggles with pride? Here are some good considerations:

Realize that it's God's love, favor, and protection which is our real treasure, not our smugness about our talents or possessions. It is enough to reflect God's power and glory.

"'My grace is sufficient for you, for my power is made perfect in weakness.' Therefore (Paul says) 'I will boast all the more gladly about my weakness, so that Christ's power may rest on me. That is why, for Christ's sake, I delight in weaknesses . . . for when I am weak, then I am strong.'" (2 Corinthians 12:9, 10).

Consider that whatever advantages or lofty position we may have in life as being ". . . all loss compared to the surpassing greatness of knowing Christ Jesus my Lord . . . I consider them rubbish that I may gain Christ . . ." (Philippians 3:7, 8 NIV).

As a practical application, take this challenging step,

"Do nothing out of selfish ambition or vain conceit, but in humility consider others better than yourselves. Each of you should look not only to your own interest, but also to the interests of others. (Philippians 2:3-4 NIV).

How can we do this? Perhaps the most important verse on overcoming pride is this:

"For who makes you different from anyone else? What do you have that you did not receive? And if you did receive it, why do you boast as though you did not? (1 Corinthians 4:7 NIV).

That's it in a nutshell, isn't it? Even if we have great abilities, intelligence, talents, gifts . . . we didn't create them ourselves. They are *gifts*. And by definition, gifts are things we receive. So anything we might be tempted to take pride in is something which God has given to us as a gift, and it is intended to glorify him, not ourselves. How absurd if I owned a Stradivarius violin and boasted that I had created it. Someone could well say to me, "You received that wonderful violin; you didn't make it. If you received it, why do you boast as though you didn't?"

One time my friend and fellow minister, Rich Bates, and I were talking to a couple of guys in a student apartment near campus. They both said they didn't really believe in God. One of them was a pretty good athlete and the other was a musician. Rich used their giftedness in these two areas to point out a pretty good evidence for God's existence. His logic was this: the guys were good at music and sports; they hadn't created those abilities themselves; they got those talents from somewhere, and, Rich said, "I believe that 'somewhere' was the person of God."

The two guys listened carefully because they knew it was true that they were gifted, and it pleased them to think that God had made them that way.

How much more pleasing and true for us who are believers and followers of the Creator to simply give credit where credit is due, to God, and just be glad that we can use what he's given us for his honor, not ours.

I'll refer to Luke 16:10 a lot, because it's an excellent approach to grow in the Christian life . . . the one who is faithful in a little thing will be faithful in the bigger things (my paraphrase). What is the first "little step" toward increased humility I can take right now?

Insecurity

Though it may seem self-contradictory, another aspect of human pride is insecurity, that is, having a poor self-image or being self-deprecating (putting one's self down). In fact, I'd say from ministry experience that more people struggle with a poor self-image than do with arrogance.

Can you think of an event or occurrence that caused you to have negative self-image? I once heard a interesting testimony by a young woman in Iowa. She said that she had developed a poor self-image as a young child from a seeming simple cause, or rather two causes: she was tall, and her last name began with the letter Z. She said that every time her elementary school class had to line up for something, or get in a group for a picture, she was always in the back or last, either because she was the tallest girl in class, or because the line formed alphabetically. This young woman laughed as she related her story, but she said it wasn't funny when she was a child. She just had it in her mind that she was "the girl who is last," and that she always would be. More about this young woman's story in a little bit.

There are a number of reasons a person might have a sense of insecurity. Look at the following verses; what do they reveal about the causes of a poor self-image?

"We do not dare to classify or compare ourselves with some who commend themselves. When they measure themselves by themselves and compare themselves with themselves, they are not wise." (2 Corinthians 10:12 NIV).

Comparing ourselves to others really isn't wise, but it's about as common an activity as breathing. Who hasn't done this at least a few times, or a few hundred times? We all know the inevitable result when we compare ourselves to others: we either feel depressed or prideful. We feel depressed if our comparison makes us feel that others are better than we are. We feel prideful if we see ourselves as better. Neither is helpful.

Here's what makes this activity so foolish for Christians: we all have the same Holy Spirit, but differing gifts, talents, temperaments, and personalities, according to God's creation and the Holy Spirit's choosing. We certainly can't compare the Holy Spirit in us to the Holy Spirit in others; he's the same.

So when we compare ourselves with others, we're just comparing what God has given us—those attributes which make us uniquely who we are—to that which God has given others. Such comparisons are really criticisms of how God has created people (or ourselves), or criticism of the purposes for which he has made each person. Whatever the reasons, comparing ourselves to others usually ends up with our feeling dissatisfied or envious; both contribute to a poor self-image.

"The Lord does not look at the things man looks at. Man looks at the outward appearance, but the Lord looks at the heart." (1 Samuel 16:7 NIV).

There's no big surprise here. People's appearances count for a lot in the world, in man's eyes, if you will. The beautiful face, the strong body, sex appeal . . . these are the values that get attention in the world of the superficial. These are the points of comparison people make which seldom lead to a healthy self-esteem.

One TV actress summed up the world's value system with this comment: "Beauty *is* important; it may be only skin deep, but it's the only part that shows." It may be the only part that shows to those for whom outward appearance is highly important, but a lot more "shows" to the Lord and those who value the heart and character of persons, not just their looks.

Here's another cause of a poor self-image.

"As (Jesus) was going into a village, ten men who had leprosy met Him. They stood at a distance and called out in a loud voice, 'Jesus, master, have pity on us!'" (Luke 17:12, 13 NIV).

These leprous men had a disease that not only caused physical suffering, but also isolation from society. Even their cry for mercy had to come from a distance. What might be the social leprosy of our day, and in our culture? It may actually be an illness, in childhood or adulthood, that separates a person from the normal life others of their age enjoy. It may be an economic or ethnic life situation that makes a person believe themselves to be unfairly disadvantaged. It may be any kind of physical difference that causes a person to see himself or herself as an outsider. It could be any of life's circumstances which cause people to suffer a sense of pain, embarrassment, or loneliness. These are serious challenges to overcome, and often result in a person believing that she or he is worth less because of the life situation.

"A soothing tongue is a tree of life, but perversion in it crushes the spirit." (Proverbs 15:4)

In the sad, tragic story of singer, Karen Carpenter, it was apparently one comment by a music reviewer that referred to Karen as "chubby" that began a long struggle with anorexia, which contributed to her early death. Words have great power to comfort and heal, or to wound and crush.

Many people can remember the words that crushed their spirit. (From the dad) "This is Ricky, my not-so-bright boy." (From the mom) "Oh, Kristen, I've told you a hundred times how to do that! Why can't you get it right for once?" (From the high school guidance counselor) "Well, we can certainly eliminate any career with math in it for you."

If there was ever an inaccurate saying, it's got to be this one: "Sticks and stones may break my bones, but words can never hurt me!" Most people would take a broken bone any day to the words that have been said to them, that have been believed by them, and that distort the truth of their wonderful worth.

Here's a good consideration:

". . . look at the birds of the air . . . your heavenly father cares for them . . . Are you not much more valuable than they?" (Matthew 6:26) and "God demonstrates His own love for us in this: while we were still sinners, Christ died for us." (Romans 5:8 NIV).

Don't think about your situations, feelings, and circumstances. Think about your value. Your value is Christ. Christ was the price paid for you; therefore, your worth is great, for the price paid for something is what it's worth.

There is another realization that can give us an accurate, healthy self-image. The young woman I mentioned above, who gave the great testimony about her own struggle with self image, said that reading and praying about Psalm 139:14 was a turning point for her.

"I will give thanks to Thee, for I am carefully and wonderfully made; wonderful are Thy works, and my soul knows it very well." (Psalm 139:14).

These were some of her thoughts.

We can thank God for the way we are, because we are made just exactly the way God wants us to be. He didn't make us carelessly, with his mind on something else. He made us carefully and wonderfully. He thinks *I* am wonderful!! He thinks *you* are wonderful! My brain and insecure feeling might be flaky, but my *soul* knows very well that I am wonderful. Believe what is true.

We may feel like there are things about ourselves that we don't like . . .

1. There are some things about ourselves that we don't like that we *should change*: our selfishness or any wrong things we do (sin).

2. There are some things about ourselves that we don't like that *we can change* if we want . . . new hair style, contact lenses rather than glasses, clothes, etc.

3. There are some things about ourselves that we might not like that we *can't change*, and shouldn't try to, because that's how God

made us and wants us to be: our temperament, personality, gifts, abilities, etc. We should thank God for being the way we are. That's what makes us unique.

Thanks to Susan Z. for these good insights.

Okay, what do we do about things that have happened to us in our lives? People may feel defeated because of hurt that they have suffered from others (young people may feel this), or guilt because they have caused hurt to others (older people may feel this).

The Apostle Paul is an example of a person to whom both of these situations apply. Paul had hurt other people.

"... not only did I lock up many of the saints in prisons ... but when they were being put to death, I cast my vote against them ... (Acts 26:10) Paul could have felt such guilt about how he had hurt others, that he might have never served God after he became a Christian. How did he overcome the guilt of the pain and loss he had caused in others' lives? Forgiveness. Paul accepted God's forgiveness for the terrible pain Paul had inflicted upon others. But Paul had also been hurt by others.

"... imprisonments, beaten times without number, often in danger of being killed. Five times I received from (my enemies) thirty-nine lashes. Three times I was beaten with rods, once I was stoned ..." (2 Corinthians 11:23–25).

Paul could have allowed anger and bitterness at the people who had hurt him to keep him from serving the Lord in ministry. How did he overcome any bitterness about having been hurt by others? Forgiveness. He forgave those who hurt him as God had forgiven him for hurting others. The answer for both guilt and bitterness is forgiveness.

"... I don't even deserve to be called an apostle, because I persecuted the church of God. But by the grace of God, I am what I am ..." (1 Corinthians 15:9, 10 NIV).

"... just as the Lord forgave you, so also should you forgive." (Colossians 3: 13)

There's a silly story about being unmerciful, or unforgiving. The story goes like this: Once, a first mate on a ship, after 20 years of an unblemished record, got a little intoxicated on shore leave and the captain caught him. The captain wrote in the ship's permanent log, 'The mate was drunk today.' The mate pled with the captain for mercy, citing his long history of faithful service, but the captain was unforgiving. He said to the mate, "We tell the strict truth in the ship's log!" The following day, when it was the mate's turn to write in the log, he wrote, 'The captain was sober today.' Ha!

Pastor Leonard Jones once said that the Lord's Prayer is a dangerous prayer, for in it we say, "Forgive me . . . *as* I forgive others . . . " Paul seemed to understand and accept God's forgiveness of him, and he could extend that forgiveness to those who had hurt him. It's and honor and compliment when God asks us to forgive someone; in a sense, he's asking us to be like him, because that's at the very heart of his nature, to be forgiving.

We will likely retain bitterness if we fail to forgive. We may struggle with guilt and depression if we will not gladly accept God's forgiveness. Is there someone we need to forgive? Is there something for which we need to ask God forgiveness?

Is there one area in our lives right now where we have an incorrect negative self-image? Give it to God. Read Psalm 139:14 and realize that you are wonderful in God's eyes. He made you the way you are on purpose. It's how he wants you to be . . . no, not the sin or bad habits, but the essence of you, who you really are, is a wonderful thing. Believe it because it's true.

Section Two

4

Principle # 2 Give Your Life to People, Not Just Your Knowledge.

"Having thus a fond affection for you, we were well pleased to impart to you not only the gospel of God, but also our own lives . . . "

—1 Thessalonians 2:8

SUPPOSE YOU WERE THE financial officer of a company, and two moneymaking options (schemes?) were presented to you. The first is that your company will receive a million dollars a day for a year. The second is that your company will receive a penny a week, doubled each week, for a year. Which option would you choose?

Ah, I couldn't trick you, could I? Even if you haven't heard one of the many illustrations of the power of multiplication (which is really just simultaneous addition), you can probably assume that option #2 is the one to pick . . . and you'd be right. Option # 1 yields, obviously, 365 million dollars for the year's time period. Option # 2 yields 20 trillion dollars in the year's time, if the penny is doubled each week. That's more than the US national debt of 2010. The yield from the million dollars a day is *less than five hundredth of one percent* of the total of the penny doubled weekly. There's no real surprise here. Pretty much everyone knows about the power of exponential math.

But here's the twist: suppose your effectiveness as a financial officer were to be evaluated six weeks into the year's period? In other words, suppose the president of the company decided to measure your money-making ability after just six weeks, and your reputation and salary depended upon your evaluation? Then what would you choose, option 1 or option 2? If you picked # 1, you'd have made the company $42, 000, 000 at the six week mark. If you chose option # 2, you'd have made the company $ 0.64 . . . yes, 64 cents.

Do you see what I'm getting at? What we choose to do, either financially or in ministry, depends a lot on whether we are thinking of short-term gains, or long-term gains. It also depends on whether we are willing to minister for the greater benefit of the Kingdom of God, even if it means we don't receive any recognition or praise for short-term impressive results.

The power of multiplication takes effect in the long-term. To continue the illustration of financial gain, a person who wishes to look good in the short term—and gain impressive amounts of cash in the short term—will choose the short-term impressiveness of addition, even though its long-term results are tiny in comparison.

But we're talking here about ministry. What's short-term ministry thinking, and what's long-term ministry thinking? As with the "finance illustration," short-term has to do with addition; long-term with multiplication.

Ministry based on the power of multiplication means individuals taking the time and care to disciple other individuals so that they could do the same with others. Dawson Trotman, founder of The Navigators, in his message, *Born to Reproduce*, said Christians can and should reproduce themselves spiritually by helping another person grow to spiritual maturity. He used the word "reproduction" rather than multiplication, but the idea is the same. Then that person, the one who has been helped to maturity, can and should do the same with another. Of course the first person can and should be doing the same thing with yet another at the same time.

Confusing? It just means this: for example, Kyle helps Jon; when Jon is a mature Christian, he finds someone to help; at the same time, Kyle finds another and helps him the way he helped Jon. Thus the multiplication, or simultaneous addition, gets going.

So, let's say you, the reader, are 30 years old, and the Lord plans on you living until 66. That gives you 36 years of ministry. Now, let's say that you meet with someone—a person who desires to grow as a Christian—for a period of two years. You help this person life-to-life to sink deep roots in Christian practices and Christ-like character. Perhaps you go through the "7 & 3" material (see previous chapter, and Appendix) with him or her. After two years, this person has a good, solid walk with God and wants to help another person the same way you've helped her/him. You both pray that God will allow her or him to find another woman/man who is serious about growing; she does, and so another discipling relationship begins. At the same time, God gives you another person to help, so then there are now four: two ministering and two receiving help. Two more years, and then there are 8, then 16, 32, 64, etc.

In the 36 years, your personal ministry could result in 250,000 people walking with the Lord. Not just saved people, but mature disciples who are joyful and committed to ministry. Lives reproduce. What you've done with them, they'll do with others. It's normal and natural for people to do the same thing that's been done with them. So two years after you've gone home to be with the Lord, there are half a million who are your spiritual offspring.

That's the wonderful thing about personal ministry. Because those we help can also help others (2 Timothy 2:2), we could very conceivably walk right past a person in the supermarket who is fruit of our ministry, and never know it. We sure won't struggle with "ministry pride" over this kind of ministry because we probably won't see those whose lives are spiritually helped by the offspring of *our* lives. But the potential of this kind of ministry to multiply and bring many to salvation and maturity is very much a reality.

This is what we need, Abrahams and Sarahs who will be the beginnings of many generations of godly men and women. It requires a radical commitment.

No, not every discipling relationship will succeed; some will lose interest and drop away. Some, for one or another reason, will not be able to disciple another. But even allowing for a fair percentage to not grow to maturity, or not be able to disciple another . . . it's still a huge number of people you have helped to joyfully walk with God and become ministers themselves. As someone once said, this is how the world got populated, not by committees, but by individuals having other individuals. It does work.

Certainly, life-to-life discipleship is not all that's needed. Large-group worship and small-group study / fellowship are crucial for joy and growth. But the individual attention is also needed and is fruitful for the Kingdom.

Does this make sense? Have you seen this kind of ministry in your part of the Christian community? Probably not. Why not? First of all, Satan, I think, hates it when lay people make disciples, so he opposes it vehemently.

Also, I'm afraid that the same kind of attraction to short-term gains takes place in the Christian world as well as in the financial world. A Christian leader may understand the *concept* of the long-term benefits of life-to-life discipling, but may feel compelled to do the usual thing, go for the short term. And since life-to-life discipleship often happens outside the walls of the local church, in living rooms and fast-food restaurants, rather than Sunday school classrooms or designated small groups, it can be puzzling to church leaders how to fit this kind of ministry into some local church models. Yet this is what Jesus asked His followers to do.

"As you are going, make disciples of all nations . . . teaching them to obey all I have commanded you . . ." (Matthew 28: 19, 20 NIV)

And in Acts 1:8, the Lord says,

". . . you will be My witnesses in Jerusalem, and in all Judea, and in Samaria, and to the ends of the earth." (NIV).

Someone once said that God is a *centrifugal* God, flinging laborers outward into the harvest fields. Some of our ministries, however, tend to be *centripetal*, bunching members tighter and tighter into the center, further and further from the harvest fields. There can be no doubt that this process of witnessing and disciple-making starts from where the followers of Christ were and moves outward.

Okay, let's go on from the concept of personal discipleship to some heart issues. Sometimes, in considering the concepts of ministry, it can make the actual people sound like numbers or work projects, which is definitely not the case. So here are some thoughts on the worth of the individual person:

The worth of the individual

The worth of the individual simply means that individuals are *worth* receiving personal, one-to-one ministry, and that individuals are *worthy* of giving this kind of help to others. It's at the heart of the reason why we say to give your life to people, not just your knowledge.

It's a simple idea—a kind of spiritual parenting—but it's one that is sometimes overlooked these days. Some may feel that personal, one-to-one ministry is just too slow or even inefficient. One man said to me, "It's too much attention given to too few people. If it's good training, why not give it to the biggest group you can?" While I understand this thinking, I feel there are some real strengths to personal discipleship.

First, in this day when many young people struggle with a good self-esteem, personal ministry demonstrates to someone that she or he is valuable. "If this Christian leader is spending personal time with me, he must think I'm worth it!" As the Apostle Paul put it,

". . . we were well-pleased to impart to you . . . our own lives, because you had become very dear to us." (1 Thessalonians 2:8).

Second, one-to-one ministry is a great way to teach principles of life, character, and ministry because the instruction, feedback, and application can be tailored to the individual. It's an answer to the old criticism of group instruction that, "Telling isn't teaching; listening isn't learning!"

Third, as stated before, life-to-life ministry can result in spiritual multiplication, a kind of chain-reaction of lives impacting others for the Kingdom. Paul implied four generations of godly people (Paul, Timothy, faithful ones, others) in writing to Timothy,

"You therefore, my son, be strong in the grace that is in Christ Jesus. And the things which you have heard from me in the presence of many witnesses, these entrust to faithful men, who will be able to teach others also." (2 Timothy 2:1, 2).

There are some important elements to the verse above. First, Paul calls Timothy his "son." Timothy's relationship with Paul was definitely a heart-felt one; Timothy was not just a 'project" to Paul, or means to achieving a ministry goal. Secondly, Paul says there are "things" which Timothy had received from him, instructions for ministry and godly living. Thirdly, Paul said Timothy was to "entrust" these things to faithful men who would be able to teach others as well.

This brings up a key consideration: how do we today know who are the faithful men and women to whom we are to entrust the "things"? Not everyone is ready, willing, or even *wants*, this kind of discipling; it's costly. Jesus said,

"Whoever would come after Me, let him deny himself, take up his cross daily, and follow Me." (Luke 9:23).

Self-denial and paying the price to follow the Lord are not at the top of the popularity list in today's culture.

The idea is that to start a discipleship movement which will spread, you begin with a few highly committed persons who will live out the ideals of the movement, and infect others with their fervor. If the first group is not radically committed, willing to live or die for the cause, the movement will sputter and fade. The assumption is that the leader of a movement will be most effective with a few proven followers because he or she can teach and motivate at an intimate level of contact.

If you go for quantity and ignore quality, you won't get either. If you go for quality you'll get both quality and, eventually, quantity.

Look at the ministry of Jesus. In John 17: 4, Jesus Christ states to the Father that he has accomplished the work for which he had been sent.

"I have glorified Thee on the earth, having accomplished the work which Thou hast given me to do."

Since the content of this chapter focuses on the Lord's requests for his disciples, not the propitiatory work of the Cross and Resurrection, we can infer that when Jesus says he has accomplished the work the Father sent him to do, it at least in part refers to the discipling of the eleven.

That Jesus makes this statement reveals the confidence he had in the principle of entrusting the ministry into the hands of the right people, faithful people. He had conducted a ministry of only three and a half years, concentrating on the twelve who were with him, yet the depth of that ministry to those few men was such that Jesus could literally transfer his earthly job description to them.

"As Thou didst send me into the world, I have also sent them into the world. (John 17:18)

These were the ones into whom he had imparted his life, and to whom he entrusted the task of reaching all mankind by continuous life-imparting discipleship. We are saved today because of this plan.

It's of real concern, therefore—and critical to the principle of 2 Timothy 2:2 reproduction—that the correct men and women are chosen into whom a life-giving commitment is given. Jesus was careful and wary in committing himself to men, including those who professed belief in him, when he could see that their commitment to him was unsure or merely curious. Look at this Scripture:

"Now when He was in Jerusalem at the Passover, during the feast, many believed in His name, beholding His signs which He was doing. But Jesus, on His part, was not entrusting Himself to them, for He knew all men, and because He did not need anyone to bear witness concerning men, for He Himself knew what was in man." (John 2: 23–25).

Jesus knew people well enough to realize that many would believe in him because of the miracles he did, but that it was probably more curiosity than commitment. He did not give himself to those people. He could see their hearts and knew they were not going to be the faithful ones whom he would select.

Even with those who did follow him, he gave opportunities to leave if they thought the cost of being with him was too high. In John 6, the Lord teaches some very difficult things to his followers, difficult both to understand or accept. It's a long passage, but here are the key points:

—"I am the living bread that came down out of heaven; if anyone eats of this bread, he shall live forever; and the bread also which I shall give for the life of the world is My flesh." (John 6:51).

—"Jesus therefore said to them, 'Truly, truly, I say to you, unless you eat the flesh of the Son of man and drink His blood, you have no life in yourselves.'" (John 6:53).

—"Many therefore of His disciples, when they heard this said, 'This is a difficult statement; who can listen to it?' . . . As a result of this many of His disciples withdrew, and were not walking with Him anymore." (John (6:60, 66).

Today, of course, we understand what Jesus was saying. We hear it every time we celebrate communion; his body broken for us is the bread; his blood shed for us is the wine. But to those early followers, it may have seemed either insane or cannibalistic. Now look at what Jesus says to the 12 "capital D" disciples:

"Jesus therefore said to the twelve, 'You do not want to go away also, do you?' Simon Peter answered Him, 'Lord, to whom shall we go? You have words of eternal life.'" (John 6:67, 68).

Do you think Peter understood what Jesus was saying about eating his flesh? I'm not sure he did. Nor do I think that when Jesus asked the twelve, "do you want to go also . . ." that he was imploring them to stay. I think Jesus wanted them to know being with him was voluntary, and that discipleship was based on knowing the Person of Christ, not on an understanding of the program or theology.

One ministry-building theory suggests that someone should have told Jesus, "Listen, if you want a big following, don't teach puzzling, difficult things, watch most of your group leave, then ask the remainder if they want to leave also!" Compare this to our "normal" ministry desire to get as large a congregation as possible, then have a fund-raising drive to build a bigger building in order to recruit an even bigger crowd. I once attended a church growth seminar which had a session titled "Closing the Back Door." Its purpose was to implement ways to keep people from leaving the local church. This thinking is good if you want a crowd. It's not good if you want discipleship and Great Commission ministry.

Selection . . .

It's important to examine the principles of selection which Jesus employed, so that we today can have good selection guidelines as well. We want to assure, as much as we humans can, that our lives will indeed result in future generations of godly women and men able and willing to do the same.

But first, let me give you a quiz. It's the "Events in the Ministry of Christ" quiz. Look at the little chart below and see if you can put these eight events in Jesus' ministry in chronological order. Match the number on the line with the letter describing the event in Jesus' ministry. Fair warning: almost no one gets this right, so don't feel badly if you're surprised at some of it.

Beginning of ministry 26 AD							the Cross 30 AD
1	2	3	4	5	6	7	8

a. raises Lazarus from the dead

b. feeds the 5,000

c. meets the first disciples

d. the "Transfiguration"

e. turns water into wine—the wedding at Cana

f. chooses His 12 Disciples

g. meets the woman at the well

    h. calls the 4 "fishers of men"

How'd you do? Here are the answers:

    1. = c Jesus meets the first disciples (John 1:35ff.)

    2. = e turns water into wine at the wedding at Cana (John 2:1–11)

    3. = g meets the woman at the well (John 4: 5ff.)

    4. = h calls the 4 "fishers of men" (Mark 1: 16–20)

    5. = f chooses His 12 Disciples (Mark 3; 14)

    6. = b feeds the 5,000 (Matthew 14: 13 ff)

    7. = d the "Transfiguration" (Luke 9: 28ff.)

    8. = a raises Lazarus from the dead (John 11: 1ff.)

Why is this difficult to do, and why is it important to notice the time frame of the Lord's ministry? It's difficult because the emphases of the four Gospels differ, so the chronology may seem confused. For example, look at the Gospel of Mark, the first chapter. In verses 12 and 13, we have the very familiar temptation of Christ out in the wilderness. We all associate this event with the earliest part of his ministry.

Now look at Mark 1: 14, the very next verse. It says,

"... after John had been taken into custody, Jesus came into Galilee, preaching the gospel of God." (Mark 1:14).

John, the Baptist, was taken into custody only once, and ended that captivity by being beheaded at the request of a dancing girl's mother (Matthew 14:3 & Mark 6:17).

So, between verse 13 of Mark 1 and verse 14 of Mark 1, there is a period of time which may have lasted as long as one and a half years. Many of the events in Christ's ministry during that period are recorded in the Gospel of John.

Yet when we read the Gospel of Mark, it seems as though Jesus called the four "fishers of men" to follow him very early in his ministry. He did not. Jesus knew these men, had spent time with them in ministry, and had carefully chosen them based upon their tested, not potential, character.

Why is this important? It's important because we need to recognize that Jesus did not select his 12 Disciples (Mark 3:13, 14, "... and He chose twelve, that they should be with Him ...) in the early stages of his ministry, but nearly *halfway* through his ministry. He took his time, and he selected them, I believe, based upon principles that we today can follow. I would not be surprised to learn that many Christians might feel that Jesus could merely look at a person with a hypnotizing stare, say, "Follow Me!" and that person would float off after the Lord like a balloon on a string. If it had happened that way, it doesn't help us much today in selecting the right people to disciple.

So here are what I see as some of the principles for selecting "faithful men and women" to whom we can entrust the precious *things* of God's plan for salvation.

First of all, Jesus did four essential "activities" in His ministry.

1. He ministered to the many ...

   - by preaching to them (Matthew 4:23)

   - by teaching them (Matthew 4:23)

   - by healing them and doing miracles (Matthew 4:23)

   - by feeding them (Matthew 14:19)

2. He selected the few (Mark 3:14)

3. He imparted His life to the few (Mark 3:14) "... with Him ... "

4. He trained the few for service (Mark 3:14) "... that He might send them out to preach ... "

Let's look at how he selected the few.

Stages of selection:

- Caution—John 2: 23–25 Remember, Jesus did not entrust himself to these curious ones.

- "Come and see"—John 1:39 This is in the early period, just after Jesus had been baptized by John, and John's disciples asked Jesus where he was staying. Jesus' statement: "Come and see," is an invitation to spend time with him, not a recruitment to ministry.

Principle # 2 Give Your Life to People, Not Just Your Knowledge.

- "Follow Me, and I will make you become fishers of men."—Mark 1:17. This stage of selection has both a challenge, "Follow Me" and a promise of ministry training, "I will make you become fishers of men."

- "... He appointed twelve, that they might be with Him, and that He might send themout to preach ..." (Mark 3:13, 14). Finally, from a larger group from which to choose, Jesus selects the 12 disciples who would become his core team, those who would be "with Him," and whom he would send out to preach and have authority.

This final stage of selection puts the disciples into a relationship with the Lord which is *on his terms*, not theirs. They were to be "with Him" from that point on; their fishing days (for fish) were over.

Principles of Selection in the ministry of Christ:

- *The time factor:* Take sufficient time to be around people, in order to get to know them personally, and to see how they react to different ministry situations. Think of all the times Jesus had with the disciples! They were in storms in boats, in wild scenes in the Temple as their "boss" tore the place apart, in events of healing, in the presence of demonic exocisms, in compassionate ministrations and confrontational encounters ... you name it, first-century-excitement-wise, and Jesus and the disciples had done it, and this was *before* he had appointed them to the core team. He knew these men and how they responded to the events of life and His ministry. He knew their strengths and weaknesses. He knew their failures of faith and appreciated their struggles to believe. And of course, they got to know and trust him.

What if Christ's ministry had *begun* at point # 5 on the little quiz chart above? That is, what if Jesus chose the 12 disciples in the very first days of his ministry? His selection of the key disciples, if successful, would have been based upon sheer luck (which doesn't exist), or some sort of supernatural insight that only he possessed. In neither instance would we today be helped in how to select correctly.

There was a time in my early Christian experience when it was popular to "have a guy" whom you were discipling. There was little thought about *how* to get the guy; it was just important that you had one. Then at a conference, Bible study, Friday night rally, or whatever ... you'd refer to "my guy, who's doing such and such." This usually didn't work too well, for a number of reasons, and "the guy" more often than not disappeared. Then you had to go find another one. This situation was discouraging and caused some real doubt about whether discipleship actually worked. Good selection is necessary for a person to stay encouraged in this business of "make disciples . . . teaching them to obey all that I have commanded." (Matthew 28:20).

If the Lord had chosen his key followers this way, we'd all be in big trouble, because the fact that we have a relationship with God today is in part a direct result of the faithfulness of those first-century disciples.

What if Christ's ministry had *ended* at point #5? In other words, what if Jesus had gone through the first two years of ministry gathering followers, but then never chose and equipped the few? What if he had not appointed twelve to be with him, twelve into whom he would impart his life and train to carry on after he had gone back to the Father? This is in essence what most local churches do, in my experience, gather a group but not help the few go on to maturity, or train them for ministry.

Well, again, we'd all probably still be lost and facing an eternity apart from God, because it was crucial that the disciples proclaim Christ. The future of mankind's redemption depended on those early followers.

- *(You) . . . be about the Father's business.*

Look at these Scriptures:

". . . And He said to them, 'Let us go somewhere else to the towns nearby, in order that I may preach there also; for that is what I came out for.'" (Mark 1:38).

"And Jesus was going about all the cities and the villages, teaching in their synagogues, and proclaiming the gospel of the kingdom, and healing every kind of disease and every kind of sickness." (Matthew 9:35).

"After Jesus had finished instructing his twelve disciples, he went on from there to teach and preach in the towns of Galilee." (Matthew 11: 1 NIV).

Did you see in the Mark 1 verse, Jesus said, " . . . for that is what I came out for."

Isn't that an amazing challenge to us? Jesus knew what he had come out for. Do we? If we know what God wants us to do, then we need to do it. If I talk about or recruit to something that I myself do not do, all I'll attract is more hypocrites, like myself.

When my wife and I began a ministry at a certain college, our ministry leadership told us, "Try whatever you want to. Be different. Make a whole new set of mistakes!" What a great freedom we'd been given!

So here's what we tried. Nancy and I decided we'd personally do two things: evangelism and Scripture memory. While the usual approach to campus ministry involved numerous fun activities such as hot dog cookouts, canoe trips, and other fellowship events, we opted for those two things. What I mean is that Nancy and I would do what we felt God had clearly called us to do, and then see if anyone else wanted to do it with us. It was one good input of the Word, and one good output.

This had some interesting results. Here's a hypothetical, but typical, phone call we'd get from students.

"Hi! This is _____. I hear that you're starting a ministry this year at ____. When's your fellowship get-together?"

"Sorry, we don't have a fellowship time."

"Oh. Well, when's your Bible study?"

"We don't have one of those either."

"Wow. What *do* you do?"

"We're doing evangelism in the dorms, and Scripture memory."

Pause in the conversation. "Oh, okay. Well . . ."

I hope this doesn't sound snobbish, but we wanted to cut right to the chase with this new ministry, and see if we could find the few students who wanted to do the tough things of ministry, not just the fun, fellowship things. At the end of the first year, we had two students, a guy and a girl, who joined us in evangelism and Scripture memory. By the end of the second year, there were about eight, and at the end of the third year, there were about 15 students, all learning to do evangelism and Scripture memory. And we never even talked or preached about those things. Just doing them ourselves had caught on. That was a highly motivated group of students. Of course, once serious students came around, we did do Bible studies and fun activities, but to serve them, not recruit them.

I see three benefits of personally doing the ministry, of being about the Father's business:

1. It accomplishes ministry work in and of itself.

2. It's obedience for me.

3. It attracts the right kind of people.

What do I mean by it attracting the right kind of people? This brings us to selection principle # 3.

- *Allow people to select themselves.*

Are they willing to pay the costs of discipleship? People's motivation for why they do things is very important. If people are externally motivated, it means that something *outside* them is what causes them to act. This outside influence is usually either a positive attraction or a negative fear. The positive attraction could be a promise of a reward ("If you sign up now, you'll get a free toaster!"), the curiosity factor of a novelty (and let's face it, Christians can be very prone to fads and novelties . . .), or the perceived pleasure of belonging to a group or movement.

The negative fear-factor can be as mild as "If you don't teach the Sunday school class, no one will." Or it can be as intimidating as the fear of not going to heaven; cults and false religions often use this kind of leverage to get people to do things.

Internal motivation, as the word implies, comes from within a person. This motivation results from a person's mind and heart responding to what he or she perceives as truth, and the commitment is a deep one. It goes "clear through to the bone," as the expression says; it's not just a coat of paint on the surface. It's this kind of motivation that the Lord sought to foster, not the shallow interest of those responding to the "carrot or the stick."

I see two approaches to finding followers: cattle-herding or ministry by "vacuum." Cattle-herding simply means rounding up the biggest number of people you can, then keeping them in the herd. Ministry by vacuum means interacting with people, then backing up to give them room to (choose to) either leave or follow. The giving people room is what I call creating a vacuum . . . it's a space or hole that people need to step into in order to follow Jesus. After all, the word "follow" implies that the person being followed is moving. I think Jesus did this.

Look at the feeding of the 4000 in. The Lord felt compassion for the crowds, and he fed them. But after he fed them, it says,

"He sent them away. And immediately He entered the boat with His disciples and came to the district of Dalmanutha." (Mark 8:1–10).

Well, that certainly wasn't a very "seeker-friendly" thing to do. There he had a crowd of at least 4000 (and probably many more), and he sends them away. That's no way to build a mega-ministry. Then, to compound the error, a little later he gives the crowd an idea of the cost of following him.

". . . He summoned the multitude with His disciples, and said to them, 'If anyone wishes to come after Me, let him deny himself, and take up his cross and follow Me. For whoever wishes to save his life shall lose it; but whoever loses his life for My sake and the gospel's shall save it.'" (Mark 8:34, 35).

It's been said that if you want to sell a product, you need to have the "three magic words" in the advertising: "Quick! Fun! Easy!" Jesus knew that such a philosophy of recruiting would result only in a crowd of curious, shallow, uncommitted fish & bread-eaters. If the true cost is communicated, it allows people to search their hearts and decide if it's bread, fish, and miracles they're interested in, or Jesus.

- *Select based upon demonstrated faithfulness, not on potential, giftedness, personality, or verbalized interest.*

Boy, is this idea beaten to pieces in the Christian community today! We tend to go for the sharp guy, the gifted woman, the person with the dynamic personality, or the one who says," Count me in!" but then doesn't show up (then we make excuses *for* him!).

What we want to do is come up with a way to allow people to *demonstrate* that they're faithful, not just say they are. And, no, this is not making people "jump through hoops." It's simply having standards for selection and holding to them. I like the idea of having one good input of the Word: ongoing Bible study, consistency in daily time with God (quiet times), or Scripture memory—and one good output, such as . . . will he come with me on evangelism? I'll admit that in one ministry situation, I was tempted to set up a bit of a hoop, but that was because I didn't see anyone in the existing group who was down to business. When we tried to find a day and time for Bible study, no one was willing to compromise their other activities, so finally I said, "Okay, the Bible study is at 6:30 AM on Saturday morning at Jerry's restaurant. I think that's an available time for any of you who want to come."

That's the idea of having a standard for selection, but rarely would we apply it to a group activity such as a Bible study or fellowship time.

Remember, this is not to select people for inclusion in the group; it's to select a person for me to disciple one-on-one. Everyone is invited to be in the large group, or the open Bible study. It is the group settings which give us a good idea of those who are more mature, ready to respond to a challenge, or willing to show their seriousness. But we can't choose everyone for individual discipleship, nor should we, for there are many who aren't ready for such a commitment, and for good reasons. There are many in a group of believers who are healing from the wounds of life, or just beginning to grow spiritually. These folks need time to heal; they need affirmation and good fellowship, not intensive discipleship or training. But to exclude selection of the few because there are many who are not ready, is a disservice to all. Selection is necessary for the Great Commission work of making disciples.

I've met Christian workers who struggle with this. They feel that singling out a few for discipling is, in a sense, playing favorites. They are often compassionate, inclusive folks who instinctively hear the word "rejection" when the word "selection" is mentioned. I understand and appreciate that compassion. Yet we know that this kind of selection (not "rejection") is a part of life. When a woman chooses a man to marry, she is not rejecting everyone else; she's simply expressing her desire to enter into a unique, intimate relationship with one special person. Without such a selection, relationships would be shallow and superficial; besides which, the earth's population might die out. (well, given the "new morality,' maybe not ...).

When a pastor, or average radical Christian, selects someone to disciple, he or she is not excluding others, or rejecting them; she or he is simply choosing to enter into a deeper, more intensive relationship so that the other person can also reproduce spiritually and add people to the Kingdom.

Question: what results from not having selection standards, or of lowering them or abandoning them? We're all familiar with how it goes. The Sunday school teacher says, "Please read 1 Corinthians, chapter 9 for next week. That'll be our text for the next lesson." What happens? Next week arrives and most of the class members haven't read the chapter. Most don't even remember they were supposed to. What does the teacher do, cancel the class? Of course not, she or he just goes ahead and teaches the lesson anyway. Mediocrity: it's how we Christians do things, and what we've come to expect.

The problem is that when standards are lowered, or abandoned, people get used to the idea that the standards are not really important. If the Sunday school teacher did indeed say, "Well, since no one did the assigned reading, we won't meet today. The assignment for next week is the same: read 1 Corinthians 9. Class dismissed," that would get people's attention. They would either storm out and complain to the Christian education director, or they'd think, "Wow, this is a serious Sunday school teacher . . . I like it!"

The point of this principle is that the best way to know who's serious and willing to be committed is to give them a chance to select themselves in or out based on Biblical standards that are established, communicated, and held to.

- *Spend extended time in prayer.*

"And it was at this time that He went off to the mountain to pray, and He spent the whole night in prayer to God. And when day came, He called His disciples to Him; and chose twelve of them, whom He also named as apostles . . ." (Luke 6:12, 13).

We don't know what Jesus prayed during that night, or even if it was prayer focused on selecting the twelve. I think we can assume that at least a significant amount of the time of prayer concerned his choosing of the twelve. We don't know *what* he prayed about the disciples on the mountain, but we do know what he valued in the lives of his disciples, as expressed in John 17:6–18

—". . . they have kept Thy word." (6)

—they received God's words, understood who Jesus was, and his being sent by the Father (8)

—they were joyful in Christ, even though the world hated them (13, 14)

—they were not worldly (16)

—they were "send-able" and able to do Jesus' job (18)

These are some good qualities to pray about when we choose those to whom we will impart our lives. Extended time in prayer is also our safeguard against choosing according to human insight rather than on

God's perspective. (I Samuel 16:7) God sees the heart, not just the external appearance.

- *Once you've selected, don't hold back.*

"It is a snare for a man to say rashly, 'It is holy,' and after the vows to make inquiry." (Proverbs 20:25).

Deliver the goods! The point here is that *after* we have chosen a person, we shouldn't question our choice or decide to lessen *our* commitment to the person. It's kind of like marriage. This commitment thing is a two-way deal. If we ask commitment from those we are discipling, we must be committed to them. Yes, there will be times when we are disappointed in them, perhaps many times, just as Jesus wondered at the lack of faith of the disciples. Yet his commitment to them was profound and faithful, even when theirs to him fell short or was "of little faith."

—in failure (Luke 9:40), when they couldn't drive the evil spirit out of the child.

—in foolish pride (Luke 9: 46–50), when they argued about who was the greatest.

—in fear and desertion (Mark 14: 27–31, 71), when their courage failed when Jesus was taken from them.

Your commitment to those you chose to disciple will give them the freedom to fail, to count the cost, and eventually to have victory. It's discipleship without divorce.

Here are some common errors in selection:

1. Selection based on potential and verbalized interest rather than demonstrated interest.

Remember, the person who looks good in the eyes of the world may not serve Christ, and the unattractive man or woman may be another Paul. Don't trust your own discernment. Set up appropriate biblical standards and select only those who meet the standards. Make exceptions only when the Holy Spirit convinces you that the standards should not apply in special cases.

2. Giving yourself too completely to the multitudes.

If we use most of our ministry strength on the groups, or people in the groups, we'll not have enough left over for the few. Spiritual multiplication is based on the few, not the many. We can't force people's commitment to us, or to Christ, by forcing our commitment on them. We'll get discouraged and burn out, and they'll feel the pressure of our over-expectations.

3. Selecting more than you can handle.

Even if you have 10 or 15 who meet all your standards, you can't give yourself to so many. Know your real capacity and select only as many as you can impart your life to. One or two is great.

4. Fear of selection at all, due to not wanting to hurt or "offend" anyone.

Without selection, our lives are limited to addition of believers, and a level of maturity (for those we help) far below biblical implications. Remember, selection means neither favoritism toward the few, nor rejection of those not selected. It means having a few proven hungry ones through whom we can reproduce our lives.

5. Selecting problem-oriented people to "fix."

2 Timothy 2:2 says entrust the precious things to "... faithful ones, able to teach others also." The idea here is that those selected are faithful, able to learn, and able to teach. We really don't help folks with significant wounds or afflictions by involving them in intense ministry training. In fact, we may possibly hurt them even more by communicating expectations they are not able to meet. I think the Lord had this in mind when he interacted with the exorcised man in the region of the Gerasenes.

"... the man from whom the demons had gone out was begging Him that he might accompany Him, but He sent him away, saying, 'Return to your home and describe what great things God has done for you.'" (Luke 8: 38, 39).

6. Holding back on those whom you've chosen.

It's a marriage without divorce. If you start to hold back, your young disciple will sense it. This will erode the trust in the relationship and damage the idea of the worth of the individual. Choose carefully, then trust God that you can give yourself away to this person spiritually. If it turns out that the person you've chosen does not want to pay the cost of discipleship, he or she will make it clear and initiate the break himself or herself.

Starting to disciple another...

Okay, let's say that you've prayed and asked God to give you one good person to disciple. You've been a part of your Sunday school class or small group for at least a year, and have seen three people you feel may be serious about their relationship with God. You talk with these three and say that you've wanted to go share your faith with some of the college students at the apartments near campus, and would they come with you? Two of them say they'll do it with you. The third says maybe sometime in the future.

So the two others and you agree to memorize the four verses to the little "SDSD, all 3" gospel illustration, and meet on Wednesday at the Heathen Glen Apartments at 6:00 PM.

On Wednesday, you and one of the two show up at the apartment parking lot. The other one texts you to say "Sorry;" I had to go to dinner with a cousin instead." So both of you, nervous as can be, go talk with students in the apartments, using the five question survey. It goes great! Both of you are amazed and grateful to God that you got to share your faith with a person who had never heard the gospel.

So you pray, "God, let this one faithful person who showed up be the one I can disciple," and God gives you peace to go ahead. Now what do you do? How do you impart your life to this person?

Ask the person if you can get together to talk about "discipleship and ministry." I'm a great fan of meeting in fast-food restaurants. It's (relatively) cheap, if you're watching your diet, most of them have some kind of salad. Best of all, it's informal and is a good setting for building a relationship. Just standing in line to get the food, and eating it, means you have time to talk about the week, the job, the family, and all the everyday issues. Take a look at the Appendix (Instructions) for some more thoughts on the setting and "mood" for these discipleship times.

The basic idea here is for you and the other person to get together once a week for the purpose of you helping him or her to have a solid walk with God. The nature of the relationship depends a lot on who you are, and who other person is. Let me explain.

If you are a mature Christian with some "credibility" like being a Sunday school teacher or small-group leader, and the other person is

Principle # 2 Give Your Life to People, Not Just Your Knowledge.

years younger than you, a "teacher-student" discipling relatonship may be ideal. It would still be very friendly, informal, and relational, but both you and the young Christian would be comfortable with you having the role of teacher.

If you and the other person are of similar ages, and you'd both feel a little uncomfortable (or a lot) with the "teacher-student" kind of relationship, you can certainly define it more as a peer-friendship relationship. In this kind of relationship, you can share the discipleship "material" with her or him, and enjoy the mutual accountability as you go along. When it comes to doing some gospel-sharing, perhaps at student apartments, you'll lead of course, and the other person will be glad to have you lead! But the basis of the discipling can be a "friendship-accountability" one. This works fine.

The balance between the friendly relationship and the actual discipleship content is important. We want enough solid structure in this discipling relationship so that the younger Christian gets to grow biblically and feel the encouragement of making progress. But if it's *too* structured, it can become burdensome or impersonal. No one likes doing studies and exercises just so she can check them off the list.

To illustrate this balance, picture in your mind the track and field event of pole vaulting. The pole-vaulter needs pretty minimal equipment. If she or he has on a suit of armor, or scuba tanks, he or she won't do very well. That would be too much equipment. Too much checklist structure in discipleship is just as hindering and clumsy, and it hurts the relationship. But the pole vaulter *does* need the pole! Too little equipment, or discipleship structure, results in vagueness and frustration.

Okay, so there you both are, sitting in the fast-food restaurant. You say "Colleen, (or Kyle) here's what I hoped we could do . . . I've been working for a while on my relationship with God, and I've come across some pretty good materials that help. Would you want to go through these discipleship plans with me? It's some basic practices of Christian living, and some Christ-like character studies. I think you'd enjoy them, and we could have some good accountability. I was thinking we could get together every Friday lunch, right here. I went through this material in about a year, so that gives a time frame. What do you think?"

That's really all the explanation you need at this point. If Kyle or Colleen says, "Let's do it!" then it's a great start. When you get together, just go through the "7 disciplines and 3 character areas," keeping it very relational, and taking all the time you want. The idea is to see young believers really build some good disciplines (i.e., godly life habits), not just zoom through the material.

Let me mention a bit of a side issue here, relating to relationship building. One of the ways we can keep our discipling relationship actually relational, is to spend time with the person we're helping in *different* situations, not just the discipleship discussion setting.

I remember years ago as I taught a Sunday school class, I found myself thinking, "I wonder what these people are really like outside the Sunday morning class; this is the only place I see them." I made it a point to just visit some of the folks at their homes and it gave me a glimpse into their lives that was wonderful in some cases, and disturbing in others. I realized that one hour a week, when people are at church, is not really representative of people's lives. I saw that I would have to get to know them in other environments as well in order to know them more fully.

Another time I was a leader in a Christian summer training program with college students. One of the young men on my team was very shy and introverted during our training sessions and Bible studies. I arranged to get some time with him with the idea that I was going to encourage him to be a bit more assertive and confident. But before our talk, which happened to be in the game room of the camp, we played a few games of ping pong. Amazing! The guy turned out to be a fire-breathing, do-or-die competitor! This young man who hardly said a word in Bible studies instantly morphed into the Attila, the Hun, of table tennis. I went from planning on giving him a confidence-building talk, to trying to calm him down after his temper outburst when he lost three points in a row! What a difference a different setting can make.

I never would have known this young man was so competitive, or that he had such a hot temper, if I had only been around him during Bible studies, where he was the proverbial lamb.

One last story. Seth was a young man who came to a student Bible study in our home. He was fun, zany, smart and caring. He, unlike the young man in the summer program, was outgoing and very transparent, so it was easy to get to know Seth. But I got to know another aspect about Seth because of his car, an ancient Pontiac that probably held the world record for breakdowns. Seth and I spent a fair number of hours changing parts on that car, or trying to get it started.

What I learned about Seth was how amazingly patient and philosophical he was about that unreliable car, and life in general. Though he was a young Christian, in terms of patience, he was ahead of us all, and it had good effect on the rest of the group. I don't think I would have ever seen this aspect of Seth just from the evening Bible studies.

I think it's valuable to figure out ways to spend this kind of time. Here's some ideas for different situations:

- fun times . . . sports, games, just goofing around

- work time . . . such as working on cars, helping people move apartments, church work days etc.

- meal times with both families, or cookouts, picnics

- in small groups together, Bible studies, seminars or conferences

- correction/ reproof times . . . hard but good, always individually & in love

Remember, this is not to find faults or weaknesses, but to get to know them better.

We'll talk more about the actual one-to-one discipleship times a little later on.

There are some good, practical ministry concepts in the first three chapters of 1 Thessalonians. In this letter to the church at Thessalonica, Paul gives us a helpful, simple picture of his approach to ministry. Let's look at what I call Paul's *goal, heart,* and *method* of ministry. Please bear with me as I ramble a bit here; it's going to take a little time to get to the focus of you and your friend sitting in the fast-food restaurant, but we'll get there. I think it's important to look at some foundational *concepts*, then we'll get to the practical steps of discipling a person.

The goal of ministry

". . . our gospel came to you not simply with words, but also with power, with the Holy Spirit and with deep conviction. You know how we lived among you for your sake. You became imitators of us and the Lord . . ." (1 Thessalonians 1:5, 6 NIV)

The first part of this passage speaks of Paul's determination to get the gospel out (see also Romans 15:20 and 1 Corinthians 2:1–5) to everyone he could. And he wanted to do it in such a way that the simplicity and power of the gospel was clear, focused on Christ, not on "clever or persuasive words." Then there'd be no confusion. Those who received it gladly got the word with the power of the Holy Spirit, with deep conviction. Paul did not want to be just another dog-and-pony show traveling through town.

Now look at the last line of the Scripture passage. "You became imitators of us and the Lord . . ." We'd probably all agree that helping people become imitators of the Lord is a pretty good summary of the goal of ministry. But what about that business of "You became imitators of us . . ."? Does that strike you as being a bit prideful, or even a bit misguided? At best, it may seem intimidating, to wish that the young believers we minister to would become like us!

It is intimidating, but it's also very exciting and motivating. It's intimidating because as we minister to people, younger Christians in the Lord, we *must* realize that they will observe our lives carefully and they *will* imitate us, to some degree and in some ways. Lives reproduce. That means we'd better be genuine Christians with pure motives, and serving the Lord, not ourselves.

The last sentence in 1 Thessalonians 1:5 points out, the people of the city observed and knew how Paul and his fellow ministers "lived among you for your sakes." It's natural and almost inevitable that people will emulate their Christian leaders if the lives of the leaders are good examples of the Christian faith. The writer of Hebrews puts it this way,

"Remember your leaders, who spoke the word of God to you. Consider the outcome of their way of life and imitate their faith." (Hebrews 13:7 NIV).

It's also exciting and motivating because we realize as well what a powerful, godly ministry force we have in the example of our own lives! It motivates us to walk closely with the Lord, to be willing to share our lives openly with people, and to have the joy (not audacity) of basically saying to them, "Be like me!" The word "leverage" may seem inappropriate in speaking of the effect we can have in the lives of people—these are persons' lives, not stone blocks—but "leverage" does express the sense of power God can have in the lives of others, through us.

Paul said "Be like me!" many times. Take a look at these amazing statements from Paul's letters:

"I exhort you therefore, be imitators of me." (1 Corinthians 4:16).

"Be imitators of me, just as I also am of Christ." (1 Corinthians 11:1).

"Brethren, join in following my example . . ." (Philippians 3:17).

"The things you have learned and received and heard and seen in me, practice these things; and the God of peace shall be with you." (Philippians 4:9).

"For you yourselves know how you ought to follow our example, because we did not act in an undisciplined manner among you . . . in order to offer ourselves as a model for you, that you might follow our example. (2 Thessalonians 3:7, 9).

Do these statements surprise you? This is an important ministry principle we don't often hear about. But what a great goal for our ministry: to see people become Christ-like (imitators of the Lord), and to see young believers become imitators of us, in terms of emulating the practices and disciplines that help us have a joyful, victorious walk. It's scary but real.

Please notice, by the way, that Paul certainly knew that there were things about his life that he didn't want others to imitate. After all, he was a sinful human (see Romans 7: 21–23) and would have hated to see his particular manifestation of the sinful nature reproduced in others. So while Paul says ". . . be imitators of me" in 1 Corinthians 4:16, he qualifies this exhortation in 1 Corinthians 11:1. "Be imitators of me, just as I am also of Christ." That's helpful, isn't it? It's the practices and disciplines of the Christian life we hope they'll imitate.

Two hearts of ministry

"But we proved to be gentle among you, as a nursing mother tenderly cares for her own children . . . just as you know how we were exhorting and encouraging and imploring each one of you, as a father would his own children, so that you may walk in a manner worthy of the God who calls you into His own kingdom and glory." (1 Thessalonians 2:7, 11, 12)

Paul says that he and his companions were like . . .

A gentle *mother*, tenderly caring for her own children.

A teaching *father*, exhorting and encouraging and imploring his own children.

I think the "hearts" of ministry are the mother's heart and the father's heart. If you've ever observed a mother with babies or very young children, you know what the mother's heart is: verbalized, demonstrated, unconditional love. Moms love their babies and every word and action expresses that love.

Obviously, we're not going to baby-talk with the young Christian we're discipling, but we sure can express and demonstrate unconditional acceptance and a genuine liking for him or her. As Paul says in verse 8 of this same passage, "having a fond affection for you . . . you had become very dear to us." Everyone loves to know that there's another person, or persons, who just likes her or him a lot, who thinks they're great! We'll forgive about anything in another person if we know they really care about us. This, I think is the heart of the mother.

Can you think of ways to let the person you're helping know that you really like her or him? While flattery is bad, praise is good. Give the person some well-earned praise. My wife and I have a collegiate Bible study in our home, and one evening the young staff man, a gifted leader, was teaching the group. He'd prepared a really good talk, but the college students that night were wound up and kind of crazy. Struggle as he might to get it under control and back on the Word, it just dissolved into chaos. The students sure had fun, but the young man leading it was discouraged. As we talked later, I looked him in the eye, and said, "I'm glad you were leading tonight and not me. I think you did a great job." The look on his face expressed it all; it said, "Thank you . . . I needed that."

The point of the *heart of the father* is to teach and admonish the young Christian. As Paul says in Colossians,

". . . admonishing every man and teaching every man with all wisdom, that we may present every man complete in Christ." (Colossians 1:28).

It's been said that Christian ministry can be summed up in two key words: truth and love. If the heart of the mother is love, then the heart of the father is truth. The "dad in us" wants to make sure that our young children in the faith know the truth and are obedient to it. In Matthew 28:20, Jesus says, ". . . teaching them to obey everything I have commanded you . . ." There's a world of difference between simply teaching a person something (imparting information), and teaching someone to *obey* something (imparting a conviction). As anyone who is a parent knows, we cannot simply say to a youngster, "Now I want you to eat those lima beans," then go off to do a household chore and expect to see the beans gone (unless it's under the table or in the dog's stomach).

Obedience has to be taught "bean by bean." The Apostle John said in 3 John 4,

". . . I have no greater joy than this, to hear of my children walking in the truth."

It wasn't just John's spiritual children *knowing* the truth, but *walking* in the truth, that brought John joy.

It's possible that this difference between teaching—and teaching to obey—is part of the problem in Christian instruction. We Christians may have fallen prey to the modern education concept, that exposing people to information is the same as people understanding that information and acting on it. It's certainly easier to merely tell people something than help them to understand and do it.

Having Biblical truth is not sufficient. *Acting* on that truth is what God requires.

Remember the illustration in Matthew 7 about the wise person who built his house on the rock, and the foolish person who built on sand. The difference lies not in one man having the Lord's words and the other not; the difference was in one man's obedience to those words, and disobedience in the other's.

"Therefore, everyone who hears these words of mine and puts them into practice is like a wise man who built his house on the rock . . . But everyone who hears these words of mine and does not put them into practice is like a foolish man who built his house on sand." (Matthew 7:24ff. NIV).

The heart of the father is to teach truth, so that the young disciple may ". . . walk in a manner worthy of God . . ."

Can you do this? Will you do this? I think it's safe to say that each one of us has a natural leaning one way or the other. You might be a compassionate caring person who struggles a bit with telling the truth to loved ones, or a confident truth-sharer who needs to remember that truth without love is like surgery without anesthetic.

We need to have both hearts, the mom's and the dad's. Whether you're a woman or a man, when you're discipling another person, you need to do both: share truth and sincerely care.

Method in Ministry

The first one is simply to *keep in touch* with your young disciple.

"... when we could endure it no longer ... we sent Timothy, our brother and God's fellow worker in the gospel of Christ, to strengthen and encourage you as to your faith. (I Thessalonians 3:1, 2).

What was it that Paul and the others could "no longer endure"? Verses 17 and 18 of the previous chapter (1 Thessalonians 2:17, 18) give us a good idea. They were eager to see the people in Thessalonica, but had been prevented from coming to see them. So finally they sent Timothy to minister to them and to bring Paul a report as to how these people were doing spiritually. Paul said he was worried that "... the tempter might have tempted you, and our labor should be in vain." (1 Thessalonians 3:5) He said the same thing to the church folks in Corinth (2 Corinthians 11:3). It wasn't that Paul viewed the church as a business venture that might fail; he loved these people and cared about them a great deal. "For you are our glory and joy." (1 Thessalonians 2:20).

No matter how difficult it is, keep in touch with the person you're helping. This sounds *so* obvious, but let's face it, these are busy hectic days in which people have very little free time. College students have more free time than most adults (though I'm not sure they'd agree!), but even then it can be very challenging to find a time and place to get with a collegian on a regular basis. And it's even more challenging to get connect with people with jobs, families (think kids' sports!), church responsibilities, etc. We must work hard to make it happen. God's enemy hates it when he senses a young believer is growing to maturity, for then that mature one can reach others. So the enemy will do anything he can to derail the growing Christian's relationship with the disciple-maker. Making it hard to stay connected is, I believe, one of the enemy's strategies.

Here's a second aspect of ministry method: *tell the truth about the Christian life* to the young Christian you're helping. To the Thessalonian believers Paul writes,

"... so that no one may be disturbed by these afflictions (which Paul and his fellow ministers were going through); for you yourselves know that we have been destined for this. For indeed when we were with you, we kept telling you in advance that we were going to suffer affliction, and so it came to pass, as you know." (1 Thessalonians 3: 3, 4).

Isn't that interesting? Paul was wise enough to realize that sugar-coating the Christian's life experience would actually be more discouraging to young believers than telling them the truth—that Christians will "... suffer affliction ..." Why? Because if we sugar-coat what the Christian life really is, then the young believers will be disturbed when (not "if") trials and suffering occur. And as 2 Timothy 3:12 says,

"... indeed, all who desire to live godly in Christ Jesus will be persecuted."

If we pretend, as I have heard some Christian speakers do, that being a Christian assures a peaceful, happy, prosperous life, then we have done a great disservice to both the young believer and the Kingdom of God.

It is a disservice to the young believer because he or she may fall away when trouble comes. Peter warns believers,

"... do not be surprised at the fiery ordeal among you, which comes upon you for your testing, as though some strange thing were happening to you ..." (1 Peter 4:12).

And it is a disservice to the Kingdom of God because when young believers are given a pleasant, but false, picture of the Christian life, it is unlikely that they will have the courage or motivation to join in the battle for peoples' souls. If the believer's life consists of comfortable socializing (aka "fellowship"), the costly actions of gospel-sharing or discipling will probably seem strange or frightening.

So Paul and his companions had been careful, in advance, to let the young Thessalonian Christians know the truth about what it meant to walk with the Lord: there was joy and victory, but also affliction and suffering.

Finally, *pray for the young Christians*, and your relationship with them.

"For what thanks can we render to God for you in return for all the joy with which we rejoice before our God on your account, as we night and day keep praying most earnestly that we may see your face, and may complete what is lacking in your faith. (1 Thessalonians 3:9, 10).

This probably seems obvious, but I'll admit that in my own ministry, I talk to people more about the Lord, than I talk to the Lord about the people. Paul prayed for the people at Thessalonica, that they would increase in love for one another, and that God would establish in their hearts "unblamable holiness." What a great prayer.

5

Principle # 3: Always Minister from the Clear Meaning of the Bible.

IN THE PREFACE PAGES of a well-known study Bible, the editor, Charles Ryrie, says this: ". . . of course, you want to hear God speak to you through what you are studying. But do not be tempted to see 'deeper' meanings or try to discover hidden ideas that no one else has ever seen! Do not invent some "message" that is not in the text in order to justify an idea you have or course of action you want to take. In the *plain meaning* of the text there is ample material for the Holy Spirit to use to speak to you and meet your individual needs."[1]

This advice is very good, and brings up our next principle of ministry: always base your ministry and teaching on the plain sense meaning of the Bible. Teach and practice the clear principles of the Bible, trusting that this faithful rule is the path to Christian maturity and victory. Don't bend the Scripture, twist it, alter it, deviate from it, exceed it, take away from it, force it to say something it doesn't, and never, never, never change the essential message of the gospel of Christ, namely . . .

- that people sin and are separated from the Holy God because of it
- that people can do nothing themselves to overcome, or pay for, their sin nature
- that people need a Savior, and Jesus is that Savior

---

1. *The Ryrie Study Bible*, NASB, p.vi.

- that people must personally receive Jesus Christ as Savior to be saved and have a relationship with God

Pretty simple, evident, truths, right? But through the centuries, much has been done to adulterate even these plain-sense basics of the Christian faith. We'll look at four big errors that those who minister to others should be aware of, in order to help folks in our ministries learn about and avoid these pitfalls.

The four big errors I'll mention are as follows:

- Legalism . . . out-Bible'ing the Bible

- Liberalism . . . loosening Scripture to excuse sin

- Mysticism . . . seeking a relationship with God in un-Biblical ways

- Universalism . . . denying God's justice and wrath, due to misguided compassion

Legalism—"out-Bible'ing the Bible"

1 Corinthians 4:6 says, in warning, ". . . do not exceed what is written."

Legalism is the one people often think of when they picture Christian doctrine in a negative sense, but really it's the least common and least dangerous (today), I think, of the classic errors. It usually means people adding restrictive rules and regulations to the Christian life that are not clearly stated in Scripture.

My observation is that legalism takes two forms: either *returning* to some Old Testament regulation, or *creating* a regulation to address some persistent social ill. For those who enact or condone legalism, it may seem easier for a Christian community to try to enforce a prohibition, than to get at the heart of the problem by getting at the heart of people. Let me use a couple of simple examples to illustrate these two kinds of legalism.

—Going back to Old Testament regulations, for example, an adherence to the Sabbath day, or an admonition to follow certain dietary procedures.

—Creating rules to address a persistent social problem, such as drinking alcoholic beverages. There are churches, denominations, and Christian schools that require students, members, or clergy to sign a pledge not to drink any alcohol.

Addressing the adherence to some Old Testament regulations, which Christ has fulfilled and are no longer required of Christians, we're aware that certain Christian communities take these regulations quite seriously. This is not a widespread situation, and those parts of the Christian world which do believe in these laws (and, by the way, can be quite biblical in other regards) are very open and blatant about these convictions. So at least there is no subterfuge or hidden agenda with this type of legalism.

Are they mistaken in adhering to such Old Testament regulations as observing the Sabbath Day (our modern Saturday), or dietary laws? I believe they are. Two verses of Scripture help clarify this issue. The first regards the Sabbath

"Therefore, do not let anyone judge you by what you eat or drink, or with regard to a religious festival, or a New Moon celebration, or a Sabbath Day. These are a shadow of the things that were to come; the reality, however, is found in Christ." (Colossians 2:16, 17 NIV).

And in reference to dietary laws:

"Such teachings come through hypocritical liars, whose consciences have been seared as with a hot iron. They forbid people to marry and order them to abstain from certain foods, which God created to be received with thanksgiving by those who believe and know the truth." (1 Timothy 4:2, 3 NIV).

It's pretty clear that observances of Jewish Law, as it pertains to festivals, the Sabbath, and abstaining from certain foods, are unnecessary for Christians, those ". . . who believe and know the truth." When Paul states in his letter to the Romans that even non-Jews have aspects of the Law in their hearts, it is implied that it is moral and ethical law which ". . . alternately accuses or else defends them . . ." rather than dietary or ceremonial regulations. I doubt a Gentile's conscience would "accuse" him if he were munching on an eel, but "defend" him about the trout.

"For when Gentiles who do not have the Law do instinctively the things of the Law, these, not having the Law, are a law to themselves, in that they show the work of the Law written in their hearts, their conscience bearing witness, ant their thoughts alternately accusing or else defending them . . ." (Romans 2:14, 15).

Principle # 3: Always Minister from the Clear Meaning of the Bible. 143

The best discussion of this is found in the book of Galatians, a letter by Paul to an early church whose members were apparently seeking to cling to Jewish law even as they looked to Jesus as their Savior

Paul instructs these Galatians that their position in Christ through faith does indeed free them from the Jewish Law, just as a child who has been under the supervision of a guardian is freed from that supervision when he/she becomes an adult. Paul is saying that people can't have it both ways: you can't be both a Christian *and* an adherent of Jewish law. Faith in Christ frees a person from Jewish law, not a freedom to sin but a freedom to be righteous (Galatians 5: 13). Here's a quick look at the crux of Paul's argument.

> "What I am saying is that as long as the heir is a child, he is no different from a slave, although he owns the whole estate. He is subject to guardians and trustees until the time set by his father. . . But when the time had fully come, God sent his Son, born of a woman, born under law, to redeem those under the law, that we might receive the full rights of sons . . . So you are no longer a slave (to the law), but a son; and since you are a son, God has made you also an heir. (Galatians 4:1–7 NIV). . . But now that you know God—or rather are known by God—how is it you are turning back to those weak and miserable principles? Do you wish to be enslaved to them all over again? You are observing special days and months, and seasons and years! I fear for you, that somehow I have wasted my efforts on you." (Galatians 4:9–11 NIV).

I encountered an instance of a mild form of legalism when I was a young Christian. It concerned the whole Sabbath day thing. The churches I attended as a new believer were quite good and encouraging to me; they taught the Bible and were warm, welcoming places. But they also adhered to a view of the Sabbath that I found confusing. I remember one church elder who emphasized the importance of not doing "significant work" on Sunday, because "it's the Sabbath, and we need to honor the Sabbath and keep it holy."

I knew enough about the Old Testament and calendars to realize that Sunday is the first day of the week, not the seventh. Therefore, to my thinking, Sunday wasn't the Sabbath. Then the movie *Chariots of Fire* came out, in which the hero, Eric Liddell, refused to run his scheduled race in the Olympics because it was on a Sunday. The elder of my church said, in essence, "See, I told you! That guy obeyed the Sabbath by not running!"

And indeed, Christians all over America made a big deal out of what a strong Christian Eric Liddell was (and I'm sure he really was, but not for *that* reason) because he "held to Christian principles" by refusing to run a race on "the Sabbath."

Well, I was perplexed. If Mr. Liddell were adhering to Jewish law, then it would have been a race scheduled on Saturday that posed a problem. If Sunday is, as some traditions state, not the Sabbath, but the Christian "first day," a day observed to commemorate Jesus' resurrection, then it has nothing to do with not working (or running a race). It can't be both ways. It's either the Jewish Sabbath day—the modern Saturday—or it's the Christian day of celebrating the Lord's resurrection.

I may be stepping on some toes here. Some folks might see the idea of Sunday Sabbath as a time-honored church tradition, and may even view discussing it's validity as being petty and picky. Or, people may reason this way, "Hey, the idea of a day of rest is a good thing, so even if the Sabbath day is a Jewish, not Christian, regulation, what's the big deal . . . where's the harm in that?" I think the answer is that while the *idea* of a day of rest may be good, the *requirement* of Christians to obey a Jewish law is not good. Even to *imply* that observance of Jewish ritual law is good for Christians is problematic. This is the very topic Paul admonishes the Galatian church about. I certainly agree with a Christian thinking, "You know, the concept of one out of seven days to rest and focus on God is good. I think I'll do that." Coming from *within* the person, based on his freedom to choose and an insight into the benefits of some Old Testament rules, that could well be a good choice, to take one day a week to rest. But if it is an external regulation, or admonition to do so from a church, then it is not a freely made choice, but adherence to Old Testament law. I believe that would be wrong. See the difference?

When Old Testament regulations were based on moral or ethical matters (lust, murder, stealing etc.), these laws certainly apply for all people for all time. Jewish ritual or liturgical law, however, does not. Even circumcision, which Genesis 17:10, 13 calls "an everlasting covenant," was ruled unnecessary by the Council of Jerusalem (Acts 15: 5, 10), and clarified by Paul in Romans:

"But he is a Jew who is one inwardly; and circumcision is that which is of the heart, by the Spirit, not by the letter (of the Law) . . ." (Romans 2:29).

Principle # 3: Always Minister from the Clear Meaning of the Bible. 145

I find it interesting that Christians even define themselves by an adherence to the Ten Commandments. Have you noticed that it is not Jews, but Christians, who defend the presence of plaques and banners with the Ten Commandments in public places such as schools and courthouses? That Christians have "appropriated" the Ten Commandments as their own is understandable; the Ten Commandments are viewed as the essence of morality and proper human behavior. It is none-the-less a mild form of legalism for Christians, in that of the ten commands, one is obsolete (Sabbath), 3 have been "upgraded" (murder, adultery, stealing), and one has been modified (we do not punish those who take the Lord's Name in vain). The Ten Commandments do not represent the heart of Christianity, but rather summarize an aspect of Jewish law.

The question is, *why* would people *want* to put themselves under the law again once they had been freed from it? Perhaps it has to do with people who don't do well with handling freedom, and yearn to again be bound by the sense of security of rules and regulations. It's a false security because it's not really safety, but slavery.

Paul told the church at Galatia:

"It is for freedom that Christ has set us free. Stand firm then, and do not let yourselves be burdened again by a yoke of slavery." (Galatians 5:1 NIV).

And remember, this freedom is not to be exploited for the sake of sin.

"But do not use your freedom to indulge the sinful nature; rather, serve one another in love." (Galatians 5:13 NIV).

The exhortation to "stand firm" implies that for some people the temptation to "wilt" by returning to the Jewish law is a strong temptation.

What about the other form of legalism: the imposition of rules to address a problem such as alcoholism? This may seem much more acceptable to many Christians, I believe, because it can be viewed as a good intention. That is, when a Christian denomination requires its pastors to sign a pledge not to drink, or a Christian college has its students sign a similar pledge, I think many people might feel, "Good for them—anything in that direction is beneficial!" In a world in which many people have suffered from family members having abused alcohol, it's understandable. But it's still a prohibition that exceeds Scripture.

Is alcohol deemed acceptable in Scripture? Remember, Paul advised Timothy to drink some wine to alleviate a stomach problem (1 Timothy 5: 23); Jesus even created wine at the wedding at Cana (John 2:9, 10) And incidentally, while some may say this "created wine" was non-alcoholic grape juice, I doubt in that case the headwaiter would have praised its quality as "the best wine." Jesus, Scripture implies, even drank wine with sinners and tax gathers (Matthew 11:19). Jesus cited his critics' reproof of his drinking as an example of the Pharisees' unwillingness to accept either him or John the Baptiser, who didn't drink. (Matthew 11:18, 19) I feel safe in saying that any denomination or Christian college which would not accept Jesus, Paul, or Timothy as student or pastor, probably needs to re-evaluate that regulation.

Yes, I would certainly endorse a college or denomination that strongly encouraged adherence to wisdom and obedience in matters such as drinking alcohol. For example, it's a bit silly for a Christian school to require signatures on a drinking pledge for students who are under legal drinking age anyway (21 in most states). That means most of the students. Romans 13:1–5 says Christians are to submit to civil law unless such laws go against God's clear mandates. That's a no brainer. If I were a college dean, I would be glad to say, "You're on your honor as a believer to obey civil laws about drinking. And even when you're of legal age, you're exhorted by Scripture not to abuse or be addicted to alcohol." (1 Timothy 3:3 Christian leaders are not to be ". . . addicted to wine . . . and . . . do not by drunk with wine, for that is dissipation." (Ephesians 5:18).

Now that seems like a helpful and non-legalistic admonition!

What is the heart of the legalist? I think it's a person for whom freedom is more of a burden than a blessing. Such folks may feel far more comfortable when freedom is restricted by Old Testament Jewish law, or man-made social rules. Paul said to the Galatians, "You foolish Galatians! Who has bewitched you? After beginning with the Spirit, are you now trying to attain your goal by human effort?" (Galatians 3:1, 3 NIV).

Paul lays the problem at the feet of some false teachers who had crept into the church to deceive the Christians. "This matter arose because some false brothers had infiltrated our ranks to spy on the freedom we have in Christ Jesus and to make us slaves . . ." (to the Jewish law) (Galatians 2:4 NIV).

To sum up, the danger of legalism is that it strikes at the very heart of one of the essentials of what it means to be a Christian . . . a freed person. Galatians 5:1 says we are to *stand firm* against any attempt by others to deprive us of that freedom. And we are to *stand firm* against any tendency in our own hearts to avoid the responsibility of our Christian freedom. What is the responsibility? To strive against the vile sin nature, not with our own strength or efforts, but the power of God through Christ ("I can do all things through Christ who strengthens me." Philippians 4:13) and have a joyful and victorious life. Then we're really a living testimony of the power of God to change lives.

Legalism hinders and even short-circuits God-powered Christian growth by taking away the freedom to trust God for victory. Legalism says, "I don't trust your relationship with God, or your indwelling Holy Spirit, to give you victory over bad behavior. So here are some rules to make sure you act properly."

Stand firm against any attempt to put you, and those you are helping to grow, under restrictions which go beyond the New Testament teachings.

Liberalism . . . loosening Scripture to excuse sin.

If the heart of the legalist is to be uncomfortable with Christian freedom, then the heart of people who advocate liberalism is to be uncomfortable with God telling them how they should live. The usual liberal approach to Christianity is to take one truth of Scripture and use it to dismiss or weaken other truths.

For example, a liberalist may highlight God's love for people, which is certainly a biblical truth, but cite this love as a reason to dismiss God's judgement on such behavior as homosexuality. I'm sorry to have to even discuss such a topic, but there is probably no clearer illustration of the destruction liberalism wreaks upon the Christian faith than this one.

The Scripture is unequivocal:

"You shall not lie with a male as one lies with a female; it is an abomination." (Leviticus 18:22).

The often-expressed liberal response to this statement is that it is an Old Testament rule which no longer applies today—just as laws prohibiting the sowing of two kinds of crops in one field, or the wearing of a garment with two kinds of material woven together—no longer apply. (Leviticus 19:19).

This kind of reasoning equates moral law, which never changes, with ritual law, which was fulfilled by Christ. It's the oldest trick of the devil there is, twisting Scripture to pervert a true meaning. So, whereas the legalist wants Old Testament liturgical law to still apply to Christians today, the liberalist wants to selectively delete even moral or ethical law, whether from Old or New Testaments.

Of course the New Testament is also clear and consistent about homosexuality. "Do you not know that the wicked will not inherit the kingdom of God? Do not be deceived; neither the sexually immoral nor idolaters nor adulterers nor male prostitutes nor *homosexual* offenders (my italics) . . . will inherit the kingdom of God. And that is what some of you were. But now you are washed, you were sanctified, you were justified in the name of the Lord Jesus and by the Spirit of our God." (1 Corinthians 6:9–11 NIV).

In this list of those who will not inherit the Kingdom of God—those called "the wicked"—homosexuals are named . . . along with other sexually immoral people. Note also that Paul says, "And that is what some of you *were*." (my italics). That is an assurance that even the sexually immoral, and sexually perverted, have the hope of sanctification and justification. But it is because they have *turned away* from immorality and perverse sexual behavior and turned to Christ. It is not justification and sanctification *regardless* of ongoing immorality or perversion. These Corinthian believers, some of them, *were* sexually immoral or homosexual, but now they are not.

I recently talked with a Christian worker who told me of a young person who professed to be a saved Christian, yet openly and proudly flaunted her Lesbian lifestyle. This expresses a position which Jesus said was not possible. In Matthew's Gospel, Jesus states:

"You will know them by their fruits . . . every good tree bears good fruit; but the bad tree bears bad fruit. A good tree cannot bear bad fruit, not can a bad tree bear good fruit . . . So then, you will know them by their fruits. Not every one who says to Me, 'Lord, Lord, ' will enter the kingdom of heaven; but he who does the will of My Father who is in heaven." (Matthew 7:16–20).

Perhaps the strongest New Testament condemnation of homosexuality is found in Romans, Chapter 1. This is a fairly long passage, but I want to cite it fully because it not only censures homosexuality, but states a cause of it as well.

> "For although they knew God, they neither glorified him as God nor gave thanks to him, but their thinking became futile and their

Principle # 3: Always Minister from the Clear Meaning of the Bible.

foolish hearts were darkened. Although they claimed to be wise, they became fools and exchanged the glory of the immortal God for images made to look like mortal man and birds and animals and reptiles.

Therefore, God gave them over in the sinful desires of their hearts to sexual impurity for the degrading of their bodies with one another. They exchanged the truth of God for a lie, and worshipped and served created things rather than the Creator—who is forever praised. Amen.

Because of this, God gave them over to shameful lusts. Even their women exchanged natural functions for unnatural ones. In the same way the men also abandoned natural relations with women and were inflamed with lust for one another. Men committed indecent acts with other men, and received in themselves the due penalty for their perversion." (Romans 1:21–27 NIV).

Note that the cause given by the Bible for this description of sexual perversion is the people's abandonment of the truth about God. It says that "even though they knew God, they did not glorify him as God ... They exchanged the truth of God for a lie." Then note carefully the phrase, "Because of this, God gave them over to shameful lusts." It's because these men and women abandoned God that they pursued shameful lusts, including homosexuality. The phrase "God gave them over to ..." is repeated, showing that apart from God, the resulting behavior is shameful, untrue, and perverse. I believe this is true today. At least one clear foundational cause of homosexuality is some people's abandonment of God.

What are liberal theologians to do with this passage? One statement I read in an article in a secular magazine, claiming to present "what the Bible really says about gays," was that the passage in Romans 1 (not quoted in the article) was not really sexual in nature, but of a "conversational interchange" between men. This is an old trick of liberalism (and Satan in Genesis 3). It's the "I know it says that, but it doesn't really *mean* that!" argument. Deceptive people have found that many people can be fooled if they are told that words don't always mean what they say.

Yet is it difficult—to the point of impossibility—for clear-thinking persons to read "inflamed with lust for one another" and "committed indecent acts with other men," and not conclude this is descriptive of homosexuality. Words do have meaning. And words clearly expressed have clear meaning. It is obvious that the behavior described in Romans

1:21–27 is sexual perversion, for that is what it is called, and it is obvious that such behavior is abhorrent to God.

Another reason liberalism-inclined people may give for the acceptability of homosexuality is that it is a genetic, not chosen, sexual orientation. If homosexuality is genetic, and God designed it that way, it is *his* plan and intention and creation (see Colossians 1:16, 17). If so, it is contrary to himself to declare homosexuality wrong and that those who practice it are "worthy of death." (Romans 1:32).

If homosexuality is genetic, but *not* the plan and intention of God, but rather an "accident" or "medical puzzle" or "random identity selection," then God is not in control of this important aspect of life. He is not sovereign. And if God is fair and reasonable, he still would not declare such random accidents "sin, and worthy of death." God can only declare something to be sin and worthy of death if it is deliberate, willful disobedience to his Word. It is the law of *mutual exclusivity* . . . if homosexuality is morally acceptable, then the Bible is wrong; it's that simple. And if homosexuality is not sin, then is there *any* sin? And if there is no real sin (moral relativity), then no One has died for sin.

Such clarity on a subject which liberals themselves have chosen as a battleground allows us one way to discern which denominations, or individual local churches, are apostate, that is, those which have abandoned the truths and principles of the Christian faith. My advice is this: unless God has clearly called you to be a missionary to an apostate church or denomination, steer well clear of them.

The issue of homosexuality is perhaps the most obvious instance of the error of liberalism, yet there are others. Liberalism is the most destructive and pervasive cancer of Christendom in the US culture today. Again, the basic premise of liberalism is to take hold of one aspect of Biblical truth and use it to pervert others. As Psalm 119:160 puts it, "the sum of Thy word is truth . . ." not just parts of it twisted to justify a sinful position.

Satan even tried this in his temptation of Christ, saying,

"'If you are the Son of God', the devil said, 'Throw yourself down, for it is written, *He will command his angels concerning you, and they will lift you up in their hands, so that you will not strike your foot against a stone.*' Jesus answered him, 'It is also written, *Do not put the Lord your God to the test.*'" (Matthew 4:6, 7 NIV).

If you come across, in your ministry, an instance in which someone is trying to excuse wrong behavior by claiming that there's a verse in the Bible that says it's okay—if that verse is "understood in a different way"—then you may have encountered an instance of liberalism. Don't let it go. Do your homework, and challenge the misuse of Scripture, and wrong behavior, with a balanced view of what the Bible says clearly about the behavior. Make sure the people in your ministry see that such twisting of the Bible is wrong, and that it can be effectively countered.

Legalism tends to be wrongly *exclusive*; that is, it wants to establish behavioral standards which exclude even biblical Christians. Liberalism tends to be wrongly *inclusive*; that is, it wants to abolish any conditions on God's inclusion of people in his kingdom, even those conditions which God himself has established. Yes, God *is* loving, but he seeks our obedience as the foundation of a good relationship with him.

Here's my overall counsel on Legalism and Liberalism:

- *Do not forbid what God permits.*"... deceitful spirits ... men who forbid marriage and ... foods which God created to be gratefully shared ..." (1 Timothy 4:1–3).

- *Do not permit what God forbids.*"... consider the members of your earthly body as dead to immorality, impurity, passion, evil desire, and greed, which amounts to idolatry ... put them all aside ..." (Colossians 3:5, 8).

- *Do not neglect what God requires.*"Be doers of the word, not merely hears who delude themselves." (James 1:22).

Mysticism ... smoke, not light.

Mysticism! This approach of trying to get close to God has been around for a long time, but it's come back into focus more in the past 30 years, perhaps because of some similarity to "new age" spiritualism. We'll define mysticism in a moment, but let's first make a distinction between *mystery* and *mysticism*.

The word "mystery" is used in the Bible to mean a truth which God reveals to the understanding of men (and angels) at certain times, and under certain circumstances. The following verses of Scripture are helpful in seeing this definition of mystery:

"... to you it has been granted to know the mysteries of the kingdom of heaven, but to them it has not been granted." (Matthew 13:11).

"Yet we do speak wisdom among those who are mature ... we speak God's wisdom in a mystery, the hidden wisdom which God predestined before the ages to our glory ..." (1 Corinthians 2:6, 7).

"... let a man regard us in this manner, as servants of Christ, and stewards of the mysteries of God ..." (1 Corinthians 4:1).

"And if I have the gift of prophecy, and know all mysteries and all knowledge ..." (1 Corinthians 13:2).

"In reading this, then, you will be able to understand my insight into the mystery of Christ, which was not made known to other generations ... to bring to light what is the administration (or careful stewardship) of the mystery which for ages has been hidden in God ..." (Ephesians 3:4, 5, 9).

"... that utterance may be given to me in the opening of my mouth, to make known with boldness the mystery of the gospel ..." (Ephesians 6:19).

In each of the Scriptures above, the phrase "knowledge of truth" can be substituted for the word "mystery," or "mysteries." So the concept of *mystery* in the Bible refers not to a vague, incomprehensible connection with God, but rather the opposite: a clear understanding of a Biblical truth because God has explained it, either through the Word or a person who is a teacher of that truth, such as Paul. And notice that the understanding of these truths, or wisdom, is for the serious followers of the Lord (as in the Matthew 13:11 verse), or to those who are mature in faith (as in the 1 Corinthians 2: 6, 7 passage).

Now let's look at a general definition of "mysticism," taken from the Grolier's Encyclopedia.

Encyclopedia Definition of *Mysticism*

> "Mysticism in general refers to a direct and immediate experience of the sacred, or the knowledge derived from such an experience. In Christianity, this experience usually takes the form of a vision of, or *sense of union*, with God. Mysticism is usually accompanied by meditation, prayer, and ascetic discipline. Mysticism occurs in most, if not all, the regions of the world, although its importance within each varies greatly.
>
> The criteria and conditions for mystical experience vary depending on the tradition, but three attributes are found almost universally.

First, the experience is immediate and overwhelming, felt to be different from "common" experience.

Second, the experience or knowledge imparted by it is felt to be self-authenticating, without need of further evidence or justification.

Finally, it is held to be ineffable, its essence incapable of being expressed or understood outside the experience itself."[2]

Examining the three attributes, or characteristics, of mystical experience given in this definition, we can see that . . .

1. The experience of connection with God, or "sense of union" as Grolier's Encyclopedia puts it, is "immediate and overwhelming." While I'm not completely sure what meaning the word "overwhelming" has here, I assume it means "emotionally overwhelming," as differentiated from, for example, physically overwhelming. There are times when I think it is true and appropriate to be emotionally overwhelmed. John surely was in his vision of the island of Patmos (Revelation 1:17) But there are other times when such overwhelming emotions can be harmful or deceiving, as with some of the people in the city of Thessalonica. These did not have the following:

". . . the love of the truth, so as to be saved. And for this reason, God will send upon them a deluding influence so that they might believe what is false." (2 Thessalonians 2:10–12)

2. The experience is defined as "self-authenticating, without need of further evidence or justification." This characteristic of mysticism should be quite troubling for Christians, and Christian leaders. It means that a mystical experience stands on its own as truth, without being validated by Scripture. Yet the Bible is our one, clear test of truth against which we are to measure anything which says it is true.

"And so we have the prophetic word made more sure, to which you would do well to pay attention, as to a lamp shining in a dark place . . ." (2 Peter 1:19).

I spoke once to a professing Christian whose father had died. The father was almost certainly unsaved, having never expressed a decision for Christ, or indeed any interest in religion at all. The person related to

---

2. Grolier Inc., p. 171.

me a dream in which the deceased father had appeared and stated that he was in heaven, and that everything was all right. I asked this person if that vision or dream seemed consistent with the Scriptures' clear teaching about salvation, and what the person knew of the father's beliefs? The answer was, in effect, that the person chose to believe the message of the dream, regardless of "matters of theology." The dream gave comfort. The Bible's position might not. The effect of this vision on the person whose father had died, was confusion, at best, and a motive to believe the dream rather than the Bible. This had serious implications for this person's future growth in faith.

Was the dream real? If so, what was its origin? I don't think its origin was from God, if indeed it was real. Jeremiah warns,

"Yes, this is what the Lord Almighty, the God of Israel, says: 'Do not let the prophets and diviners among you deceive you. Do not listen to the dreams you encourage them to have. They are prophesying lies to you in My name. I have not sent them, ' declares the Lord." (Jeremiah 29:8, 9 NIV).

Our safeguard for what is true is to test all things with the Word of God.

3. The experience is "held to be ineffable, its essence incapable of being expressed or understood outside the experience itself." The word *ineffable* means "incapable of being expressed in words." Well, this makes whatever is learned through a mystical experience, by definition, unable to be passed along to help anyone else. Even further, if the experience is incapable of being understood or expressed outside the experience itself—and we all think and learn by means of words—one has to wonder what benefit, other than emotional, the experience has even for the one who has experienced it.

Here is an except from a paper I came across which may help illustrate one approach to what I consider to be modern-day mysticism. It is titled *Centering Prayer*, and is printed under the banner of The Youth Ministry & Spirituality Project.[3]

> "*Centering prayer* is a particular method of contemplative prayer. Contemplative prayer is the full opening of heart and mind, soul and body—our whole being—to the Spirit of God, the ultimate

---

3. *Centering Prayer*, leaflet.

mystery, utterly beyond thoughts, words, and images. We open our awareness to God, whom we know by faith, hope, and love (sic) is dwelling within and around us, closer than breathing, closer than thinking, closer than choosing, closer than consciousness itself. We train our eyes, ears, minds and hearts to attend to God's "inner voice of love" calling out to us and reminding us of our original name as Beloved, in whom the Creator takes delight.

The Guidelines
1. Choose a sacred word or phrase as the symbol of your intention to be open to God's presence and action within you (examples might be "Jesus," "Love," "Holy Spirit.") Once you choose a word or phrase do not change it, but consistently use the same word throughout the prayer.

2. Sitting comfortably and with eyes closed, settle briefly into the presence of God by taking a few deep breaths and letting go of all thoughts and distractions. Begin silently to repeat your sacred word or phrase as the symbol of your consent to God's presence and action within your heart. Continue this prayer for twenty minutes. Do this once a day, preferably in the morning.

3. When you become aware of thoughts or distractions during the prayer, return ever-so gently to repeating the sacred word or phrase.

4. At the end of the prayer period, remain in silence with eyes closed for a couple of minutes and close your time with God by reciting the Lord's Prayer."

In some ways, this doesn't seem that harmful; it seems rather gentle and calm. A verse of Scripture I have heard referenced in regard to this sort of experience is in Psalm 46:10,
"Be still and know that I am God." ((Psalm 46:10 NIV)
"Cease striving and know that I am God." (NASB version).
Even though the context of this brief Psalm seems to indicate a cessation of striving from warfare, rather than an admonition toward meditative stillness, I don't think anyone would object to the idea of prayer in a calm, peaceful setting . . . or even taking a deep breathe before praying. But having a time of prayer free from noise and distractions is quite different from the description above of "settling briefly into the presence of God by taking a few deep breaths and letting go of all thoughts." Strong caution should be exercised by believers when we see the phrase "letting

go all thoughts," or "empty your mind." This is a form of mysticism called transcendentalism.

The repetition of the "sacred word or phrase" is similar to the "mantra-chanting" practice of the Hindu sect of Hare Krishna (International Society of Krishna Consciousness). In this approach to the supernatural, the literally mindless repetition of a word, phrase, or set of phrases, is intended to "transcend" the obstruction which the human mind presents. In other words, thinking is seen as a hindrence to a relationship with God, not a help. This may be seen as desirable to a Hindu person; it is not desirable to a Christian, for whom the use of the mind is essential to a clear understanding of the Christian faith.

". . . do not be conformed to this world, but be transformed by the renewing of your mind, so that you may prove what the will of God is, that which is good, and acceptable and perfect." (Romans 12:2).

In general, the problem I have with this kind of thing is that, like hyper-emotionalism, it produces, I believe, an unhealthy attitude toward Christian growth. Rather than doing the hard (though immensely satisfying) work of Bible study and obedient prayer, people instead seek the ease of entering into the "ineffable experience" of mysticism. As for being still and quiet, I agree that quietly meditating on the Word is good. (Joshua 1:8 ". . . meditate on it day and night that you may be careful to do everything written in it . . .") Searching out the mysteries of the knowledge of truth of the Word is good indeed. But to resort to trying to transcend a state of conscious reasoning is not good; that is more Hinduism than Christianity. If mysticism is a significant part of a Christian's life, I believe the results will be as follows: a diminished interest in personal Bible study or intercessory prayer, a more casual attitude about strict obedience to the Word (due to the vagueness of the mystical experience), unhealthy introspection, and a seeking for greater and greater emotional experiences.

My conclusion is this: if a person is not reading the Bible and praying coherent thoughts with the conscious mind, then that person does not have a meaningful relationship with God, no matter how comfortably he is sitting, no matter how many deep breathes he takes, and no matter how many times he repeats a word or phrase.

Principle # 3: Always Minister from the Clear Meaning of the Bible.

Universalism . . . compassion without truth.

What is universalism? In its simplest, most sweeping form, it's the idea that a loving God would never really send anyone to hell, and so everyone goes to heaven. That's the basic concept, but there are a number of variations or modifications on this theme. They all have this in common, I believe; they're based on a mis-guided sense of compassion, that is, an unwillingness to accept that "good" people might incur God's wrath and end up eternally lost. It may be as uncomplicated as an emotion such as "My grandma didn't believe in Jesus, but she was a wonderful person. Don't tell me *she's* in hell!" Or it can be as complicated as an extensive rewriting of the gospel message in order to erode the biblical premise of people separated from God because of their sin.

Let's take a look at two kinds of universalism.

The "Tash/Aslan" form of universalism.

This is based upon the C. S. Lewis *Chronicles of Narnia* book, entitled *The Last Battle*. Let me preface my remarks by saying that C. S. Lewis was a brilliant thinker and apologist for Christianity, and is solid, in most every other way I can think of, in his presentation of Biblical theology. But I do see in *The Last Battle* a tendency toward the sort of compassion, or yearning for redefined fairness, that is puzzling and confusing at best.

For those who have not read these books, the scene of this excerpt is this: Emeth, a young soldier who had served the false god, Tash, comes face to face with the true "god," Aslan, the Lion. Here's the interaction between the young man and Aslan:

> "Then I fell at his feet and thought, Surely this is the hour of death, for the Lion (who is worthy of all honor) will know that I have served Tash all my days and not him . . . But the Glorious One bent down his golden head and touched my forehead with his tongue and said, Son, thou art welcome. But I said, Alas, Lord, I am no son of thine but the servant of Tash. He answered, Child, all the service thou hast done to Tash, I account as service done to me. Then by reasons of my great desire for wisdom and understanding, I overcame my fear and questioned the Glorious One and said, Lord, is it then true, as the ape said, that thou and Tash are one? The Lion growled so that the earth shook (but his wrath was not against me) and said, It is false. Not because he and I are one, but because we are opposites, I take to me the services thou hast done for him. *Therefore if any man swear by Tash and*

> *keep his oath for the oath's sake, it is by me that he has truly sworn, though he know it not, and it is I who reward him.*"[4] (my italics).

Do you see the problem in this passage, assuming that the analogy is to Christianity versus a false religion? The sentence I emphasized is key. The clear implication of this sentence is that if a person follows another god with sincerity of heart, then the sincerity is seen as loyalty to Christ (or Aslan, as Christ is portrayed in the Lewis books) and qualifies that person for salvation. In other words, it is the sincerity of heart, not the god whom they serve, which is important. This modified form of universalism opens the door for the inclusion of many more people into the Kingdom of heaven than the Bible does, those whose intentions are good, even though they have not received forgiveness of sins by receiving Christ.

Is this allowed Biblically? I believe it is not. These Scriptures point to the unique position of Christ as the only way to God:

"... as many as received Him, to them He gave the right to become children of God, even to those who believe in His name." (John 1:12)

"Jesus said to him, 'I am the way, and the truth, and the life; no one comes to the Father but through Me.'" (John 14:6).

Clear enough. Yet the puzzle and the confusion of the C. S. Lewis passage comes from this idea: that maybe the atoning death and resurrection of Jesus Christ covers people who have not even heard of him, and thus, of course, have not received him as Savior. So, because of some factor other than personally receiving Christ, they are none-the-less saved by Christ. Indeed they would not even *know* they are saved by him; as the Lewis quote above states, "... it is by me (Aslan, the Christ figure) that he has truly sworn, *though he know it not*..."(my italics) This is a bit hard to follow—and explain—so bear with me a bit.

What Lewis is seems to be implying is that the *other* factor—other than personally receiving Christ as Savior—is sincere obedience to whatever god is being followed:

"... if any man swear an oath by Tash (the false god) and keep his oath for the oath's sake (i.e., sincerity and integrity toward the oath to the false god), it is by me (Aslan, the true god) that he has truly sworn."

Then, even if "he know it not," the sincere person is saved, and enters into a relationship with God. While there is a certain attractiveness

---

4. Lewis, *The Last Battle*, pp. 204–205

Principle # 3: Always Minister from the Clear Meaning of the Bible. 159

in this position—because it has a faint flavor of compassionate fairness to it—it is not a Biblical position.

Look at this well-known passage in Romans, Chapter 10.

"'Everyone who calls on the name of the Lord will be saved.' How, then, can they call on the one they have not believed in? And how can they believe in the one of whom they have not heard? And how can they hear without someone preaching to them? And how can they preach unless they are sent? As it is written, 'How beautiful are the feet of those who bring good news!'" (Romans 10:13-15 NIV).

This passage of Scripture is clear and consistent with other Scripture which state that those who have not heard of and believed in and called on, Jesus . . . are not saved. But it is not their ignorance (of Christ) which condemns them; it is the consequence of unforgiven sin which does.

Those who have had the good news of Jesus Christ preached to them, have heard and believed and called upon Jesus . . . are saved. That is why the passage ends with the statement that those who bring the good news of salvation through Jesus Christ, are said to have "beautiful feet," that is, what they have done by going (on their feet, i.e.) to tell the lost about Jesus is a beautiful thing!

The passage gives no room for any possibility that those who haven't heard or believed can somehow be saved anyway. I know of no Scripture which allows such a possibility.

One helpful test on all these kinds of universalism is to ask the question: "If this is true, (the non-orthodox presentation of salvation) then is it *better not to even tell people* about Christ?" If they are saved by their sincerity, or because of a kind of all-inclusive love, it is a disservice to them to tell them about Christ, thereby giving them the choice of rejecting their salvation.

Evangelism then becomes a bad thing to do. If I tell someone about Christ who is already saved, though ignorant of his salvation, I'm really causing him to have a chance of losing that salvation if he should make a decision to reject it. And, of course, we are then faced with the frustrating dilemma about what to do with the commands in Scripture that we *should* preach the Gospel!

How absurd to pose such a foolish situation. If it is logically harmful to tell the lost about Christ, then Paul's cry of, ". . .woe is me if I do not preach the gospel . . ." (1 Corinthians 9;16) seems like nonsense. Of course it's not nonsense for Paul to feel this way, because God is not contradictory. We *are* told to preach the good news of Christ, because that is how people get saved, and it is joyful obedience for us.

You may not see in your own ministry an example of something as blatant as the Tash/Aslan portrayal of universalism. But there is another kind that shows its face now and then. It's a subtle modification of the universalism discussed above, but with an even more expanded view of who is saved.

The "separation is myth" universalism.

A few years ago, a staff director of a Christian youth ministry asked me to read some papers written by another staff person of the same ministry. The papers were quite wordy and abstract, pedantic but not scholarly; the writer was confident in his assertions, but neither biblical nor logical. The essential point was this: that sin does not separate people from God, and that telling young people that sin separates them from a loving God is wrong. Here are the main points of the argument these papers presented:

- Because God is a loving God, he would never allow himself to be separated from the people whom he loves, because of something *they* do, i.e., sin.

- Therefore, all people are already in a relationship with God; no gospel message of sin and decision is necessary. The only real purpose of ministry is to "announce" to people that they already are in a saved relationship with God, and to help them "embrace that relationship."

- Sin is redefined as a conscious rejection of one's "already existing relationship" with God.

- Those people who reject or deny that relationship are the only ones who "go to hell."

- The key value established is the "right of belonging" which all people have in their relationship with God.

- The idea of separation from God due to one's sins (Isaiah 59:2 NIV ". . . your sins have made a separation between you and your God.") is referred to as a "myth."

- No understanding of the concept of sinfulness, or a decision to seek forgiveness for sin, is necessary to have a full, meaningful, and eternal relationship with God.

The writer of these papers vehemently denied that this position was universalism. The writer stated several times that it was something "between" universalism and limited atonement. Here is where this kind of thinking (using that word loosely) falls apart, because there is no such position as somewhere "between" universalism and limited atonement. The very concept is literally nonsensical: the definition of universalism is that all people are saved; limited atonement means that *not* all people are saved. The literal explication of "limited atonement" is that atonement—Christ's payment for sins to allow an "at one" relationship with God—does not automatically include all people.

We know this is true Biblically from such passages as Matthew 7:13, 14:

"... for wide is the gate and broad is the road that leads to destruction, and many enter through it. But small is the gate and narrow the road that leads to life, and only a few find it." (NIV).

We also know that one's personal response in faith, or not, is important. The following Scripture clearly states this.

"For we also have had the gospel preached to us, just as they did, but the message they heard was of no value to them, because those who heard did not combine it with faith." (Hebrews 4:2 NIV).

The only real argument or question here is *why* all people are not saved. Those of one persuasion will say that not all people were chosen, or predestined, by God for salvation. Those in another camp will say that for whatever reason, people choose to turn away from the offer of salvation, even those who heard (Hebrews 4:2) Others might point out that many have not heard the message of salvation and are therefore lost, not due to ignorance directly but for the consequences of un-forgiven sin. Whatever the reasoning, if limited atonement is true, then it means just that, that not everyone is saved. There is absolutely no scripture in the Bible that states or implies that people are already saved and only by rejecting their salvation can be lost.

There is a very strong warning which Paul gives to those who change the clarity of the gospel message. This warning is found in Galatians, chapter 1.

"... Evidently some people are throwing you into confusion and are trying to pervert the gospel of Christ. But even if we or an angel from heaven should preach a gospel other than the one we preached to you, let him be eternally condemned! (... a good verse for Mormons to consider ... ref. the "angel") As we have already said, and so now I say again: if anybody is preaching to you a gospel other than what you accepted, let him be eternally condemned." (Galatians 1:7–9 NIV).

Paul's statement pulls no punches. Those who pervert the gospel message deserve condemnation. This is so because people's eternal destinies depend upon a clear presentation of the gospel: people sin, they are separated from holy God because of it, there is forgiveness for sins through acceptance of Christ's free gift of eternal life because of his having paid for the sins.

Paul's challenge to the Galatian church also shows that he trusted that those Christians could discern what the true gospel was, and which gospels were perverted. This is encouraging for us today. It is as much a heart's discernment perhaps as intellectual, but the discernment is possible and needed in order to combat the false gospels.

So, why do people do this? Why do people pervert the gospel, or in the case of legalism, put restrictions on God's grace and freedom? I certainly don't feel confident in offering a definitive answer, but here are some observations I've had over the years in ministry:

First, I have sensed in some people an anger at the idea of God as judge. The idea of God as a loving Father is gladly accepted, but thinking of God as judging and punishing people for their behavior is not acceptable to some. That was the tone of the emotions at the religious seminar I attended entitled, "Where Then is the Judgment?" Those leading the seminar rejoiced in John 3:17:

"... God did not send the Son into the world to judge the world, but that the world should be saved through Him."

But they dismissed the truth of the very next verse.

"He who believes in Him is not judged; he who does not believe has been judged already, because he has not believed in the name of the only begotten Son of God." (John 3:18).

These are folks, I think, with a fondness for the concept of God as all-loving—a kind of jolly old Santa whose worse judgements and punishments fall into the "naughty or nice," and "gift, or lumps of coal" verdicts.

Principle # 3: Always Minister from the Clear Meaning of the Bible. 163

Secondly, some people may have what I call a "Systematic Spectrum of fairness." This means that they feel few people are bad enough to deserve the lake of fire described in Revelation:

"The devil . . . was thrown into the lake of burning sulfur, where the beast and the false prophet had been thrown. They will be tormented day and night for ever and ever . . . If anyone's name was not found written in the book of life, he was thrown into the lake of fire." (Revelation 20:10, 15 NIV).

They may agree that the lake of fire is literal, but seem compelled to believe that it establishes only the extreme end of a spectrum, with most people being in a far less painful place. Hitler in the lake of fire . . . yes; my sweet, non-religious grandma in the lake of fire . . . no.

So they modify, or tone down, both heaven and hell. Heaven is viewed as a place in which people's earthly selfish pursuits are somehow made virtuous and magnified. That is, it's like American suburbia without mortgages or car problems. Hell is seen as a place that is definitely not nice, but no worst than an unpleasant business office. One pastor described hell as a place where there was "a lack of blessings." Hummm . . .

Third, and most commonly, I think some people alter the truth and clarity of Biblical salvation and the Christian life from a misguided kind of compassion. They just hate the thought of the nice dad or sweet aunt being in the lake of fire, so in their own minds it is comforting to create alternatives to the Bible's depiction of the human condition and eternal conclusions.

What do we look for in our ministries to make sure that we stay on track? Very quickly, be on the alert for these symptoms:

- Non-biblical, or contrived, emotionalism . . . yes, emotions are God-given and wonderful when they express our feeling about, and focus on, what God is doing in our lives. King David is a good example. He was a very emotional person, but his emotions involved his relationship with God, and the trials and victories he experienced. Emotionalism is not healthy when it focuses on itself, in other words, as one of the college students in ministry laughingly put it, "How do I feel when I feel the feelings I'm feeling?" Emotionalism for the sake of being emotional, like mysticism, can lead to stunted growth as a Christian.

- Odd applications of Scripture . . . someone may find an obscure passage or concept and insist on its application in the ministry. An example of this occurred many years ago in a ministry I was involved in, in which one of the ministry folks emphasized the casting out of demons as an activity we ought to be doing in our ministry. Was this a biblical concept? Yes. But I recall the confusion in the group when we wondered how to do this, and especially where we should go to do it. Our leader wisely concluded, after we'd all had a chance to discuss it, that should we find demonic possession to be a normal situation on the campus where we were ministering, that we would seriously commit ourselves to learning how to deal with it. It was good counsel, and the person who had brought up the issue accepted it graciously. But had we pursued the exorcism aspect of ministry to the extent the person wanted it, I think it would have been a pretty significant distraction from the evangelism, discipleship, and dorm Bible studies that were the usual focus.

- Departures from the grass-roots essentials of ministry (such as evangelism and discipleship) because a novelty comes along, or the leader seems to have become bored with the basics. Let's face it, some Christians love fads. And the Christian world is filled with them! Sometimes, it's many years into ministry that the oddities and out-of-balance preferences creep in. I can think of more than a few Christian leaders who started well, but then got off track. Why this happens probably has many reasons, but the key is this: it is crucial to stay solidly based on the clear, uncontroversial facts and practices of the Christian faith as expressed simply in the Bible. Do not change or exceed what is written.

And that brings us to our next principle . . .

6

Principle # 4: Never Stop Personally Doing Ministry ... in Spite of the "Killer D's" of Distraction, Dissipation, Discouragement, Doubt

> "After Jesus had finished instructing his twelve disciples, he went on from there to teach and preach in the towns of Galilee."
>
> —Matthew 11:1 NIV

THIS SUBJECT MIGHT SEEM a bit strange to be talking about—not quitting personal ministry—when we've just been discussing how to get started. But having experienced and struggled with all four of these Killer D's, let me put some red flags on these things in order to try to save you some time and frustration in advance.

I think the first two D's, Distraction and Dissipation tend to trouble younger people more than older, and the other two, Discouragement and Doubt, are more likely to be felt by older people. That's a sweeping generalization, of course, but I think the sheer, raw strength and energy of youth makes them more prone to the first two. Younger people may feel they have the energy to take on lots of projects, both Kingdom work and otherwise. Older folks may not feel this.

Is it wisdom that permits older Christians to keep from being distracted or dissipating their efforts? Possibly, but it's just as likely to be tiredness. Our lessened energy level (yes, I'm an old guy . . .) makes us more likely to pick our fights carefully and avoid distractions, but we *are* more likely to become discouraged, or wonder about God's ways (doubts), as we get older.

Distraction . . .

There can be a lot of projects or activities in a Christian's world that compete for time and attention. And I don't mean the things we *have* to do to live and take care of our families. Let's face it, the vast majority of hours in a week are taken up by activities we must do: our jobs, getting to and from the job, fixing the car, fixing the roof, paying the bills, sleeping (not really an "activity" but necessary), playing with our kids, and helping them with homework (joyful necessities!), etc. I would even classify some kind of recreation and relaxing as necessary. With the time remaining, we want our ministry to be as effective as possible. We want to bear as much fruit for God's Kingdom as we can and thus please the Father.

"By this is My Father glorified, that you bear much fruit, and so prove to be My disciples." (John 15:8).

What do we do with the hours we have free? Well, there's the matter of *wasted* time . . . I'll let you decide what that is for yourself, but my watching five straight hours of the Masters golf tournament probably qualified! (TV always comes to mind.) But there are the things that we do in our discretionary time that may be productive, but still distract from our ministries.

"No soldier in active service entangles himself in the affairs of everyday life, so that he may please the one who enlisted him as a soldier." (2 Timothy 2:4)

I certainly don't know what kind of everyday affairs Paul had in mind when he penned that analogy, but our world today is one of great "plurality," of affairs (to use the sociologist's term) in which we can involve ourselves. So what kinds of things are distractions? My observation is that they tend to be things we don't really plan on doing, but agree to do when someone asks us. They may seem like good things to do, but don't directly relate to the ministry of evangelism or discipleship. It takes some good discernment and an ability to say "no" to requests for your time. We have to have a clear ministry goal in mind, and evaluate how we spend our discretionary time by asking ourselves this question, "Does this directly contribute to my ministry goal?" If "no," say "No."

Question: "Do you want to be on the church softball team?"

Evaluation: "That sure would be fun, but does it contribute to my ministry goal of sharing the gospel, and discipling? Maybe being on the city-league softball team could be an opportunity for relational evangelism, but the games I've watched don't seem to lead to good chances to share. Everyone just takes off the minute the game's over."

Question: "Can you commit to ten weekends to help build the homeless shelter?"

Evaluation: "That's certainly a good project, but does it directly contribute to my goal? I don't know. I'll need to ask the project leader who's going to be working on it. If it's all church people, it wouldn't be fruitful for evangelism, and there's not really time for discipleship. If it's not church folks, it might not be a good environment for sharing the gospel. I'll need to ask a lot more questions before I can make such a costly commitment"

Question: "Could you come with us to the Navy base and teach the chaplain's staff how to share the gospel with sailors?"

Evaluation: "This is a pretty big commitment; it'll take at least six weekends because I'll want to take the chaplains out for real training, not just do a seminar or workshop on it . . . Hummm . . . But, I think it sure fits in with my ministry goals because it's not only evangelism, but teaching others how to share. I'll do it."

What are some activities you might be asked to do? How would you evaluate them?

I believe another distraction that causes people to stop doing ministry is success in their ministry. What?! Yes, the problem is that when a person succeeds in ministry focused on evangelism and discipleship, that person runs the risk of being tempted to "turn pro," that is, go from doing ministry to talking about how to do ministry. The person who has been courageous in sharing the gospel and helping people grow, may be asked to teach others how to do it. This can be good if that means taking others along as you do it, but sometimes you're asked to lead that most dreadful of all educational devices: the seminar.

The moment we stop actually doing ministry in order to talk about it, we lose the powerful leverage of our life-in-action. Then those we have around us observe in our lives, that the talk is more important than the doing. That's not what we want our lives to communicate. It's not that seminars are basically wrong, if they are given *in addition* to doing ministry. But seminars are not good if they are given *in place* of doing ministry.

In the Matthew 11:1 (NIV) verse quoted above . . . "After Jesus had finished instructing his twelve disciples, he went on from there to teach and preach in the towns of Galilee," Jesus had just instructed his twelve disciples before sending them out on a solo mission assignment (see Matthew 10:1–5ff.). Then Jesus went off (by himself?) to teach and preach in the towns in Galilee. He didn't stop ministry himself once he got some others doing it. He didn't found a seminary to teach the disciples ancient languages or how to give sermons. He didn't formulate a seminar. He sent his disciples out to minister, and then he went out himself to minister.

Does this have application for you? It might. You may not think you'll ever be so "successful" in ministry that you'll be tempted to "turn pro." (By the way, the word "amateur" means a person who does something out of *love* for it.) But it is true that when you've been sharing your faith and helping younger Christians for a while, it'll attract some notice. Your enthusiasm and commitment will communicate. That's when your church or ministry organization may ask you to give a series of workshops on evangelism, or go to the different Sunday school classes or small groups and teach them about evangelism or discipleship.

It's possible that this could be good, if the small group or Sunday school class is serious about learning, and *doing*, e.g., evangelism. But more often than not, it's just another 13 weeks (i.e., a Sunday school "quarter") of material covered in the class or small group. Rarely, if ever, is any application made to material presented in these kinds of formats.

Save your good stuff for the life-to-life training where people actually go out and do it with you. I once showed a pastor the "7 & 3" content, with the idea that he and I could meet and do it, then he could pass it on to some key people in his church. He said, "Wow, this is great! Can I take it and show it to my church leaders?" I said "Sure," and when I next talked with him a few weeks later, he said, "Oh, I'm using your material for my Sunday school class. What a blessing. Thanks. I had no idea what to do this term." I was disappointed, for I knew that an opportunity had been lost. Doing real, application-intended discipleship training in a class setting lessened the chance that those folks would be motivated to be serious about it later. "Oh, I've already been through that stuff," is a normal response of people who've seen training content in a non-training setting.

So, my advice is this: don't let yourself get distracted from the important activities of ministry: sharing the gospel and helping others to grow. Remember, lives reproduce, and if you're doing these essentials, others will too. If you get distracted from doing the essentials, others will conclude that actually doing ministry is just not too important.

Dissipation . . .

By dissipation, I simply mean spreading yourself too thin, even in good Kingdom work. If distraction is getting off track by doing activities that don't really focus on your ministry goals, dissipation is trying to do *too many* things that do focus on your goals. For example, to try to disciple 15 people, life-to-life, is just too many. Even the Lord didn't take on that many. (Though what a wonderful problem *that* would be, to have that many people serious about growing!)

My personal learning curve on this issue was tough. I just couldn't seem to say "no" to any ministry opportunity that came along. It wasn't that I was reluctant and wanted to say "no" but couldn't; I was glad to grab at anything that seemed like it might be good for the Kingdom. And since I had lots of energy in those days, it worked for a while. Somehow when you have lots of energy, everything seems easy.

Max Weighmink, the man who was discipling me, said to me once, "Cunneen, you're all over the place!" I think he told me that when I mentioned to him that I'd spoken at two Unitarian Universalist churches that month on the topic of "Real Existentialism and Real Christianity." Max was wise enough to let me go so I could learn how to limit myself to the "pure gold" activities, but it took a while.

What finally convinced me to pull back from participating in so many activities—even evangelistic activities—was an awareness that I wasn't doing a good job with the couple of guys I met with for discipleship. I knew I needed to prepare well, and pray, for these guys before I met with them, but I wasn't. I was winging it. I'd jump in the car, shoot up a prayer that the time would go well, look over a page of notes, and then meet with one of the men at a restaurant.

It wasn't good. The worst moment came when the guy I was meeting with, quietly said, "We went over that last week." That's how unprepared I was; I couldn't even remember what I'd done with the guy. And this one-to-one discipling was the most valuable thing I was doing for the Kingdom, and I knew it. So, I learned to say no to some invitations, and I did a better job of working on the essentials.

I'm not sure that the following Scripture addresses this issue directly, but the principle of it is helpful, I believe.

"Everyone who competes in the games goes into strict training . . . Therefore, I do not run like a man running aimlessly; I do not fight like a man beating the air." (1 Corinthians 9: 25, 26 NIV).

I think the idea of strict training in order to run the race well, or minister effectively, implies having the discipline to focus on what's essential. This becomes, I feel, more important as the years go by and we lose strength and energy. If we are used to being involved in many activities, we can become so used to it, that we try to keep it up long past our ability to do it. Then we either become used to mediocrity, or we become discouraged and weary. Please don't dissipate your energy, but rather ask God to give you discernment about which things in your ministry are essential, then focus on them.

Discouragement . . .

There I was, sitting in the fast-food restaurant and I just *knew* the young man I was waiting for wasn't going to show up. This was the second time this week I'd been in this same restaurant waiting for someone who forgot about meeting with me. A restaurant employee whom I knew well (I spend a lot of time in fast-food restaurants) walked past and cheerfully said, "Looks like you got blown off again!"

It had been one of those weeks. A few days before, a small group Bible study I was leading had met, and though I had prepared what I thought was a pretty interesting study, the whole group seemed comatose. There had been much yawning and checking of watches!

So I left the fast-food place and went home, and my wife Nancy said as I came in the door, "I hate to tell you, but I think we have a plumbing leak again." Agh!

Discouragement. No matter how gifted you are, no matter how hard you work, no matter how encouraging ministry usually is, there are times when it seems as though nothing goes right. When you share the gospel, people aren't interested. When you lead a Bible study, people are bored. Even the ones you've prayed about and chosen to disciple life-to-life forget to meet with you, as if they're saying, "This stuff isn't all *that* important or interesting . . ."

Discouragement comes from the feeling that our ministry is too slow, too few people seem interested, and that too many of our efforts fall flat. It's disheartening.

Well, to coin an absurd phrase, the "encouraging thing about discouragement" is that it's a normal part of ministry, and the Bible has some good advice for getting past it. Someone once said that of all Satan's tricks to get people to stop doing ministry—second only to temptation—he uses discouragement the most. So let's look at some good verses of Scripture on this subject.

Talk about frustration and weariness; Moses had them.

> ". . . Moses was troubled. He asked the Lord, "Why have you brought this trouble on your servant? What have I done to displease you that you put the burden of all of these people on me? Did I conceive all these people? Did I give them birth? Why do you tell me to carry them in my arms, as a nurse carries an infant, to the land you promised on oath to their forefathers? Where can I get meat for all these people? They keep wailing to me, 'Give us meat to eat!' I cannot carry all these people by myself; the burden is too heavy for me. If this is how you're going to treat me, put me to death right now . . ."
>
> —Numbers 11:10–15 NIV

Even the prophet Elijah became weary and discouraged.

". . . he went a day's journey into the desert. He came to a broom tree, sat down under it and prayed that he might die. 'I have had enough, Lord,' he said. 'Take my life . . .'" (—1 Kings 19:4, 14 NIV).

Oddly enough, the background for this glimpse into Elijah's life is that he had just had a tremendous victory over the 450 prophets of the false god, Baal. (see 1 Kings 18) Why then would he be so depressed and discouraged? One of the unusual aspects of ministry I have observed is that sometimes we can be discouraged and vulnerable right after something good has happened. Once, after working hard, participating in a Christian conference, I was exhausted and kind of depressed, even though the conference had gone really well. Perhaps Elijah experienced something similar. He also thought he was all alone in following the Lord, and was afraid because Jezebel had vowed revenge on him.

"He replied, 'I have been very zealous for the Lord God almighty. The Israelites have rejected your covenant, broken down your alters, put your prophets to death with the sword. I am the only one left, and now they're trying to kill me too.'" (1 Kings 19:14 NIV).

I doubt we will ever be in a situation quite like Elijah's, but there can be times when we feel as though we are alone, and face the discouragement that comes with that feeling. God reassured Elijah that he was not alone, that God still had ". . . 7000 in Israel, all whose knees have not bowed down to Baal . . ." (1 Kings 19:18 NIV).

God gives us such encouragement too. And while it's true that even Paul expressed his frustration with the Christians in Galatia: ". . .I fear for you, that somehow I have wasted my efforts on you." (Galatians 4:11 NIV), he also said to a bunch of Christians who were even weaker (the believers in Corinth) ". . . Therefore, since through God's mercy we have this ministry, we do not lose heart." (2 Corinthians 4;1–4 NIV).

Isn't that good? Paul realized that God has given us this ministry, and that even if we share the gospel with people who seem uninterested, it's because ". . . the god of this age has blinded their minds . . ." (2 Corinthians 4:4), not because we're ineffective in ministry. Therefore, *we do not lose heart*. It's God's power and his ministry, and we can be encouraged that whatever happens, we're doing what is pleasing to him.

What's the best counsel the Bible gives us on overcoming discouragement? I think it's these two verses that let us know that the work we do for God will have good results, whether we see those results right away or not.

". . . you know that your labor in the Lord is not in vain." (1 Corinthians 15:58 NIV).

"And let us not lose heart in doing good, for in due time we shall reap is we do not grow weary." (Galatians 6:9).

Don't give up. Don't lose heart. Don't be discouraged. God is in control and he will give a harvest at the proper time.

Doubt . . .

If discouragement comes from how long ministry seems to take, and how unresponsive people seem to be, I believe that doubt comes from long-term situations for which we have prayed and trusted God, but nothing ever appears to change. It may be that we have prayed for years for family members to come to Christ. We might have prayed to be effective in ministry, but consider ourselves unsuccessful. We may have prayed for loved ones' healing, physically, emotionally, mentally, spiritually . . . yet nothing apparently happens in answer to those prayers. We may begin to doubt God's activity, or interest, in these people's lives. This is a very serious challenge for men and women who are committed to ministry because it strikes at the very heart of the message we preach to others: God loves you and will take care of you, and that God calls you to ministry and will cause you to be fruitful.

Consider these situations:

- The young woman whose sister became addicted to pain killers, and now the sister has a police record, a child born out of wedlock, and a sense of hopelessness that borders on despair. The parents, who have walked with the Lord for many years, and prayed unceasingly for their daughter, rely on the younger daughter for their only encouragement. The younger daughter is 20; the sister is 32. The young woman feels overwhelmed with dealing with her own sadness about her sister, and the burden of trying to continually cheer her parents. The young woman's comment is this: "I don't think I'm losing faith, but where *is* God in all this?"

- The middle-aged couple whose mother, age 93, has been institutionalized for over 18 years with severe dementia, of a kind which causes profound distress and a tendency to violent outbursts for the patient, and even greater distress for the couple. And though they love the mother, they have begun to pray that God would just take her home to him.

- The family whose teenaged daughter has been struggling with profound depression, self-loathing, and suicide attempts.

- And in a different vein, the doubt that can creep into our hearts as we work very hard at ministry, especially in the local church, and never seem to get anywhere. We may begin to gradually doubt that the discipling ministry really works, especially as lay people with little "credibility," and especially in the modern US culture in which many people just seem to be set against commitment, even to following the Lord. We may feel, "If it doesn't work, why even bother. But *why* doesn't it work? God said it would."

Are all these situations part of living in a fallen world? Yes. But the young woman with an addicted sister has a question that perhaps many of us ask at one time or another in our Christian lives: "Where is God in all this?"

Look at these Scriptures about others who have struggled with doubt concerning that question, "where is God, and his mercy, in all this?"

"The arrows of the Almighty are in me, my spirit drinks in their poison; God's terrors are marshaled against me . . . Oh, that I might have my request, that God would grant what I hope for, that God would be willing to crush me, to let loose His hand and cut me off." (Job 6: 4, 9 NIV).

Job's terrible situation was one of both physical suffering and spiritual despair. Remember, although Job was not sinless, he was a righteous men, even in the estimation of God (Job 2:3). So Job was dismayed by the suffering which had come to him, because he was confident of his innocence. The suffering, therefore, was agonizing to Job because he didn't understand why it was happening. He even says, perhaps in dramatic exaggeration, "O, if only God would give me my wish, and kill me!"

The following verses describe Job's sense of helplessness and frustration:

> ". . . Who can say to him, 'What are you doing?' . . . How can I dispute with him? How can I find words to argue with him? Though I were innocent, I could not answer him; I could only plead with my Judge for mercy. Even if I summoned him and he responded, I do not believe he would give me a hearing. He would crush me with a storm and multiply my wounds for no reason. He would not let me regain my breath, but would overwhelm me with misery. If it is a matter of strength, he is mighty! And if it is a matter of justice, who will summon him? Even if I were innocent, my mouth would condemn me; if I were blameless, it would pronounce me guilty" (Job 9:12b, 14–20 NIV).

Can we relate to how Job feels, that God is not only *not* helping us, but is a contributor to our pain? I think we can at times. The writer of Psalm 77 certainly did, saying, "Will the Lord reject forever? Will he never show his favor again? Has his unfailing love vanished forever? Has his promise failed for all time? (Psalm 77:7, 8 NIV).

Perhaps the death of Lazarus is one of the most dramatic events in which people doubted the Lord's concern. John's Gospel, chapter 11, relates the occurrence.

"Now a man named Lazarus was sick. He was from Bethany, the village of Mary and her sister, Martha . . . so the sisters sent word to Jesus, 'Lord, the one you love is sick. . .' Jesus loved Martha and her sister and Lazarus. Yet, when he heard that Lazarus was sick, he stayed where he was for two more days. On His arrival, Jesus found that Lazarus had already been in the tomb for four days. 'Lord,' Martha said to Jesus, "if you had been here, my brother would not have died.'" (John 11:1, 3, 5, 17, 21 NIV).

Martha's comment may seem disrespectful. Of course, Martha was not one to hold back from plain speaking. In Luke 10: 40 she also complained that Jesus didn't seem to care that she was doing all the work! But here, I think she is not reproving the Lord, but expressing her heart's belief that Jesus could have saved her brother. In a way, this is real faith, even if it's disappointed faith.

I believe the first step in overcoming our doubts about God's "unfailing love" and his promises (Psalm 77:7, 8) is to be very honest about what we're feeling. This can be scary, for none of us likes to admit to doubts. It's kind of a badge of honor among Christians to have unflagging faith even during the toughest times. And that is indeed good, unflagging faith. But we may have to do a bit of soul-searching and growing to get there.

I think overcoming doubt really amounts to *learning to live in the Sovereignty of God,* or, more simply, learning to trust God in anything and everything. What do I mean by this?

The word "sovereign" means "ruler who is supreme in power, position and authority." To illustrate this, picture in your mind, if you will, a round table with three legs. Let's say the table is about waist-high, and sitting on top is a goldfish bowl, filled with water. The water in the bowl represents our faith. If the table is solid, the faith is secure. If the table collapses, our faith goes with it.

Say, each leg is one of the attributes of God which help define his sovereignty. Again, this is a simple analogy. There are many attributes that together define the sovereign rule of God, but we'll focus on just these three: love, power, wisdom.

So each leg supporting our round table represents one of those attributes. If we are to really trust God, living in faith under his sovereignty, we have to believe he is perfect in these three attributes. Take any one leg of the table away, and the table will collapse, spilling the faith.

- His love: "The steadfast love of the Lord never ceases; His compassions never fail; they are new every morning. Great is Thy faithfulness." (Lamentations 3: 22, 23 RSV).

- His wisdom: "For as the heavens are higher than the earth, so My ways are higher than your ways, and My thoughts than your thoughts." (Isaiah 55:9).

"All the days ordained for me were written in your book before one of them came to be. How precious to me are your thoughts, O God! How vast is the sum of them! If I were to count them, they would outnumber the grains of the sand." (Psalm 139:16–18 NIV).

"... Great is our Lord ... His understanding has no limit." (Psalm 147:5 NIV).

- His power: "For by him, all things were created; things in heaven and on earth, visible and invisible, whether thrones or powers or rulers or authorities; all things were created by him and for him. He is before all things, and in him all things hold together." (Colossians 1:16, 17 NIV).

"... with God all things are possible." (Matthew 19:26 NIV).

We can be sure of His love; it is steadfast and unfailing. This unfailing love in part defines God's faithfulness.

We can be sure of His wisdom, especially about us. He knows our cares and concerns better than we know them ourselves.

We can be sure of His power, which is infinite and unlimited. Christ holds the very atoms of the universe together.

What if we were to doubt God's power? Then we'd have a pathetic deity who is all-knowing and loving, but unable to help us when we need it most. What a foolish image, God wringing his hands in heaven as he looks down on one of his loved ones suffering and crying, "Oh, I wish I could help, but I just can't do anything in these kinds of situations!"

What if we were to doubt God's wisdom? It brings to mind an equally ridiculous picture of deity who loves us and is all-powerful, but is simply not too bright, or is clueless about peoples' life conditions. "Oh, wow! I never saw *that* coming to those folks! I'd have prevented that if I'd only known!"

What if we were to doubt God's love? Then we'd have all-powerful and all-knowing deity who would understand everything about us, be able to do anything he wanted, but wouldn't help because he didn't care.

Put in these terms, it appears foolish indeed not to trust God with all that happens in our lives, and the lives of those we love. But doubt still confronts us, and the logic of the of the impossibility of a weak, stupid, or uncaring God gets us only so far.

Which of those three attributes do you think people doubt the most when they are struggling to trust God? I believe it's his love, e.g., "If only God would have some good things happen to my son (or daughter)! It just seems like my son's life is so hard. Sure, some of it is from the consequences of his own bad decisions, but it seems to me like God beats up on him too. No wonder my son isn't sure if God really cares about him."

My experience is that Christians don't often question God's wisdom or power, but they do wonder about his care and concern in hardships that last a long time.

What's the Bible say? How can we overcome our doubts about the character and nature of God when we are losing heart? It's an important question, I believe, because if we are to minister to others, we must believe in our hearts that the One we proclaim is truly the God, of love, power and wisdom.

Let's think about a few reasons why God might allow, or even bring about, some of the difficult life situations which could cause us to doubt. Look again at the situation of Lazarus' death. Martha's statement, "If you'd been here, my brother wouldn't have died . . ." implies at least a hint of doubt about Jesus' love for her brother. Yet we see in several verses in that passage evidence of Jesus' love for Lazarus.

First of all, John in writing the account states it in verse 11:5, "Now Jesus loved Martha and her sister and Lazarus." Also, look at the following passage:

"When Jesus therefore saw Mary weeping, and the Jews who came with her, also weeping, He was deeply moved in spirit, and was troubled, and said, 'Where have you laid him?' They said to Him, 'Lord, come and see.' Jesus wept. And so the Jews were saying, Behold how He loved him!" (John 11:33–36).

Isn't this amazing! Jesus deliberately delays coming to Lazarus so his disciples, and Martha and Mary, would see and believe that he had the power over death. (And what more convincing way could there be than to resurrect a dead person!) He waits for Lazarus to die, and tells his disciples, "... Lazarus is dead; and I am glad for your sakes that I was not there, so that you may believe ..." (John 11:14, 15).

Yes, all this makes perfect sense from a strategic standpoint, but it seems rather heartless. Yet now we see Jesus, fully knowing that he is going to raise Lazarus from the dead, weeping because of the pain Martha and Mary are suffering. Isn't that what we deeply hope and pray God feels about us and our life situations? Aren't you glad to think of Jesus being deeply moved in spirit and sorrowful about the pain we, his children, have to endure? Doesn't that help us as we wrestle with doubts: knowing that even though God is allowing us live through long periods of pain, emotional or physical, we *know* that he loves us?

What's another reason? I believe one of the simplest to state, but hardest to understand, is that God will not violate peoples' ability to choose, even when they make the wrong choices. Romans, Chapter 1 is pretty clear. When people abandon the truth of God and choose lies and sinful behavior, God allows them to sin. Paul says,

"... although they knew God, they neither glorified him as God, nor gave thanks ... Therefore God gave them over in the sinful desires of their hearts ..." (Romans 1:21–24 NIV).

We can pray, and often do perhaps, "Oh, God, please stop my ... child, mother, father, brother, friend ... from making such bad decisions! Keep her/him from the path of sinfulness that she's/he's on!" But I know of no Scripture which says that God will *make* a person live rightly. Yes, there are times when he may intervene, protect, steer or guide people in ways that may not have been their normal path, but not, I think, in violation of their ability to choose.

Here's another reason that God may allow people to go the wrong way: to give them enough liberty to sin that they might "come to their senses" as a result of experiencing the garbage they've chosen. The best example of this that I know is the story of the prodigal son (the word "prodigal" by the way, means "wasteful" or extravagant").

You remember this story in Luke 15. The younger son asks his father for his share of the inheritance, goes off to a distant land, wastes the money on "loose living," and then, when his so-called friends ditch him because his money is gone, he finds himself tending pigs that are eating better than he is. Now comes one of the most beautiful phrases in the world, "... he came to his senses ..." (Luke 15:17). Isn't that wonderful! How many people have you prayed would "come to their senses"? A lot, I imagine. The father of the story allowed the son to go and sin, suffer, come to his senses, and return a changed person.

Another reason that God may allow you to suffer is in order to benefit others. Of course, the suffering, humiliation, and death of Jesus Christ is the supreme example of this, in that it brought salvation to all who accept it. Paul is another example of this principle. His imprisonment not only caused him to write the letters to churches and individuals which comprise our most comprehensive body of doctrine and guidance, but his imprisonment actually gave courage and boldness to Christians who were *not* in prison.

"Now I want you to know, brethren, that my circumstances have turned out for the greater good of the gospel, so that my imprisonment in the cause of Christ has become well known throughout the whole praetorian guard and to everyone else, and that most of the brethren, trusting in the Lord because of my imprisonment have far more courage to speak the word of God without fear." (Philippians 1:12–14).

And what about that "obnoxious kid with the colorful coat" ... Joseph? He was thrown into a pit by his brothers, sold into Egypt, imprisoned under false charges, yet he ends up telling his brothers, as he makes provision for their families,

"... as for you, you meant evil against me, but God meant it for good in order to bring about this present result to preserve many people alive." (Genesis 50:20).

The final consideration I can think of is the one that is, at the same time, the most comforting and hard to bear. It's this: there are many times when we just don't know the reason for God's allowing us to suffer, and we may never know.

For 37 chapters of the book, Job works up his courage to ask the Lord, what basically amounts to this question: "Lord, do you know what You're doing to me?" God's answer is this:

"Who is this that darkens counsel by words without knowledge?" (Job 38:2)

Translation: "Job, you don't even have a right to ask your question." Then God uses five chapters to illustrate that Job is a man, and God is God. At one point God says,

"... you instruct Me. Will you really annul My judgment? Will you condemn Me that you may be justified? (Job 40:7, 8)

Job's response:

"I know that you can do all things, and no purpose of yours can be hindered ... I declared what I do not understand ... Therefore, I retract (my question). And I repent. (Job 42:2, 3, 6 NIV).

Why does God seem so severe about Job's question, a question that may seem quite reasonable to us? I believe it's because the most solid foundation for trusting God is to realize and accept that he is God, and ultimately, he does not answer to us about his doings. With that foundation, we can also come to see that he is loving and kind.

- So we can cry out to God from our hearts.

"Why are you in despair, O my soul? And why have you become disturbed within me? Hope in God, for I shall again praise Him for the help of his presence." (Psalm 42:5)

- We can search for the truth of God in His Word.

"... examining the Scriptures daily, to see if these things were so." (Acts 17:11)

- We can remember how he has loved and cared for us in the past.

"I shall remember the deeds of the Lord. Surely, I will remember Thy wonders of old." Psalm 77:11).

- We can accept the truth of this statement.

"... for he who comes to God must believe that he exists, and that he rewards those who earnestly seek him. (Hebrews 11:6 NIV).

- And so we end up, peacefully, accepting the simple words of the Lord, himself:

"Let not your heart be troubled; believe in God, believe also in Me." John 14:1 (NASB).

Don't ever quit. We can train ourselves to stay on track, to seek encouragement in fellowship, prayer, and the Word ... and overcome doubt as we simply believe that God is wise, loving, and powerful.

7

Principle # 5: Don't Hesitate to Lead, When Leadership is Needed.

Yes, leadership is one of the spiritual gifts (Romans 12:8), but it is also a function. It's something that needs to be done, even if there are no "gifted" leaders around. People need and benefit from good leadership. The big question is, when should we take the leadership role, or when should we not?

Let's consider a hypothetical situation. You're part of a good local church, and the pastor has expressed an interest in forming an evangelistic outreach team. This is just what you've been praying God would put on the pastor's heart, so you're very glad. The pastor calls together a group of the "more mature" believers, and says this, "Who'll lead this team?" And a long pause follows.

In the group called together by the pastor, there are several people who've done some kind of evangelism in the past. But you also know that most of the people have not, and that among those who have done evangelistic outreach, much of it was years ago, and of a type that is perhaps too "churchy" for today's secular culture. That is, it was more of a "visiting the church visitors" program than an outreach to the mainstream community, and more of "Are you ready to renew your walk with God?" than "Do you believe there *is* a God?"

What do you do? Do you volunteer to lead the group? Do you let someone else do it, perhaps someone not as well qualified as you? Where does humility come in? Where does one's temperament come in? If you do take the leadership, will others in the group think you're doing it to seek honor for yourself? Should you speak up and say "Yes." Should you just keep silent and see if the rest of the group acknowledges that you're probably the best one to lead, and nominate you without you saying a word? What should you do!

Thoughts race through your mind as you try to figure out how much time would be required to lead the team, how it would affect your relationships in the group, what kind of training it would take, etc. etc.

And while you're agonizing about all this, the worst thing possible happens. The one person who probably shouldn't even have been invited to the meeting volunteers to be the leader! No one says a word. No one dares say a word. And the evangelistic outreach you'd prayed for will almost certainly follow a familiar trajectory . . . a series of meetings to discuss which "evangelism program" to use, selection of the most irrelevant, least biblical one (won't offend anyone!), and a seemingly endless discussion about what kind of kick-off dinner to have. All during which time, you'll be thinking, "Oh, man! Why didn't I just jump in and lead? Now the moment is lost, because the way this thing is now, it's hopeless."

Have you ever been in such a situation? Does my hypothetical situation seem harsh on the person who volunteered to lead? He or she probably did it from good intentions, and since no one else spoke up to take the leadership, it's not really the fault of the unqualified person who did. She or he was probably not even aware he/she was unqualified.

What are the reasons people hesitate to take leadership? What are the reasons they do lead? Of the reasons people hesitate to lead, humility is the good reason; laziness or indifference are the bad. Of the reasons people *do* take on leadership roles, seeing the Kingdom of God benefit is the good reason; arrogance or unwillingness to follow other's leadership are the bad. What I would like to encourage in this chapter is for each of you who are qualified to lead, in different situations, to be *willing* to say, "Yes, I'll do that. I'll take the responsibility of leadership for this." Whether you're appointed to lead or not is another issue, but at least be *willing*.

So, let's look quickly at what Biblical leadership is (which is a *huge* topic, but this will be simple). First of all, Christian leadership is not like secular leadership, or even the kind of leadership seen in other religions.

"Jesus called them to Himself, and said, "You know that the rulers of the Gentiles lord it over them, and their great men exercise authority over them. It is not so among you, but whoever wishes to become great among you shall be your servant, and whoever wishes to be first among you shall be your slave; just as the Son of Man did not come to be served, but to serve, and to give His life as a ransom for many." (Matthew 20:25, 26).

That distinctive difference between Christian leadership and other kinds is a wonderfully freeing difference. It's freeing because we can set aside any false modesty, or worries about promoting ourselves, by taking a leadership role . . . for the simple reason that leadership is not "lording it over" others, but serving others. Most of us would say to ourselves, "Hey, I sure don't mind serving in this deal. I'm just nervous about being the boss." Well, the good news is, it's more serving than bossing, so we can be at peace agreeing to lead. Here are three characteristics of biblical leadership:

Be a servant . . .

Most Christians I know wouldn't mind at all being *called* a servant, but not everyone likes to be *treated* like a servant. This aspect of leadership takes humility.

A Christian college student at the school where I taught once told a funny story about this to our Bible study group. Wanting to please the Lord, he tried to serve his parents when he was at home. He said that he and his mother and father loved grapefruit, and every morning the three of them had a half grapefruit each. Of course this meant that one of the halves was a day old and a bit dried out. So Charlie, my college student friend, who really was a very humble guy, always grabbed the old half as a small way of serving his parents. Then one day he slept later than usual, and when he came to breakfast, his mom had given him the old grapefruit. Charlie laughed and told us that for some reason it really bothered him.

Charlie's analysis of this little incident was that though he wanted to be a servant, when his parents treated him that way, it hurt his pride. It was a good teaching point, and sure impressed the rest of us in the group, because Charlie was by far the most serving person in our bunch.

Here's a good verse from the Gospel of Luke that expresses the heart of a servant. It's a pretty common-sense sounding idea and not very "spiritual," but is quite helpful.

"So you also, (Jesus instructed His disciples) when you have done everything you were told to do, should say, 'We are unworthy servants; we have only done our duty.'" (Luke 17:10 NIV).

It's like the man who found a wallet and returned it to its owner. Though some might call this as a good deed worthy of praise, the man had only done what he *ought* to do. This heart attitude is excellent as we seek to serve as leaders, because "pride in serving" lurks just around the corner in every ministry, and we need to fight it off.

This next Scripture gives more good counsel: that we serve to please Christ and not ourselves.

"For we do not preach ourselves, but Jesus Christ as Lord, and ourselves as your servants for Jesus' sake." (2 Corinthians 4:5 NIV).

Isn't that a wonderful verse? We are to serve other people, for Jesus' sake. This not only takes the focus off us, and our service, but it makes us realize that the one whose appreciation really counts is the Lord's. *That* is an appreciation we can receive and enjoy.

One of the best examples of serving in ministry I've ever seen was a couple named Dave and Bev. (And Dave and Bev, if you ever read this, don't cringe at the praise, because you guys deserve it!) I saw this couple only about once or twice a year at a ministry conference in Florida. But it was for quite a few years, so I felt I got to know them pretty well. And though these conferences tended to be discipleship oriented, Dave and Bev usually brought at least a few of what I'd call hurting, afflicted people. I was always impressed with the love and humility they showed for these folks, and I hung around them as much as I could. It was such a delight to see. In the eyes of Bev and Dave, these people were precious—and of course they were. In several years, I cannot ever remember seeing either Dave or Bev eating a meal; it seemed like they were always standing in the cafeteria lines and carrying trays to their guests. How Dave and Bev ever paid the conference fees for these folks, I can't imagine, but year after year, there they were, the dear funny bunch with their servants, Dave and Bev. And I'd bet a million dollars that Bev and Dave never thought of themselves as anything special or noble. What a joy that there are such people.

Paul once made an amazing statement (Romans 9:2,3) that he'd even give up his own salvation if his brothers, the Jews, would repent and come to Christ! Of course, Paul knew this wasn't good theology, but it did express his heart. He served to please God and for the sake

Principle # 5: Don't Hesitate to Lead, When Leadership is Needed. 185

of people. He told the people in Corinth, "I will very gladly spend for you everything I have and expend myself as well." (2 Corinthians 12:15 NIV).

Another point . . . our serving has a Kingdom goal:

"I have made myself a slave (servant) of all, that I might win the more . . . I have become all things to all men, that I may by all means save some." (1 Corinthians 9:19, 22).

The point here is clear. Paul's serving people had a clear purpose. He did it so that some of the people would be saved. Have the goal of your ministry effort or project clearly in mind. This is one of the most important parts of leading, and sometimes one of the easiest to forget about. In the business of everyday life, and even the activity of ministry, people can lose track of what the Kingdom goal is. Some folks really struggle with this. At Florida State University, one young man often asked me, "Tell me again where we're going with this?" He wasn't being a wise guy; he was working hard to keep our ministry goals in mind, because he didn't want to waste time and effort getting sidetracked. Good man.

How can we be sure we will not serve others in order to serve our own self-esteem? I think the answer is our own security in our relationship with God. Look at John 13:3. In this famous passage in which Jesus humbles himself and washes the feet of his disciples, it first says this:

"Jesus knew that the Father had put all things under his power, and that he had come from God and was returning to God." (NIV).

Simple as that statement is, it summarizes what we too can realize and hold on to. We have come from God; we are returning to God; and while we are on earth, God will give us the power to do what we must do. What a profound security there is in those truths.

Serve from a heart of obedience, to please Christ, to increase God's Kingdom.

Be diligent (work hard) . . .

". . . if it is leadership, let him govern diligently . . ." (Romans 12:8 NIV).

Boy, is this ever true! Being a good leader is hard work. Paul says of his ministry goal in Colossians, ". . . that we may present everyone perfect in Christ. To this end I labor, struggling with all his energy, which so powerfully works in me." (Colossians 1:28, 29 NIV).

Where does the hard work of leadership come in? I think it is the sheer labor and number of hours spent in coordinating a ministry effort. There can be a maddening complexity to even trying get people together. Someone said that directing a ministry team was the same as trying to keep fifty ping pong balls under water in a bathtub. Move the tiniest muscle, and ten pop to the surface. It sometimes seems that way when you're attempting to arrange a time and place for the team to meet in order to agree upon the goal and activities of the ministry.

It's difficult enough wrangle schedules so that three people can get together; try it with seven or eight people. In view of the number of calls you'll be making, you might as well duct tape that cell phone to the side of your head.

An excellent model of a hard-working leader is Nehemiah. If you remember the story, about 450 BC, Nehemiah was the cup-bearer, or court official, to King Artaxerxes, of the Persian throne. This king had already allowed Ezra to take a large number of exiled Jews back to Jerusalem, and thus Nehemiah got news of the state of the city: the wall and the gates of the city had been destroyed. Here's a brief look at how God used Nehemiah as a leader:

- Nehemiah receives word that ". . . the wall of Jerusalem is broken down, and its gates are burned with fire." (Nehemiah 1:3) Thus, the *goal* is established, rebuild the wall and gates, for their ruin was a source of shame for Israel.

- Nehemiah's response to this news: ". . . I sat down and wept and mourned for days; and I was fasting and praying . . ." (1:4) Nehemiah begins working toward his goal with *prayer*. He prayed for four months!

- Nehemiah claims God's *promise* concerning the goal. ". . . Remember Thy word . . if you return to Me and keep My commandments . . . I will return (you) to the place I have chosen to cause My name to dwell." (1:9).

- Nehemiah, who could face death for this audacity, goes before the king with this request, ". . . If it please the king . . . send me to Judah to the city of my fathers' tombs, that I may rebuild it." (2:5) This is the beginning of Nehemiah's *plan*. The king agrees and gives Nehemiah permission and resources.

- Nehemiah *gathers information* about the situation before he recruits a team or explains the goal. " . . . a few men with me. I did not tell anyone what God was putting in my mind to do for Jerusalem . . . So I went out at night . . . inspecting the walls of Jerusalem which were broken down . . ." (2:12, 13) Know the task before you, and know it well, so the goal is always clear in your mind. This is a key to good leadership.

- Nehemiah *builds a team* by explaining the goal to be achieved. "Then I said to them . . . 'Come, let us rebuild the wall of Jerusalem, that we may no longer be a reproach.'" (2:17).

You probably know the rest of the story, the people respond and, with a sword in one hand and a trowel in the other, they rebuild the wall and gates. They fight off opposition and discouragement, and complete the goal in 52 days!

This describes the amount of hard work, both in prayer and planning, that the leader in ministry needs to do. Let's take a look at one more aspect of leadership, then we'll see what this might look like in our hypothetical situation.

Be an example.

There's an old joke about leading: "Oh, there go the people. I must hurry and lead them!" That might describe some political leadership, just trying to get in line with where the people are heading anyway, but not Christian leadership. We must lead by example, being in front of the people, doing what we want them to do, and showing them how.

"Be shepherds of God's flock that is under your care, serving as overseers . . . not lording it over those entrusted to you, but being examples to the flock." (1 Peter 5:2, 3 NIV).

If it's occurred to you that although serving and working hard are needed, they still don't really provide a leader to follow, this aspect—being an example—does. When we lead by setting an example, we provide a model for others. When we set an example of obeying Scripture, especially in an endeavor like evangelism, our life becomes an authoritative model. It is our *doing* something that gives us our authority as Christian leaders. If, in addition to actually living out our stated conviction, we can demonstrate and teach an effective method of doing it, other people who want to obey will follow. It does not take a dynamic personality to be a good leader as much as being an obedient, effective example.

One last benefit of leading, for the leader, is a little-known secret. It's this: when a person is leading, she or he seldom thinks very much about herself or himself. It's such a responsibility, and joy, to lead a team of willing Christians in a biblical endeavor, you'll find you just don't worry about yourself. You may worry about how the others are doing and feeling, or about whether you're making progress toward the goal, but you'll rarely think much about yourself.

What would this kind of leadership look like in the hypothetical situation above?

Okay, let's say you're back in that meeting the pastor called, and he's just said, "Who'll lead this team?" You stand up and say, "I think this is a great thing for our church to be doing, and I'd be glad to help coordinate it if you'd all like me to." You *know* that several people in the room just breathed a sigh of relief, some because they didn't want to have to take responsibility, and some because they're grateful a qualified person's going to lead.

Now what? If you are confirmed as the leader, let's learn from Nehemiah and apply some of the principles from his approach.

Goal...

Let people know that they need to be serious to consider being part of this team. Make two things clear: (1) that you're going to actually go out and meet people in the community at large and share Christ with them; it's not just a church visitation program, and (2) that you will be responsible for training them and taking them out with you (and any other who's experienced) so that they won't be just expected to do it "sink or swim."

Prayer...

Ask for a few people who will pray, right after the present meeting, for this effort. Ask them to keep praying in the days to come for God's leading.

Promise...

It is important to claim God's promises concerning evangelism, like Isaiah 55:11, "So shall My word be which goes forth from My mouth; it shall not return to me empty, without accomplishing what I desire, and succeeding in the matter for which I sent it."

Gather info . . .

Now pick one or two of those most able and confident, and go out with them into the neighborhoods, or apartment complexes, where you plan to go to share Christ, and do some reconnaissance. This is just what Nehemiah did to figure out what the real nature of the project would be. Find the places that are best. You'll be amazed at how good a "feel" you'll have for which areas and neighborhoods would be appropriate for your team to go.

Build a team . . .

This step is costly: meet with each person who volunteers to be on the team . . . individually. This is part of the hard work. Really interact with each one and determine who's where in ability and confidence as far as evangelism. Begin to build a real strong bond between you and each team member. This will really distinguish the outreach from any other church program they've been a part of, and it will definitely establish you as the leader. Plus, it builds the comradeship of satisfaction and joy of those who are working together on an eternally significant goal.

What I'm going to say next may surprise you. Have only two meetings, or three at most, to train people how to share the gospel. Why so few? First of all, the gospel illustration (remember, "SDSD—all Chapter Three") isn't that difficult to learn. Secondly, they'll be with an experienced person who'll do all the talking anyway . . . for the first few times. Thirdly, amazingly, the more people "practice" sharing the gospel with other Christians in meetings, the more scared they get. Really. Just going out and doing it, with a seasoned veteran along, is the least intimidating and most confidence-building way there is to do this. You may have only you and one other person who's capable and confident to be the one who shares the Gospel. In that case, go slowly. By that, I mean, just have two "rookies" at a time go out. After a few times, they may feel they can go out by themselves, then you can take another beginner. Don't feel you have to rush things, and have the whole team of volunteers going out in just a couple of weeks.

Okay, now just go do it. Nehemiah and his workers had trowels in one hand to build the wall, and swords in the other hand to fight the enemy. You'll have the power and authority of the Word of God, and the presence of Christ "And surely, I am with you always . . ." (Matthew 28:20 NIV).

Make sure each person on the team is safe, physically and emotionally. There's two goals here, share the gospel with non-believers, and give courage and confidence to those who are learning to share. Your team members will be glad for your leadership.

Women as leaders . . .

There is another question that I think should be clarified. That question is this: what is the role of women in Christian leadership? What guidelines does the Bible give for this issue? I know this can be a very sensitive concern for women and men, and I'd like to briefly give what I feel are considerations of this issue as it relates to our topic of "Don't hesitate to lead."

First of all, I don't believe the spiritual gift of leadership is sex-specific. That is, Romans 12:8 (". . . if it is leadership, let him do it with diligence . . .") does not state, nor imply, I believe, that the spiritual gift of leadership is for males only. The "him" there is just the old-fashioned grammatical convention of using the masculine pronoun. I would say there are many times and situations in which women can and should lead.

Secondly, I am convinced that the essential work of the "Great Commission" (term for evangelizing and disciple-making of all nations) is not only *inclusive* of both women and men, but is a *command* for both sexes. Much of Scriptural teaching and exhortation is addressed to mankind: male and female, the creation of God, in the image of God. So the critical ministry of evangelism and discipling is something both women and men can do, and should do.

The tension, if you will, of the differences in the roles of men and women comes from a few passages which I'd like to look at and discuss. Allow me to approach this discussion with a little story.

I was once asked if I would meet with a small group of graduate student women in the university where I taught, who referred to themselves as feminists. They had somehow heard that I was a Christian, and they wanted to hear my thoughts on the Christian's view of feminism and equality of the sexes. There were seven or eight women, all but two working on their doctorates, so it was a pretty impressive group, brainpower-wise. I was a little nervous as we started talking, but I was soon amazed at how much common ground we shared.

Our first point of common ground was to agree on the definition of "equality." The dictionary defines "equality" as sameness in . . .

- Size or quantity

- Position

- Value or quality.

This was a great starting point because the women all agreed, for themselves and (as one put it) for "99% of all women", that the size issue was irrelevant. They felt very few women wanted to be the same size as men. There's not that great a discernable size difference today anyhow, at least between college-age men and women. But even if the world statistics showed that men are on average 15 pounds heavier than women, or an inch taller, or whatever . . . the group of women I was talking to said that didn't matter. Not many women really want to be large enough to try out successfully for offensive line for the Green Bay Packers' football team.

I turned then to the issue of value, or quality. This is the factor that has enormous importance for Christians, because it can be clearly evaluated, but is less clear or important for the secular world. The Bible is absolutely crystal-clear that all human beings have the same value.

"There is neither Jew or Greek, there is neither slave nor free man, there is neither male nor female; for you are all one in Christ Jesus." (Galatians 3:28).

That's as direct a statement on this topic as we could wish. All are of one value in Christ. Each has the same exact value as any other one. The price that was paid for every human being who claims salvation through Jesus Christ was identical, whether they're slaves or free, women or men. In business terms, a million dollars worth of diamonds is the same *value* as a million dollars worth of plywood, though the two items are quite different.

So equality in terms of size and value are addressed. The one doesn't matter (size) and the other is biblically established. The area of tension comes with the third aspect of "equality:" position.

I suggested to the group of women that for both non-Christians and Christians, the issue of positional differences was probably the battleground. They agreed. I presented them with an analogy based upon the position each of them found themselves in as graduate students. I asked if any of them felt inferior to their professors. There was much laughter. The answer was, "Of course not!" I concluded a few of them did not have a very high opinion of the intellectual abilities of some of their professors.

"Why not?" I asked them. "I mean, not only are you positionally under your professors' authority, you even pay a lot of money to be there."

Their answer was good, and amounted to this, "First of all, it's for our benefit; with our degrees, we can get excellent jobs. And secondly, it's temporary. Even if some of the profs are obnoxious, we'll be done in another two years."

Taking that comment, in conjunction with a key verse of Scripture, gives us an amazing and profound truth: that people of identical, equal value can be positionally different. It has nothing to do with superiority or inferiority. The Scripture is 1 Corinthians 11:3 (NASB) and says, "But I want you to understand that Christ is the head of every man, and the man is the head of a woman, and God the Father is the head of Christ."

This chapter in First Corinthians deals with positional differences and the order of authority. It is very important passage, summarized in verse 3, because I think it equates Christ's positional relationship with the Father with women's positional relationship with man. Say what!? Hang on now. When Jesus was on earth, he did the will of the Father. (". . . Yet not what I will, but what you will." Mark 14:36 NIV) It's absurd to imagine Jesus saying, "Why do *I* have to be in subjection to the Father and do *His* will all the time? Why don't I get to be the Head sometimes!?"

And while our understanding of eternity in heaven is somewhat conjectural, Jesus is referred to as "sitting at the right hand of the Father." (Mark 14: 62) So there is at least an inference that Jesus' positional relationship with the Father is eternal.

Can we accept that God the Father and God the Son are perfectly equal in Godhood, yet positionally different? Yes. To imply that the Father and the Son hold the same position denies the essence of the Trinity, that is, the distinctive Persons of the triune God. To suggest that the Son is somehow "less God" than the Father, or inferior in any way to the Father . . . is blasphemy.

Can we accept that the positional roles of men and women—during our time on earth—are different without in anyway diminishing either sex? Yes. Are women or men in any way inferior to the other sex because of a positional difference? Emphatically NO! And not only that, for Christian men and Christian women, the difference is only temporary.

There is no positional difference in heaven based upon one's sex that I am aware of. Jesus told the Sadducees that in heaven people are like the angels in that regard. I don't know if sexual distinctiveness is evident in heaven or not, but I know there is no marriage, a key aspect of human sexuality. (Matthew 22:30).

The key to being at peace with all this is, I believe, to realize that one's *position*—in relation to other people—is not important. One's *value* is what is important. The world, without the affirming equality of Christ's valuation of people . . . (His own life given for them . . .) cares only about positional battles, for position is what gives people of the world their sense of value. And, believe me, the battles are not for equality, but for supremacy.

The most difficult passage of Scripture in this regard is probably 1 Tim 2:12-14 (NIV) The Apostle Paul is writing to Timothy concerning church procedures. The passage says, "I do not permit a woman to teach or to have authority over a man . . . For Adam was formed first, then Eve. And Adam was not the one deceived; it was the woman who was deceived . . ."

What are we to make of this teaching today? Is it cultural? Is there anything to tie it to Paul's culture but not ours? If it *is* trans-cultural (that is, *not* pertaining only to a specific time or place), then what is its extent and application? Would it apply in all areas, e.g., secular jobs, or not? Would it apply to all instances in which teaching is practiced, or not?

Okay, here's a couple of bits of obvious logic. If I lock my keys in my car and a woman happens to come by and says, "I know how to pop the lock on this model car . . ." do I shun her help because I, as a man, am not allowed to be taught by a woman, or do I say "Please show me how!"

Or if my family and I am on a sinking cruise ship, and the trained lifeboat master happens to be a woman, do I go down with the ship so as not to be under the authority of a woman, or do I follow her orders?

Agreed, these are absurd examples. But I believe the context of the 1 Timothy 2:12-14 passage relates to church authority and the teaching of Christian doctrine. I wouldn't feel comfortable extending this admonition to secular situations; for one reason, the world, generally, does not follow Christian principles, and for another, I don't believe the context allows it.

Does this mean then, that the 1 Timothy passage has no relevance for us today? I believe it does, because from a hermeneutical standpoint, the passage is clearly trans-cultural. That is, it is not a teaching which pertains only to Paul's day and situation. What are the elements which make it trans-cultural? First of all, Paul's explanation for giving this rule goes all the way back to Adam and Eve, and the position of precedence of Adam. ". . . For Adam was formed first, then Eve." This is, to coin a word (?) "trans-temporality" or transcending the *time* Paul spoke. This addresses the authority, or headship, issue. Is Paul saying that women would not be good in positions of authority or headship? No. But as the 1 Corinthians 11:3 verse states, there has to be headship, and it is appointed by God to the man, in the man/woman context. This is no big deal, in my estimation. Somebody has to do it, and it's best done as God directs. As the old saying goes, "Anything with two heads is a monster, and anything with no head is dead."

Then there is another element, and please forgive me if I express this poorly. Verse 14 of 1 Timothy 2 says, "And Adam was not the one deceived; it was the woman who was deceived . . ." This trans-cultural aspect concerns susceptibility to being deceived, a consideration which would affect the teaching of doctrine. And while we may think that Adam and Eve sinned the same sin, Eve's was to be deceived (2 Corinthians 11:3); Adam's was to knowingly join Eve in the sin.[1]

Now this seems such a harsh accusation against Eve, and women, but sin is sin, and Adam's sin is, if anything, worse than Eve's. However, in today's culture, which so admires the sleazy rascal rather than the gullible nice person, Eve's transgression seems more embarrassing, or demeaning.

Yes, we all know men who are the very essence of gullibility . . . they buy stuff advertised on TV at 4:00 AM of the "But wait! There's more!" variety. And we all know women who are as shrewd and wise as Solomon. But, again, the authority *must* be assigned for church order and discipline to be maintained, and so God assigns it to men. Who could possibly make such distinctions between men and women in churches on a daily basis? And once Christians submit to God's way and will, he

---

1. By the way, please note that though Eve and Adam both sinned, Adam got the blame from God for it. Why? Because he was the head. ". . . sin entered the world through one man and death through sin . . . death reigned from the time of Adam . . . even over those who did not sin by breaking a command, as did Adam . . . (Romans 5:12–14).

assures such obedience is honored, and even though the not-too-smart man is the head of the brilliant woman, there is peace in the Kingdom.

And remember, this is not man saying this, but the Word of God. My feelings about it may or may not be in agreement with the Scripture, but that does not alter the teaching.

What's my point in all of this? That women can and should lead women in the essentials of Great Commission ministry, and in godly, victorious living. Men can and should lead men in the same. In those instances in which there is a ministry team made up of both sexes, a man should lead. A woman in authority over men, in either a church denomination or para-church organization, is, I believe, contrary to the instruction of 1 Timothy 2:12. While I do not think Romans 12: 8 "leadership" is sex-specific, I would say that the positions of church authority detailed in 1 Timothy 3 and Titus 1 are sex- specific, applicable to men only.

But really, it is my *deep conviction* that it is relatively unimportant who is coordinating such a team, or whose name is on the sign outside the church, or denominational headquarters. The heart of the ministry of Jesus Christ is done by women and men as they share Christ and disciple others. That is what is important.

To serve the Lord with all our hearts means to do so from a foundation of security in Christ, and humility. To me, battling over positions or titles in the church, or bitter confrontation over the female/male issue, reveals an insecurity which Jesus loves to resolve as people grow closer to him.

Conclusion: People benefit greatly from solid leadership. When a situation arises in which it seems leadership is needed, ask yourself these questions:

- Am I qualified to lead in this situation?

- Am I familiar with and experienced in the required activity?

- Do I have a good biblical understanding of the goal?

- Can I lead a team to the goal with clear Scriptural principles?

- Is my motive to see success so the Kingdom benefits?

- Am I biblically permitted to lead in this situation? If I am a woman, would I have men under my authority?

- Do I have the health, time, and energy to take on this task?

- Would my leading result in hardship for my family?

- Would my leading in any way be a bad testimony?

If, after thinking about these considerations, you feel it would be good for God's Kingdom for you to lead . . . please do it.

8

Principle # 6: Don't Use People to Build Your Ministry. Use Your Ministry to Build People.

THIS IS A FAIRLY simple principle to present, but it can be difficult at times to resist the temptation to go against it. The principle is this: the people God entrusts to your shepherding care are to be valued and helped, not used.

"Be shepherds of God's flock that is under your care." (1 Peter 5: 2 NIV).

As this verse points out, the people are God's flock, not ours. We are entrusted to be their shepherd; they are under our care. This seems so utterly clear and uncomplicated, yet I have seen it violated numerous times in Christian ministry.

How are people abused? By doing ministry jobs they are untrained for, or jobs which detract from their own spiritual growth, or by being asked, inappropriately, to recruit others to come be part of the ministry. I think this happens for a couple of reasons.

How growth is viewed . . .

One reason I've observed is that the ministry leaders (or the ministry strategies of the organization) may not view individual growth to spiritual maturity as a realistic or desired goal, but instead have goals in which the largeness of its groups is seen as desirable. Obviously, *groups* do not "grow in Christian maturity;" it is individuals within the group which do that. But there are some organizations, I believe, which see ministry as an effort have as many people involved as possible, and that those, in turn, would attract or recruit even more.

This results in what I call a "Baby World" ministry. Lots of immature believers whose essential role is to bring even more babes, or be part of providing the activities and entertainment which are a key attraction of these kinds of ministries. The "maintenance" if you will, of large groups of immature Christians normally uses up all the resources of the ministry, so that rarely are there provisions, time, or plans to help young believers who want serious growth.

Does that mean that large ministries or churches are unfruitful in the Great Commission? The answer is "yes" if simply being large is the main goal. The answer is "no" if there is an intentional, carefully thought-out plan to disciple and equip individual members of the group. Then its large size is seen as an opportunity to help people walk joyfully with the Lord, and be able to minister to others.

It really depends on how *growth* is viewed. If growth is seen basically as the *numbers of people* increasing, I think it's not good. If growth is seen as helping *individual persons* to grow spiritually, I think it's good. Mere addition of babes and more babes to the group is not the Great Commission ministry of making disciples of all nations. In fact, I feel that when babes are expected to reach more babes, it's a violation (to employ a term in an absurd way) of child labor laws . . . or even "baby labor laws."

Don't put your babies to work! Care for them and feed them. Then, when they come healthily to maturity, they can reach and disciple others. I call this the big "flip-flop." It's the time when those who have been loved and helped want to do the same for someone else. Together with that person, you can pray, "Oh, Lord, give Kyle or Kristen a person to help!" The sheep, fed and cared for, becomes a shepherd. This kind of growth is wonderful! This is multiplication, not mere addition.

And remember, while it may be that the Lord causes a big group of mature disciples to remain together, He may also send them out into other ministries. According to Acts 1:8, ". . . in Jerusalem, in all Judea, Sameria, and to the ends of the earth." God seems more of a centrifugal srategist than centripetal. That is, laborers are more likely to be flung out than clumped together. The implication of this is that even effective, biblical ministries can tend to remain quite small. As my friend and mentor, Ron Shimkus, told me once, "Most real discipleship is dinky." Can we live with this humbling situation? Yes, with great joy.

Leaders' self-esteem issues . . .

Another reason people in ministry may be inappropriately used is to bolster the self-esteem of the ministry leader(s) as reflected by his or her "success." And sadly, success in ministry is usually measured in numbers: numbers of members, attenders, givers, programs, etc. of the ministry.

Let's take campus ministry as an example. The Christmas conference, or in some cases, the spring conference, is the big deal of the year. Every campus minister hopes to have a large group of college students going with her or him to the conference. And of course, the master of ceremonies always says, "Hey, who's here from the University of Wherever?" There are yells and cheers from the 50 students from U of W! Then the MC says, "And who's here from Smallstuff College?" Smallstuff is your college ministry. Two students shyly answer "Us." You feel like a failure.

So, in the embarrassment of how pathetic your think your ministry is—based on the setup of the conference—you vow that next year you'll have at least twenty students at the conference, or die trying. So next year, you get your few committed students out trying to recruit others to go to the conference. It doesn't matter who, as long as they're breathing and have a pulse. The problem is, all this takes manpower, hours, and effort. And the limited time your students have for Bible study and personal time with the Lord is used up in the big recruiting outreach. Being college students, with their proverbially enthusiastic attitude and energy, they agree to do it.

But everyone loses in the end. Yes, a few more bewildered students go to the conference, but the original, committed ones begin to feel as though it really wasn't worth it. They feel the loss of the excitement of personal growth they experienced the previous year, and worst of all, the first seeds of doubt about their leader's concern for them begin to take root.

Of course, this situation applies not only to campus ministry, but to local churches as well. We call church folks who are burned out with all the activities "crispy critters." These are people who believed their leaders that "you are just *the* person for the finance committee!" and served for two years, but silently vow never to raise their hands again when the urgency of filling positions comes around again.

This reality presents pastors and church staff with a dilemma, because there *are* indeed jobs in the local churches that have to be handled by volunteers. But the question the pastor should *always* ask himself first is this: "If I ask Karen to be the church treasurer, even though she's a CPA, will it hurt her personal spiritual growth?" To not ask this question is to abandon the shepherd's duty, in favor of the CEO's labor requirements. In some ways, local churches are famous for "eating their seed corn." By this I mean, that when a person in a church begins to grow spiritually, and shows enthusiasm, the church leaders may notice and grab her up, putting her to work on a church job that may be needed, but never-the-less often short-circuits the young Christian's growth. So the person, like the kernel of corn, is used immediately rather than being "planted." (See John 12:24) If the seed is planted, it brings forth an entire corn plant, with several ears and many kernels. That's Kingdom growth.

Challenging Christians to take the next appropriate step in their spiritual journey is good. Exploiting them as a labor force is bad. This is pretty simple to determine. If I challenge a person to do something for his or her own spiritual growth, it should not be primarily for the benefit of me or the group. In fact, it often means more work for me to come along side him and help him take on the challenge.

Before we philosophize much more, let's look at Scripture. This whole thing is addressed in Chapter 34 of the book of Ezekiel. God speaks about good and bad shepherds.

> "... prophesy against the shepherds of Israel, prophesy and say to them: 'This is what the Sovereign Lord says: Woe to the shepherds of Israel who only take care of themselves! Should not shepherds take care of the flock? You eat the fat, clothe yourselves with the wool and slaughter the choice animals, but you do not take care of the flock. '... You have not strengthened the weak or healed the sick or bound up the injured. You have not brought back the strays or searched for the lost. You have ruled them harshly and brutally. So they scattered because there was no shepherd, and when they were scattered they became food for all the wild animals ... They were scattered over the whole earth, and no one searched or looked for them.'" (Ezekiel 34:2–6 NIV).

Let's look at the key points. God describes bad shepherds in the following way:

- they eat the sheep
- they fleece them
- they kill the choice animals (for profit?)

- they neglect feeding, strengthening, healing the sheep under their care

- they don't look for lost or straying sheep

- they allow the wandering sheep to become prey for wild animals

In brief, what bad ministers do is use the people in their ministry for the profit of the minister or ministry to the detriment of the people, and neglect to feed or heal them. If they stray off, they're not sought after, and become pray for the "wild animals" of this world.

God concludes His assessment of these bad shepherds by saying, "I am against these shepherds and will hold them accountable for my flock. I will remove them from tending the flock so the shepherds can no longer feed themselves... I will rescue my flock..." (Ezekiel 34:10 NIV).

Then God describes his own portrait as a *good shepherd*.

> "For this is what the Sovereign Lord says, 'I myself will search for my sheep and look after them. As a shepherd looks for his scattered sheep when he is with them, so will I look after my sheep. I will rescue them from all the places they were scattered ... I will bring them into their own land ... I will tend them in a good pasture, and the mountain heights of Israel will be their grazing land. There they will lie down in good grazing land, and there they will feed in a rich pasture on the mountains of Israel. I Myself will tend my sheep and have them lie down, ' declares the Sovereign Lord. 'I will search for the lost and bring back the strays. I will bind up the injured and strengthen the weak ... '" (Ezekiel 34:11–16 NIV).

Isn't this a wonderful description of ministry? Key points:

- Search for lost sheep. One campus staff said it took him a whole year to find all the students who'd left the ministry during the time of a bad shepherd. They were happy to be found and reconnected.

- Tend them in good pasture, providing safety and food. Give the folks in your ministry the bread of the Word of God, teaching and exhorting, and tend them by praying for them and "carrying" them spiritually. Jesus asked Peter to do this for him: "... feed my lambs ... take care of my sheep." (John 21:15, 16 NIV)

- Tend the injured and weak. To the best of your ability, heal those who have been wounded by life or people, and help those who are weak—emotionally, spiritually, intellectually—to gain strength.

There's a kind of logic to this principle (to not use people to build your ministry). The logic is this: if I improperly use a person in my ministry to build my ministry—that is, use a person to reach other people so the ministry is bigger—then I have de-valued the first person, the person I used. And why would the second, twentieth, or fiftieth, person be any more valuable than the first? If I devalue the first, I really don't really value *any* one.

Let me give an illustration. Let's say I'm a person who loves and values Stradivarius violins. I own one "Strad" and would love to have more. Now let's say a strange person comes to me and says, "If you'll ruin the Strad you have, I'll give you two more Strads." Should I do it? And if I do agree to this bizarre bargain, would I then ruin my two Strads to gain four? Do you see the perverse nature of this kind of thinking? If I destroy something I claim to love in order to have more of them, I really only show that it is the numbers of violins that I love, not the violins themselves. If I really value the violins themselves, I would never destroy the one I have in order to get more, then ruin those to get even more. Each Strad violin is precious in itself. To destroy one to get more is a horrible self-contradiction.

To *not* value and shepherd one person, but instead use that person to get others, is the same perversion of ministry. It reveals, not a love for people, but rather a love of numbers.

Conclusion . . . you may be a pastor or ministry leader who has many in your flock, and perhaps several of them are capable of ministering to others. Thus, you have considerable resources to reach the lost and disciple the hungry. On the other hand, you may be the only person in your group who is at a point of maturity to be able to feed and care for others. Then your ministry resource is one: yourself. In that situation, be content and use your 'sole resource" to shepherd your flock. The point is this, please employ in ministry only those for whom the challenge to work is a benefit to them. Love and minister to the others with the resources you have, feeding and caring for them.

9

Principle # 7: Be Gracious, Yet Wise, in Your Relationship with Your Local Church as You Disciple.

PRAISE GOD FOR GOOD local churches! Not only are they the physical locations where God's people gather to worship and celebrate the sacraments, they are the home bases from which most average, radical Christians will do ministry. While there will be quite a number of folks called to campus ministries, overseas missions, or other specific-group works, the majority of serious believers will find their best opportunity to contribute to the Kingdom of God within the context of their local church.

The key point of this chapter, or ministry principle, is that we would be appreciative and gracious, but also wise, as we relate to our particular local church. There are great blessings to be had as we seek to make disciples within the framework of our church, but also some challenges.

Let's consider some of the many good things that local churches do. And please remember, we're talking here about solid, Bible-believing, Bible-teaching churches, not those whose liberalism or other deviation from Scripture has caused them to abandon orthodox Christian truths.

First of all, good local churches have some really wonderful people in them. There are many members of the congregation, church staff and pastors who are the kind of folks you'd love to have as neighbors. It's no secret that the number one attraction for a lot of new believers, seekers, and even non-believers to a local church is that the people there are just so nice. The worship services and small groups are usually friendly, welcoming, and non-judgmental. People just feel safe and happy to be around such people. Someone has accurately said that the "radiation" given off by good Christian fellowship is one of the most valuable assets of the Christian world. As one young professional put it, "It's the best place I've ever found to make friends!" For people used to the fragile, even treacherous, relationships often found in the world, the local church environment is a haven. It's a place where they feel they can be themselves and build trustworthy relationships with others. Sure, Christians aren't perfect, but compared with the "two ticks, and no dog" relationships of everyday life (each one looking to get needs met from the other), being part of a Christian group and having Christian friends is an amazing treasure. Good local churches give a place for people to belong, and feel safe belonging.

And, speaking from my own experience, I feel one of the big positives of being in biblical fellowship is that we can become secure enough to see other's viewpoints, or perspectives. This is a good benefit of being in a small group Bible study. We get to hear other peoples' thoughts and insights on a common subject, and it's amazing how varied those can be.

Here's a classic case of different perspectives . . . when I was visiting friends in Africa, we went on a car trip through a game preserve. I pointed to an animal and asked, "Is that a Thompson's gazelle?" Our Kenyan guide smiled and said gently, "Well, *we* don't call them that." Aha! Long before the Scottish explorer presumably "named" the animal, Africans already had a name for it. What a good perspective changer.

Then there is the fact that the gospel is preached in good churches, and it's not only the gospel that's taught, but biblical truths that address many issues pertaining to everyday life and godly living. In many churches there is also a Biblical call to foreign missions and full-time ministry. What a benefit to be able to receive good teaching from the Scripture.

Another thing that local churches do really well is provide resources and people power for charitable work in the community. Shelters and food for homeless persons, financial help for such things as rent, utilities, child-care; these are all part of the benevolence budget of just about every good church I know. There are also counseling, legal, and shelter services for abused women and children; there is grief counseling, hospice care, pastoral counseling for folks struggling with many, many issues. This is a list that could go on, literally, for pages. Again, I'll say it. Praise God for good local churches!

The important function which many local churches do not do (in my experience), however, is *equip and train* lay people for Great

Commission ministry . . . the ministry of effective evangelism and discipleship. Because of this, you may encounter misunderstanding, confusion, or perhaps even some opposition as you work on making disciples in your local church.

Why is this such a tough issue for local churches? The first is, again, the unfortunate clergy/laity distinction common in our Christian culture. Just the idea of a lay person being involved in the very heart of ministry (witnessing and discipling)—perhaps even more than the pastors—can be very unsettling for some. So when we introduce the idea of lay people doing this most essential work of biblical ministry, it can be a tough sell. The clergy / laity distinction is so ingrained, that to go against it, even in such a gentle and inoffensive manner as one church member helping another to grow, is to risk a bit of a negative reaction.

Seminaries may unknowingly contribute to this clergy / laity distinction, to the detriment, I believe, of the Great Commission. The "ordained" minister takes that ordination seriously, as well he should. But "ordination," which simply means "ordered," (or the "conferring of holy orders") is something that applies to every Christian. We are *all* ordered, commanded, to make disciples of all nations. The special-ness, if you will, of "ordained clergy" is, I believe a man-made distinction that only serves to separate further the roles of pastors and lay people.

Perhaps another reason some local churches have a hard time with personal discipleship is an *over-emphasis* on community and an *under-emphasis* on individuality. In our culture today, and especially in the Christian culture, the word "individualism" often has a negative connotation. It sounds like "lone-wolfism," or a maverick who doesn't want to be a team player or part of a group. There can be that connotation, but I mean the term in its most basic definition . . . the saved individual who is building a strong, personal relationship with God, and wants to serve in a significant way.

It's quite understandable for church leaders to desire a strong sense of community in their church. Fifty years ago, at least in rural America, the churches were often the social focus of the town, as well as the spiritual focus. Everyone who attended a particular church probably knew each other, and the church activities of a social nature—picnics, potluck dinners, weddings, holiday services and musicals—formed a strong bond of unity. It's perhaps hard for some pastors not to wish for that kind of bond in their churches today, though it is perhaps counter to the reality of modern culture.

Yes, a group of people can join together to put a new roof on the homeless shelter, but a *group* does not have a personal relationship with God. A *person*, by definition, has a *personal* relationship with God. If the individual, and her or his relationship with God, is the primary "unit," if you will, of the local church, then I firmly believe that the church *and* the community will be stronger and more effective in ministry. That is because each person is in a relationship with the Lord, and the joy and victory in life that results from such a relationship will make the community more vital and joyful. Real fellowship and ministry will result, not just socializing.

If the corporate community is primary, then people who do not have a personal relationship with God, or a weak one, are still part of the group, but their main relationship is not with God, but rather with each other and the activities of the church. That is more descriptive of Judaism than New Testament Christianity.

And obviously, a person without a good personal relationship with God is not going to be interested in discipling another person, because having a strong relationship with God is what discipleship is.

With life-to-life discipling, the focus is on the few serious ones to disciple, and, to begin with, the numbers are miniscule, the progress slow, the multiplying effect long-term, and the evaluation difficult. It's much simpler to ask "How many came?" than "How *is* that man's walk with God?"

It's also more traditional and familiar to administer programs, and their outcome, than personal discipleship. When a person begins her or his unique relationship with the living God, who knows where it will lead? When persons begin to share their faith and help younger believers to grow, it may or may not be within the context of their own local church. It may not be, initially, in the context of *any* church. That scenario may not produce happy thoughts for some church staff.

It's understandable for pastors to feel that the traditional model is the safest way. Wouldn't we all? But it makes it tough, in some cases, to establish a life-to-life disciplemaking ministry in a few local churches. There can be resistance to lay personal ministry even though personal discipling within the church really doesn't cost anything financially, and rarely negatively affects anything else the church is doing.

I have encouraged pastors that one-to-one discipleship can fit into any church, and the church can continue to do all the other programs it's always done. Nothing needs to be "cut" in order to include discipleship. It's the leaven hidden in the measures of meal. (Matthew 13:33) It can be so low-key as to be hidden, yet still be effective. I've been encouraged with some pastors' response and understanding of this concept, but there have been other times when the response was not so positive.

* * *

Note: Let me offer these thoughts to pastors. Pastors, in reality, you are often the key to Great Commission ministry in your churches. You have the knowledge, the concern, and perhaps most important, the credibility, to lead and model in this important work. If you *do* want to break out of the clergy/laity mold, you *must* do what you wish the people in the church would do. (Remember Principle # 1: *Be what you want others to be; do what you want others to do.*).

- If you want them to share their faith, you must. And I don't mean from the pulpit; I mean in real life, outside the walls of the church, with the non-Christian friends you have made.

Do you have any non-Christian friends? I hope so. One evangelical denomination stated that, to their shame, "the higher up in the denomination our pastors are, the further they are from the harvest field." If the church lay people really are "entrusted with the gospel," (1 Thessalonians 2:4); if they really are ambassadors for Christ," (2 Corinthians 5:20); if they really have "this treasure in earthen vessels," (2 Corinthians 4:7), then lead them in outreach to the lost around them. It's not enough that they invite people to church. It's not enough for them to say to others, "Come to a place where there's an earthen vessel who can tell you about Jesus."

- If you want them to study and apply the Bible, you must. And I don't mean "sermon prep." Lay people don't do sermon prep.

- If you want them to disciple another, you must. And no, that doesn't mean having a monthly meeting of the board of elders.

Pastors, get a guy or two and meet with them individually once a week at the fast food restaurant near the place that they work.

Admonish them and teach them (Colossians 1: 28) how to study the Word, how to memorize it, how to share the gospel, and how to help another. Take them with you as you do evangelism, to college apartments or the neighborhoods around the church. Or arrange with a non-Christian friend of yours to meet for lunch at the fast food place, and have your young disciple join you and watch as you graciously share the gospel. This is ministry training, not just information dispensing. Get out of the church building, and into the real world and those you disciple will do the same.

Jesus chose His disciples to be "with Him and to send them out,"(Mark 3:14) not just to hand them three-ring binders of "discipleship material."

* * *

Here are some ways your local church might respond if you introduce the idea of personal discipleship for lay people:

- Best situation . . . The pastor heartily agrees with your desire to see one-to-one discipleship in his church, and he wants to do it too.

- Next best situation . . . The pastor is excited by the concept of discipleship, and will endorse it in the church with enthusiasm. But he does not see himself doing it, for he feels that would be showing favoritism by the "shepherd" who proverbially loves and treats everyone the same. But he will support your effort, and he "appreciates your passion" for this ministry.

- Kind of okay situation . . . This is what I call the Gamaliel response. Remember when the disciples got into trouble (Acts 5:34—40) for preaching Jesus. (Acts 5: 28) ". . . We gave you strict orders not to continue teaching in this name . . ." They got hauled before the Council of religious leaders, and the high priest and others wanted to put them to death. But a Pharisee named Gamaliel said this to the Council,

"Take care what you do to these men . . . I say to you, stay away from these men and let them alone, for if this plan should be of men, it will be overthrown; but if it is of God, you will not be able to overthrow them; or else you may be even found fighting against God." (Acts 5: 35, 38, 39).

That's pretty clear, isn't it. It's a kind of "wait and see" position. If what these men are doing is of God, we sure don't want to oppose it.

And if what they're doing is just another scheme of men, it'll fail anyway. Some pastors will take this stance. They won't really go out on a limb and endorse discipleship, but they'll not oppose it. One church leader said to me, "I don't think this is going to raise much interest, but if it does, we'll put some resources into it next year."

How can we best minister within our churches? The bare bones plan is pretty simple:

1. Join a Sunday school class or small group if you're not already in one.
2. Volunteer to lead it if that's a possibility. This gives you credibility.
3. Look for one or two in the group who are obviously hungry and serious about the Word and learning. This is pretty easy to discern.
4. Ask if you can get with them to go through discipleship together. Use the 7 & 3 discipleship material. (See the Appendix for this material in a "ready-to-share" format.)
5. Disciple that person.
6. Then pray together that she or he can do the same for another.

That's it.

Okay, if this principle is be gracious but wise, what's the gracious part? It's pretty simple. Romans 12 gives good advice:

"Let love be without hypocrisy ... Be devoted to one another in brotherly love; give preference to one another in honor ... If possible, so far as it depends on you, be at peace with all men." (Romans 12:9, 10, 18).

Keeping good relationships with others in your local church, even if they're not really supportive of your discipling ministry, is probably much more important than "being right," or feeling you have to defend this kind ministry. These church folks may not get what you're doing, but they are your brothers and sisters.

Plus, I think in most cases, you'll be able to disciple within your church anyway. Real life-to-life discipleship is so low-profile, it's not going to raise alarm with the vast majority of people. It really depends on God leading you to a few who are eager to grow and do ministry, and as we know, nothing is impossible with God.

What's the wise part? Let's take a look at a man with a real "attitude" concerning his relationship with church authorities, the Apostle Paul.

> "But from those who were of high reputation (what they were makes no difference to me; God shows no partiality)—well, those who were of reputation contributed nothing to me. But on the contrary, seeing that I had been entrusted with the gospel to the uncircumcised, just as Peter had been to the circumcised . . . and recognizing the grace that had been given to me, James and Cephas and John, who were reputed to be pillars, gave to me and Barnabas the right hand of fellowship, that we might go to the Gentiles, and they to the circumcised. They only asked us to remember the poor, the very thing I also was eager to do" (Galatians 2:6–10).

I think what's important in this description of Paul's interaction with the church leaders in Jerusalem is that he, Paul, knew what God had asked him to do and he was going to do it, whether "those of reputation" understood it or agreed with it. Yes, I think Paul was a bit harsh in his somewhat irreverent assessment of the "pillars" of the Jerusalem church, but it shows his clarity about his mission, and his determination to do it. In the last verse cited, at least Paul found some agreed-upon-concern with Peter, James, and John.

This passage gives a good insight, I believe, into our position as lay ministers in the local church. Just as Paul's going to the Gentiles with the gospel was something the Jerusalem church leaders probably wouldn't have done, and were not called to do, so too our mission of making disciples, life-to-life with a multiplication goal, is something that many in the church will be puzzled by. This shouldn't discourage us from doing it.

Wisdom is that you not be discouraged if you encounter opposition, or less-than-enthusiastic reception as you begin to minister in your church. Don't allow other's doubts or misunderstanding about what you are trying to do to keep you from pursuing what you believe God has put on your heart.

What would cause us to hesitate? I think it's quite normal for even strong Christians to feel that . . . "If *so many* Christians aren't doing this—making disciples—then there must be something wrong with it, or me!" It's the nagging doubt of "Can all of them really be missing the key point of the Great Commission? What arrogance for me to think that I'm right and they're wrong!" But hold fast to what you know is true;

God has asked believers to make disciples. It is wise to accept the fact that many do not, but that you will not permit their inaction to dissuade you from your obedience to the Great Commission.

You're really going to have to pray and seek God's peace that life-to-life disciple-making is Biblical and important. I encourage you to keep 2 Timothy 2:1, 2 in mind. It is clear and courage-imparting. Here's that powerful passage, with my parenthetical comments:

"You then, my son (it's a relationship, life-to-life), be strong in the grace that is in Christ Jesus (it's a personal relationship with God). And the things you have received from me (there's structure and content to discipleship) in the presence of many witnesses entrust to reliable men (selection of the right ones to disciple is important) who will also be qualified to teach others." (2 Timothy 2:1, 2 NIV).

You must be convinced, very convinced that this ministry is something God wants you to do.

10

The Challenge—Will You Do It?

WILL YOU MAKE DISCIPLES? It won't always be novel or thrilling. It will be day-to-day obedience to help another, and there will be problems and aggravations along the way. But, like raising children, it is a joy and delight. As Paul says to the people whom he loves in Thessalonica, "For what is our hope, our joy, or the crown in which we will glory in the presence of our Lord Jesus when he comes? Is it not you? Indeed, you are our glory and joy." (1 Thessalonians 2:19, 20 NIV).

And it's scary. It's a big risk. This is a difficult thing to do, to step out in faith and trust God that he will do this through you. Look at the amazing story of Jonathan and his armor-bearer for your inspiration. What a risk they took, but what a victory God gave. The story is found in 1 Samuel 14:6–23, "Then Jonathan said to the young man who was carrying his armor, 'Come, let us cross over to the garrison of these uncircumcised (Philistines); perhaps the Lord will work for us, for the Lord is not restrained to save by many or by few.' And his armor bearer said to him, 'Do all that is in your heart . . . here am I with you . . .'" (vss 6, 7).

This is the world's smallest army ever: one general and one brave, willing soldier! As you begin your venture in making disciples, it's great to have another with you.

"Then Jonathan said, 'Behold, we will cross over to the men (the Philistines) and reveal ourselves to them. If they say to us, 'Wait until we come to you;' then we will stand in our place and not go up to them. But if they say, 'Come up to us,' then we will go up, for the Lord has given them into our hands; and this shall be the sign to us.'" (vss. 8–10).

This is interesting. Jonathan actually makes the worst possible battle situation—to have to *climb* up to the enemy—the sign of God's giving them the victory. Talk about trusting God! Do we look for easy success in ministry as a sign of God's approval, or are we willing to go ahead even when it's difficult?

"And when both of them revealed themselves to the garrison of the Philistines, the Philistines said, 'Behold, Hebrews are coming out of the holes where they have hidden themselves.' So the men of the garrison called to Jonathan and his armor bearer and said, 'Come up to us and we will tell you something.'

And Jonathan said to his armor bearer, 'Come up after me, for the Lord has given them into the hands of Israel.' Then Jonathan climbed up on his hands and feet, with his armor bearer behind him; and they (the enemy) fell before Jonathan, and his armor bearer put some to death after him." (vss.11–13).

When God gives the sign for Jonathan and his armor bearer to go ahead, then they do what they know to do, fight for the Lord, even though it's against overwhelming odds. Having this confidence, they crawl and climb into the battle.

"Then Saul and all the people who were with him (back in Israel's camp) rallied and came to the battle . . . Now the Hebrews who were with the Philistines previously . . . even they also turned to be with the Israelites who were with Saul and Jonathan. When all of the men of Israel who had hidden themselves in the hill country of Ephraim heard that the Philistines had fled, even they also closely pursued them closely in the battle. So the Lord delivered Israel . . ." (vss. 20–23).

It took only two people to win the battle. Jonathan and his armor bearer were willing to fight for the Lord against seemingly impossible odds. When these two brave people began to fight, it gave courage and confidence to others . . . to the Israelites in the camp of Saul, to Saul himself, to the Hebrews who had fearfully joined the enemy, to people hiding in holes all over the hills of Ephraim. When Jonathan trusted God, and acted with courage, it changed the entire outcome of the battle.

You can be a Jonathan and climb into battle, trusting that God will give you the victory. And when you do, it will give courage to others. They will follow your lead and join you.

You can do it. And remember, Jesus promises (Matthew 28:20 NIV), that as you make disciples, "... I am with you always, to the very end of the age."

Will you do it?

Appendix

"THE 7 & 3 ... PLANS FOR DISCIPLESHIP"

OVERVIEW—LIFE TO LIFE DISCIPLESHIP

This material is the content of an approximately one-year discipleship process. It is intended that it be used in a person-to-person (one-on-one) context, because *application* of the material covered is of primary importance, and this is best achieved with the encouragement and accountability of a one-to-one relationship. Please read the "Instructions for Discipleship Plans" carefully for more details.

The goal of the discipleship process is raise up godly men and women, of Christ-like character, who are solid in their walk with God; and who are committed to, and trained in, discipling others who in turn can do the same. (2 Timothy 2:1, 2).

OVERVIEW OF THE MATERIAL:

Seven Disciplines of the Christian Life

1. Assurance of Salvation: The *Tripod* Illustration.

    To help the young Christian have confidence that she/he is indeed saved and a child of God, so she or he can draw near to God with joy and assurance. The *Tripod* illustration presents three distinct ways a person can know from the Bible that he/she is a Christian. The 3 ways are as follows:

    - God says it! (1 John 5:11–13)

    - Inner conviction. (Romans 8:16)

- Outer Evidence (Galatians 5:22, 23)

2. Quiet Times: The *Best Friend* Illustration.

    To help the young Christian develop a personal relationship with God through brief daily times in the Word and prayer. The 6 points of this topic are as follows:

    - Best friend illustration
    - How 2-way conversation works
    - Examples from the Bible of Quiet Times (Mark 1:35, Psalm 5:3)
    - 2 Benefits of Quiet Times (John 16:33, Acts 4:13)
    - The 1% principle
    - Psalm 1 as a "practice" QT

3. Prayer: Forget smelling roses; take time to pray!

    To help the young Christian develop the habit of praying, to strengthen her personal relationship with God, and to see godly effect in peoples' lives through intercession. The structure of this content is as follows:

    - Three *kinds* of prayer
        1. Chatting with God
        2. Extended time with the Lord. (Psalm 51&73)
        3. The "work" of prayer: praying for others by using a prayer list. (1 Samuel 12:23)
    - Three *benefits* of prayer
        1. Answers (John 16:24)
        2. Freedom from fear (Romans 8:15 & Psalm 34:4)
        3. Forgiveness (1 John 1:9)
    - Three *Conditions* on Prayer
        1. Honesty (Psalm 66:18)

2. Believe God will answer (James 1:5–7)
3. Correct motives (James 4:3)

TOM = daily application: *T*hanks for something; *O*thers, *M*yself

4. Fellowship: *Brothers and Sisters* illustration.

To help the young Christian experience and benefit from the wonderful provision of Christian fellowship. The four aspects of Biblical fellowship discussed are as follows:

- Encouragement (Hebrews 10:24, 25)
- Learning and sharing with others (Ephesians 4:11–14)
- Protection (Ecclesiastes 4:9, 10)
- Correction (Hebrews 3:13)

5. Bible Study: "Truth shall set you free!" *Handcuffs* illustration.

To show the young Christian how to go to the Scriptures with confidence in order to seek God's truth—through topical Bible study and passage analysis Bible study—as follows:

- Topical Bible study using a concordance and a cross-referencing technique
- Passage analysis Bible study using

    Observation . . . what's it say?

    Interpretation . . . what's it mean?

    Application . . . how do I do it?

6. Witnessing: The *Courtroom Trial* illustration.

To encourage the young Christian to overcome his/her nervousness about sharing Christ with others. This is done by explaining concepts, tools, and techniques in witnessing; and by actually involving the young Christian in evangelistic situations as you demonstrate and coach her/him. This is a topic that's fairly easy to present, but it may take a couple of months to do the "field practice." The content is as follows, with lots of Scriptures:

- 3 facts and 1 conclusion
- Logic loop ... regarding the Biblical motivation to witness.
- What hinders us from witnessing?
- 3 stages of growth in witnessing: able, avail-able, account-able.
- The three tools:

  —survey
  —"SDSD, All 3" gospel illustration
  —relational evangelism

7. Scripture memory: (no illustration for this topic)

   To help the young Christian store God's Word away in her/his heart through a Scripture memory process, so that he can

   —guard himself against sin (Psalm 119:9, 11)
   —minister the Word to others (2 Tim. 2:15)

Three Character Areas

These are the "opposite attributes" of the three sin areas spoken of in 1 John 2:15, 16 (lust of the flesh, lust of the eyes, the boastful pride of life). The character areas are covered by doing a Bible study with the young Christian on each area. The studies are self-explanatory. The three studies are as follows:

1. Purity and holiness ... freedom from the "appetite sins" (sexual sins, food, etc.)
2. God's perspective on money and stuff ... freedom from greed or anxiety. Plus, principles about giving to God's work.
3. Humility ... freedom from over-estimation of self, or self-deprecation. Also covers these two aspects of self-acceptance:

   How to over-come bitterness or anger about hurt and pain others have done to you.

   How to overcome guilt about hurt and pain you have caused to others

INSTRUCTIONS FOR DISCIPLESHIP PLANS

The purpose of these follow-up plans is to help a young Christian to grow toward spiritual maturity by incorporating godly disciplines into his/her life, and understanding and working toward the Bible's standards in three areas of Christ-like character.

The follow-up plans are designed to be presented and discussed in a one-to-one context, that is, one person to one person, not in a group setting. I recommend a fast-food, or other inexpensive, restaurant setting as a good place to meet someone for personal discipleship. Getting something to eat, and eating it, gives good time for casual talk and relationship building. The actual content-imparting time usually takes about a half hour (longer for topics such as Bible study; less time for topics such as Assurance of salvation).

When you're ready to do the Bible content/ message to motivate, get right to it; don't beat around the bush; when it's one-to-one, there's no need for worrying about "smooth transitions." Just say, "Okay, let's get our Bibles out; I want to talk about Quiet Times," (or whatever the topic is . . .).

The format of each follow-up plan is the same. I learned this format from Navigators Larry Whitehouse and Ron Shimkus. There is (1) a written goal (2) a brief "message to motivate" (3) something to get her started (4) a list of resources or helps to keep him going (5) an evaluation section, both objective and subjective. The format is not discussed with the young Christian, only the "message" and concepts.

For each topic:

Goal:

Clear, simple definition of what we want to see in the person's life.

Message to motivate:

Often starts with a question to introduce the topic, an illustration to help visualize the concept, Bible examples, verses on benefits and or conditions concerning the topic, and a brief idea of how to do it.

Get her started:

A practical way to begin to *do* the Christian discipline which has been introduced and discussed. The key to growth is *application* of Bible truths, not just understanding.

Keep him going:

Simply a list of other resources which relate to the topic/discipline. Other Bible illustrations, booklets, tapes, mature believers with appropriate testimonies, etc. are all helpful for times in the months to come when the young Christian has doubts or problems in the areas of discipline or character.

Evaluation:

A basic tool to help us understand how a young Christian is doing in a particular area, in order to encourage her/him or adjust our leading him/her in this issue.

—objective evaluation: based upon easily measured criteria, e.g., did he write down any Quiet Time thoughts?

—Subjective evaluation: how do I *feel* the person is doing?

It's okay to alter or personalize any or all of these discipleship plans. Ministry combines relationship and structure. Structure is like a skeleton; the relationship is like the flesh and blood. "Bones is bones." As long as the structure of the follow-up discipling is biblical and well thought out, you can do with it as you will. Just don't leave out important stuff, and don't put in excess baggage. I suggest you use the following plans pretty much as they are at first, however, until you are comfortable and confident in life-to-life discipling, *then* make alterations. A strong, trusting relationship with the person you are helping is very important.

DISCIPLESHIP PLANS

PLAN ONE: ASSURANCE OF SALVATION

Goal:

To bring the young believer to an understanding and sureness of his eternal life, and that he/she can verbalize this conviction using at least two references/Bible concepts. This topic is presented to assure a person who has received Christ as Savior that he or she can go into the presence of God and grow in her/his relationship with God through Christ. It is not intended as a doctrinal answer to the question of whether a person can lose his or her salvation.

Message to Motivate:

Ask this question, "How do you know for sure that you're a Christian?"

Emphasize that Christianity is a relationship with God through Jesus Christ, not really a "religion" (man's attempt to get to God through his own efforts). Have him or her read John 17:3 . . ." This is eternal life, that they may know Thee, the only true God, and Jesus Christ whom Thou hast sent."

Use the *"Tripod"* illustration as a good way to know for sure from the Bible that he has eternal life. A tripod is a very stable device for it has three legs firmly planted on the ground. This "spiritual tripod" has three distinct truths (legs) firmly planted in the Scripture that describe our assurance of salvation:

God's enemy loves to plant doubts in our minds about many truths, and this is one of them. If we have only one way we believe that we're Christians, for example, "I just know it in my heart!"—a kind of a monopod of assurance—then the enemy can suggest, "But that's only an emotion." Let's go for the tripod, and look at three good ways to know we're saved.

Picture a tripod in your mind. Here are the three legs:
Tripod leg # 1 . . . (1 John 5:11–13) "God says it!"
Tripod leg # 2 . . . (Romans 8:16) "Inner conviction."
Tripod leg # 3 . . . (Galatians 5: 22, 23) "Outer evidence."

Leg 1—God says it!

". . . that you may *know* that you have eternal life . . ." (1 John 5:11–13). Emphasize the truth that people who *have the Son, have life,* and that they can know that they have eternal life.

Leg 2—Inner Conviction!

"The Spirit Himself bears witness with our spirit that we are children of God." (Romans 8:16). Emphasize that this is not merely an emotion, which changes from day to day, but a deep inner conviction from God's Holy Spirit.

Leg 3—Outer Evidence!

"But the fruit of the Spirit is love, joy, peace, patience, kindness . . ." (Galatians 5:22, 23). Emphasize that these are life qualities which become more and more evident as that person develops a close walk with God. The world has fake qualities which correspond to these qualities: e.g., lust vs. love; fun vs. joy . . . but only God can build the real things into a life. Ask the young Christian to pick one or two of these qualities that she/he would especially like to see become more evident in his/her life.

Get him/her started:

Ask her/him to try to remember the "tripod" illustration. Tell him/her that you're going to check on her/him by asking the same question:"How can you know you're a Christian?" the next time you get together.

Keep him/her going:

(This amounts to a list of resources on the topic).

Share that although we have a new life in Christ (2 Corinthians 5:17), we still live in a world with problems, temptations, and pain. We are to see these challenges as opportunities to walk with God and grow. Go through James 1:2–4 with her. "Consider it all joy when you meet various trials . . ."

Review the gospel with him, and have him verbalize his understanding of it with you. Indian-giver principle: give it to him and have him give it back; this reveals her understanding or lack thereof.

Ask about any positive changes he's seen in his life since making the decision for Christ.

Have her talk to someone with a good, clear testimony about security and sureness of salvation, yet can relate to her early doubts.

Evaluation:

Subjectively: was she/he excited, puzzled, or bored by this information?

Objectively: can he/she state a week later two of the three legs of the Tripod illustration, and verbalize his/her confidence in his salvation?

Quick Summary
Tripod Illustration:
Leg 1—1 John 5:11–13   God says it!
Leg 2—Romans 8:16   Inner conviction!
Leg 3—Galatians 5:22–23 Outer evidence!

DISCIPLESHIP PLANS

PLAN TWO: DAILY TIMES WITH GOD (QUIET TIMES)

Goal:

To have the young Christian grasp the importance of daily, consistent time with the Lord in prayer and Bible reading in order that he/she might get to know God personally (John 17:3). To have her/him establish a consistency of five days per week. To have him/her verbalize the impact of these Quiet Times on her life in at least one area ... e.g., purity of thoughts, lessened worrying, etc.

Message to motivate: (6 points)

1. "Best friend" illustration: ask her/him who his best friend was in college or high school. Ask how this person became a good friend (answer is usually that they spent time together on a frequent basis, and talked together). Tell him/her that building a relationship with God is similar to the way they got to know the person who became their friend ... spending time together and talking. Being willing to share openly, and listening and understanding when the other one shares, establishes trust and closeness in a relationship. Jesus has said he would like to be our friend (John 15:15)

2. Two-way conversation: talk about how good conversation works, with both persons sharing with, and listening to, the other. It's not good relationship building if only one talks all the time, and one only listens and doesn't share. Prayer is talking to God about what's on our hearts, and reading his Word is listening to his voice.

3. Some biblical examples:

    —Mark 1:35 ... Jesus gets up before daylight to meet with the Father, before all the people come looking for him with their needs and demands.

- —Psalm 5:3 . . . David says he prays in the morning, and eagerly watches for how God will answer.

- —Proverbs 8:34, 35 . . . Here the man who seeks God's wisdom daily is called blessed.

4. Benefits of Quiet Times: (3 mentioned, but many more possible)

    - —John 16:33 . . . Peace of heart and mind in a stressful world.

    - —Acts 4:13 . . . Confidence (courage) and focus in a confused world.

    - —1 John 1:7 . . . Better relationships with people in a mistrusting world.

5. Amount of time a Quiet Time takes: The 1% Principle

    - —A day has 1440 minutes. One percent of a day is 14 minutes. Or, even more realistically for people just beginning, a half of one percent is about 7 minutes; a few minutes to read some Bible and a couple of minutes to pray to God about what you've read. Consistency is the key! Make the amount of time short enough that anyone can do it pretty much every day if he really wants to. Many short times in the Word and prayer build a better relationship than extended time once a month. Giving the Lord one percent of the day can result in a solid, personal relationship with him.

    - —Suggest a morning time rather than the end of the day . . . fresher and we can pray "preventively" about the day rather than praying "repentively" at the end of the day.

    - —Suggest he pray to God about the passage of Bible he just read, rather than about some unrelated topic or request. This reinforces the idea of two-way conversation.

6. Psalm 1 as an example:

    - —6 verses . . . have him read three verses; you read three, then briefly discuss any questions or impressions.

—Pray back those thoughts and questions to God, first you, then him.

—Thank God for showing you both some great truths in this short passage of Scripture, e.g., that we shouldn't get counsel from the ungodly, that we should be like trees planted near water (i.e., spend time with God in His Word), that we got to ask him what it means to always be "green, but fruitful in season."

Get him or her started:

In a sense, you just did get him started by doing a little "time with God" with him. The very best thing at this point is to ask if you could get together sometime in the coming week before work, for just a few minutes, and have another "time with God" together. People are much more likely to actually do something if it's been demonstrated to them. It's important that she/he sees how you do it; this can reproduce into his life.

Keep her/him going:

Give him or her encouraging booklets such as, e.g., *Appointment With God* (NavPress)

Suggest several books of the Bible for him to have QT's in; work in variety to avoid the mini-legalism of trying to read Bible from start to finish. Talk about what to do when QT's get dry.

Do little message on Luke 10, the Martha and Mary story; Mary chose the better part, sitting at Christ's feet, rather than letting busyness distract her from spending time with the Lord.

Talk about Quiet Times in the group or team meeting, and have others interact with him or her about how they do their daily times with God, and some good things they've gotten from them.

Evaluation:
(subjective = "feeling" & objective = "measurable")

Did he meet me for QT?

When is he doing his QT? How many times did he have a QT?

What is he verbalizing about his times with the Lord . . . excited/interested, or is he just going through the motions to please me?

How does he do during vacation time, or during breaks from his normal life routine?

Quick Summary

1. "Best friend" illustration
2. Two-way conversation with God, praying and reading Bible
3. Examples from the Bible:

    Jesus—Mark 1:35

    David—Psalm 5:3

    Proverbs 8:34

4. Benefits of having Quiet Times:

    Peace—John 16:33

    Confidence—Acts 4:13

    Better relationships—1 John 1:7

5. The "1%" principle (or 0.5%)
6. Psalm 1 as an example

DISCIPLESHIP PLANS
PLAN THREE: PRAYER

Goal:

That the young Christian would learn that prayer is the way he/she talks with God . . . that he'd understand the benefits and conditions of prayer . . . that she'd develop a simple prayer practice based on TOM . . . that in a few months time, she'd be having consistent prayer times.

Message to Motivate:

"The message of 3's" (3 *kinds, benefits, & conditions* of prayer)

Illustration: One of the big milestones in a child's development is when she/he begins to talk. The parents are delighted. It's a significant turning point in the relationship of the parents to the child, because now there is communication. The child can express his thoughts and feelings, and the parents can respond. It's not that the parents don't know what the needs of the child are; they do, probably better than the young child. But the ability of the child to talk with the parents establishes a bond of love and trust. The sign of a problem in children (especially teens) is when a child stops talking and sharing openly with the parents.

Our talking to God in prayer is similar. We pray, not so much to tell God what we need (Matthew 6:32 says he already knows), but to get to know him better. The heavenly Father, like all good parents, loves to hear us talk with him about what's on our hearts, about questions we may have, and about our joys, pains, worries, and fears.

Three kinds of prayer:

- Informal . . . chatting prayers (in car, etc.) prompted by some stimulus that jogs our minds and reminds us to pray about something. This kind comprises probably 90% of what most Christians do in prayer.

- "pour out your heart to God" prayer . . . this is extended time with the Lord in prayer, maybe only once or twice a year. We want to get with God for perhaps a half day when we face a major decision or have an overwhelming worry, fear, or guilt about sin (Psalms 51 and 73 are good examples). Find a place where you can be undisturbed (park, empty church on Saturday, e.g.). Think through on what the issue is. Become quiet and try to settle down; this is hard to do in our culture, and may take some time. Then just talk to God from your heart about the issue.

- Structured prayer . . . praying through a prayer list. This is what some Christians call the "work of prayer." This is the kind of prayer that is hard to do, perhaps because it is carefully planned rather than spontaneous. 1 Samuel 12:23 puts it this way: ". . . far be it from me that I should sin against the Lord by ceasing to pray for you . . ."

Three benefits of prayer:

(put whatever you have found to be the best benefits of your own times in prayer)

- Freedom from fear . . . Romans 8:15 & Psalm 34:4

- Forgiveness... 1 John 1:9
- Answers... John 16:24

Three conditions of prayer:

- Be honest in your prayer... Psalm 66:18 If I cherish some secret, favorite sin in my heart, God will not respond to my prayers.
- Believe that God can and will answer... James 1:5–7 If I pray just as a last resort, and don't really think God cares or will do anything, then "... let not that man expect that he will receive anything from the Lord." James 1:7
- Pray with correct motives... James 4:3 If I regard God as a mere catalog to order stuff from for my own sinful pleasure, he won't honor those prayers. "You ask and do not receive, because you ask with wrong motives, so that you may spend it on your pleasures." (James 4:3)

Get him/ her started:

Using the Lord's Prayer as a model (Matthew 6:9), encourage him/her to write out a simple prayer list. An index card is a handy size. Have a maximum of five headings on this list:

- Praise or thanks expressed to God "... hallowed by Thy Name."
- Seek his will for your life regards decisions and choices (John 7:1 The one who'll do God's will shall know it) "... Thy will be done, on earth..."
- Ask forgiveness for any known sins. "... forgive us our trespasses..."
- Pray for other's needs... Matthew 9:36, 38
- Pray for my own needs and concerns "... give us this day our daily bread...."

An even simpler beginning for developing a prayer life is to pray every day according to the acronym "TOM." This stands for:

T = Thanks... gives thanks to God each day for something!

O = Others . . . pray for other people's needs before your own.

M = Me . . . finally, talk to God about your needs, fears, hopes.

Keep him/her going:

Do a little Bible study on prayer, looking at prayers such as Elijah's in James 5:16–18.

Ask a real prayer warrior to come have lunch with you and your young Christian, to share his/her excitement about prayer and answers to prayers.

Best of all, get together with her or him and have a time of prayer, for others and yourselves. Keep the prayers quick, simple and real.

Evaluation:

Objective: did she/he make up a prayer list (card), or is doing "TOM" daily?

Subjective: pray with the young Christian; does it seem he is really talking with God from his heart in a genuine way (even if awkward), or does it seem to be an imitation of real prayer?

Quick Summary
Illustration: parent's delight at a child talking with them
Three kinds of prayer:
Chatting
Pour out your heart (Psalm 51, 73).
Structured, prayer list (1 Samuel 12:23).
Three benefits of prayer:
Freedom from fear (Romans 8:15 & Psalm 34:4).
Forgiveness (1 John 1:9).
Answers (John 16:24).
Three conditions of prayer:
Honesty (Psalm 66:18).
Believe God will answer (James 1:5–7).
Correct motives (James 4:3).

DISCIPLESHIP PLANS
PLAN FOUR: FELLOWSHIP

Goal:

That the young Christian would meet regularly with other believers for the purpose of encouragement, instruction, and opportunities to serve God. That he/she would understand the Scriptural basis of fellowship (and how it differs from socializing), and be able to verbalize two or three reasons why he feels fellowship is important.

Message to Motivate:

Illustration: role of siblings in the family—to keep us honest, keep us from taking ourselves too seriously, teach and train us in sometimes sensitive matters, stick up for us—mostly, encourage us! Differs from a parental role, which is like discipleship (1 Thessalonians 2:7, 11) "... you know how we were among you, as mother ... and father ..." Discipleship involves taking parental responsibility for the well-being and rearing of the child. Fellowship involves the brother/sister caring (but not parental responsibility) of one another as members of the same family.

Christians are part of the same family, and God has given us a wonderful resource in our fellow brothers and sister in the faith. (1 Timothy 5:1, 2). Here are four ways that real Christian fellowship benefits us, and why we ought to take advantage of this provision of God.

- Encouragement (Hebrews 10:24, 25) ... for one another; to learn to love Christ and each other, and to serve him with good works. Encouragement is both comforting for past pain or failure, and challenging to meet goals which lie ahead. Among the many ways Christians encourage (means literally to impart courage) is by sharing about their own struggles and how they trusted Christ to help overcome them. Young believers need to know that many people struggle with similar issues, and that God is able to not only help us with the struggles, but to do it in a way that our faith actually grows. (1 Corinthians 10:13 & James 1:2–4)

- Learning and sharing (Ephesians 4:11–13) ... that we could learn from each other; this is one of the best ways that God has given us to be teachable and learn. We're in a cultural time in which there is much insecurity and poor self-images ; this may make young Christians wary and unteachable in some situations in which a person in authority is the teacher. But young people are often willing to learn from peers, making the value of fellowship sharing even more crucial.

- Protection (Ecclesiastes 4:9, 10) ". . . woe to the one who falls when there is not another to pick him up!" This is not so much a matter of protecting from a sin problem (see *correction* below) as much as a matter of a young Christian being misled by false teachings, doctrinal stands which "exceed what is written," or lack of balance due to the young believer's own natural leanings or strengths.

- Correction (Hebrews 3:13) ". . . lest anyone be hardened by the deceitfulness of sin." We all need the accountability of our brothers and sisters in Christ to prompt us to live rightly by pointing out (in a loving way) areas of our lives which are not conformed to Christ. Even seemingly insignificant sins, if habitual, have a hardening effect on our desire to live holy lives. This is an ongoing battle because we live among a "perverse generation," and James 4:4 (NIV) strongly emphasizes that ". . . friendship with the world is hatred toward God." All of us have blind spots, and our fellow Christians can serve as mirrors to help us see and correct sin which occurs in those blind spots.

Get him/her started:

If she's not getting regular time with other Christians in a situation which focuses on the Word & biblical encouragement, and/or if the friends he looks to for group support are non-believers, then warmly encourage him/her to come to your Bible study or fellowship group. (You *must* have something with genuine fellowship to invite him to; if you don't, work hard on creating it!). It could be the Sunday School class, the small group Bible study, the after-church lunch at Denny's, etc., any activity in which he/she can be around other Christians and get to know them as friends. It should be a time which permits good interaction, not just socializing. (Movies are lousy for fellowship; meals are good.)

Try to encourage the young or new believer to come to a fellowship activity which you personally know is good, hopefully one you're a part of. Sometimes as a young Christian begins to grow, she/he is motivated to go back to her old childhood church, and this is not always a healthy decision. If he/she insists on going back to the old church, go with him and check it out. If it's not good, don't criticize it, but gently encourage him to come to your church. Pray the Spirit will prompt him to do this.

Keep him/her going:

Here are some mini-messages from the Bible: 1 Peter 4:2–4 . . . fellowship helps the young Christian avoid the temptation of falling back into the old world of sin, usually at the prompting of old friends. Fellowship gives the young believer an alternative, a new set of friends to encourage the new man or woman. (1 Corinthians 15:33 ". . . do not be deceived; bad company corrupts good morals . . ." and 2 Corinthians 6:14 ". . . do not be unequally yoked . . ."). But, remember, we don't want her/him to despise the old friends, for Christ loves them too. Non-Christian friendships can and should be maintained so that the old friends have greater opportunity to come to the Lord themselves. We just don't want the old friends to adversely influence the young believer.

Talk more about the Ecclesiastes 4:9, 10 passage, especially if the young Christian is experiencing discouragement, depression, or has a deeply ingrained habit of sin.

Do mini-message about Proverbs 27:17 "As iron sharpens iron, so one man sharpens another."

Talk about fellowship as a preparation for service to God. (2 Corinthians 4:5).

Have him or her talk to someone who'll give a good testimony about how he/she benefited from fellowship, and do it on some specific area in which the young Christian is having some struggle. Remember, all young Christians have struggles; this should not discourage the disciple-maker . . . it's just part of normal growth.

Evaluation:

What was his/her response to the motivational message . . . interested, indifferent?

Has he expressed any negative feelings about experiences with Christians in the past? This is all too common. Talk through the issue with him. It's possible the negative experience was with a "religious person," who did not accurately reflect Christ-like values.

Does she seem to resist the idea of changing her relationship with her old friends, or express an interest in still looking to the old friends for counsel or support?

Did he offer any thoughts that he himself recognized the need to spend more time around other Christians?

Did she come to the fellowship activities you recommended?

Has he sought out fellowship from any of the other people in the Bible study, the Sunday school class, etc. at his own initiative?

Can he give you two Scriptural reasons why he'd benefit from having regular fellowship?

Quick Summary
Illustration: the role brothers and sisters play in our lives
Four benefits of Biblical fellowship:
Encouragement (Hebrews 10:24, 25).
Learning & sharing with others (Ephesians 4:11–13).
Protection (Ecclesiastes 4:9, 10).
Correction (Hebrews 3:13).

DISCIPLESHIP PLANS

PLAN FIVE: BIBLE STUDY

(Hang on, folks . . . this is a long discipleship plan!)

Goal:

That the young Christian would grasp the importance of regular, consistent study of God's Word as a lifestyle. That he/she would come to see that understanding and application of Scripture results in freedom from slavery to sin and many of life's entanglements. That she/he would be excited about seeing the Bible yield real guidance and clear answers for daily living. That the young believer would seek to study and apply the Bible as a key means of deepening his or her relationship with the Father and Christ.

Appendix

Message to Motivate:

The key concept of this study is "freedom."

Illustration: *"Handcuffs"*—the Bible is the key to getting free and staying free from sin.

Enslaved to sin

The truth shall make you free . . .

Scriptures about freedom:

"It was for freedom that Christ set us free; therefore keep standing firm and do not be subject again to a yoke of slavery." (Galatians 5:1 NASB).

"For sin shall not be master over you, for you are not under law, but under grace." (Romans 6:14).

". . . If you abide in My word, then you are truly disciples of Mine; and you shall know the truth and the truth shall make you free." (John 8:31, 32).

The powerful idea here is that Christians are made free by Christ, not free to sin but rather free not to sin. But it's hard to overcome the habit of sinning, and there's even a perverse pleasure in returning to old ways, being . . . subject again to a yoke of slavery to sin. The Galatian Christians were having a hard time standing firm in their freedom and were foolishly returning to the yoke of slavery from which Christ had set them free. Sadly, a lot of Christians today do the same thing, ignore their freedom and live just as they used to before they became Christians. The answer is to "abide" (live) in Christ's Word . . . to know the truth and be free from old sin habits.

Ask the young Christian what he/she thinks are some areas of sin that are good to be freed from:

Areas of enslavement:

To anger

To lust
To greed
To selfishness
To insecurity and fear
To bad relationships
To . . . (what are some others?).

Results of a commitment to Bible study:

- Closer relationship with God (John 14:21)

- Answered prayer (John 15:7)

- Spiritual fruit in our lives (Galatians 5:22, 23)

- Knowing how to *use* the Word in ministry (2 Timothy 2:15)

- Instruction for our own lives (2 Timothy 3:16)

- Knowing the purpose of your life (1 Peter 2:9)

- Christian maturity!!! (Ephesians 4:14 & Hebrews 6:1)

Read each of these verses together, then discuss what seems most encouraging to the younger Christian.

Get him/her started:

There are bascially two kinds of Bible study: topical and passage analysis. Emphasis here is on *self-discovery* of truths in Scripture. Accordingly, gently discourage the use of "under the line" commentaries (in most study Bibles), editor's notes, commentaries in general, or computer generated searches which deprive the young Christian of finding the books of the Bible for himself and thinking for herself. It's okay to look at what other Christians have said about a topic or passage (commentaries or editor's notes) *after* the young Christian has looked into the Bible for herself and arrived at conclusions and applications on her own. Leaders, don't give ground on this one. It goes against the current Christian education trend (of finding out what others have said first), but self-discovery promotes application. It is difficult to apply to my life someone else's Bible study.

—Topical Bible study: see Examples A and B

—Passage analysis Bible study: see Example C

Keep her/him going:

Resources to help keep him/her studying the Word:

Testimony of someone who has gotten victory over some area of sin as a result of being in the Word.

Discuss other types of Bible study helps: Nave's Topical Bible, Strong's Concordance, R.A. Torrey's *Treasury of Scriptural Knowledge*, etc.

Invite her to a more advanced Bible study meeting—as a guest—to see other, older, Christians being excited by the Word. This is a great resource!

. . . other resources of your own.

Evaluation:

Subjective and objective

Does he seem to grasp concepts in Scripture as we study together? (both subjective and objective)

Did she work hard on her Bible study in preparation for our getting together? (objective : study done and lots of notes = diligence).

Does he seem application oriented? (subjective). Does she talk about how the Bible relates to her own life? Has she actually applied something from either the topical or passage Bible study? (objective).

Are her questions in the Bible study group honest and prompted by a real desire to know . . . or are they Pharisee-type questions?

Does he just bluff his way through the study, i.e., wants attention or socializing, but no real desire to study? (subjective, but easy to recognize).

Quick Summary
"Handcuffs" illustration
Scriptures on Freedom
   Galatians 5:1
   Romans 6:14
   John 8:31, 32
Areas of enslavement to sin
Benefits of Bible study
   Closer walk with God
   Answered prayers
   Spiritual fruit

Knowing how to use the Word
Instruction for our own lives
Knowing our life's purpose
Christian maturity

Example A: Topical Bible Study Using the Concordance

The topic: "What is a person's *soul*?"

Note: the first step in doing a topical Bible study is to *ask a question*, as in the topic above, which defines the quest of the topic. This narrows the scope of the topic and gives a clear, simple goal for the study: to try to answer the question.

The simplest and most accurate way to determine God's teaching on any topic is to find as many verses or passages in the Bible as possible which relate to the topic. The best commentary on the Bible is the Bible itself... that is, other relevant verses.

The most basic form of topical Bible study, and the best starting point, is simply to look up a key word in the topic, e.g., "soul", in the concordance in the back of your Bible. Most Bibles have concordances; some are quite good, and others are not so good. But a simple concordance is still the best starting point for a topical study. You can also buy an inexpensive concordance on-line or at a Christian bookstore.

In my Bible's concordance (NASB), I found these verses in which the word, *soul*, appears:

a. Deuteronomy 4:29—..."search for (God) with all your heart and all your *soul*."

b. Psalm 16:10— "... Thou wilt not abandon my *soul* to Sheol..."

c. Psalm 23:3—"He restores my *soul*."

d. Psalm 24:4—"... (he) who has not lifted up his *soul* to falsehood ..."

e. Psalm 42:1—"As the deer pants for the water brooks, so my *soul* pants for Thee, O God."

f. Psalm 103:1—"Bless the Lord, O my *soul*; and all that is within me ...

g. Proverbs 24:12—"... does He not know it Who keeps your *soul*?"

h. Ezekiel 18:4—"Behold, all *souls* are Mine; the *soul* of the father as well as the *soul* of the son is Mine. The *soul* who sins will die."

i. Matthew 10:28—"And do not fear those who kill the body, but are unable to kill the *soul*; but rather fear Him who is able to destroy both *soul* and body in hell."

j. Matthew 16:26—"For what will a man be profited if he gains the whole world, and forfeits his *soul*? Or what will a man give in exchange for his *soul*?"

k. Luke 1:46, 47—"And Mary said, 'My *soul* exalts the Lord, and my spirit has rejoiced in God my Savior.'"

l. Acts 4:32—". . . those who believed were of one heart and one *soul*."

m. I Thessalonians 5:23—"Now may the God of peace Himself sanctify you entirely; and may your spirit and *soul* and body be preserved complete without blame at the coming of our Lord Jesus Christ."

n. Hebrews 10:39—". . . those who have faith in the preserving of the *soul*."

o. James 1:21 & 5:20—". . . which is able to save your *souls* . . . save his *soul* from death . . ."

p. 1 Peter 2:11—". . . abstain from fleshly lusts, which wage war against the soul."

On this topic there are many different possible definitions for *soul*, so it is helpful to try to categorize the different meaning. These different category headings are just to help, not determine doctrine for the ages. It's an excellent exercise in self-discovery to begin thinking about Bible meaning in this way without worrying about "being wrong."

Possible categories for meaning of "soul"

Heart or passion, intense emotion	Inner person or "spirit"	The eternal part of a person that gets saved or condemned	Mind, intellect, personality, choice-maker
Deuteronomy 4:29 Psalm 42:1 Psalm 103:1 Acts 4:32 Luke 1:46, 47	Psalm 23:3 1 Peter 2:11 Proverbs 24:12 (?) 1 Peter 2:11	Psalm 16:10 Proverbs 24:12 (?) Ezekiel 18:4 (?) Matthew 10:28 Matthew 16:26 Hebrews 10:39	Psalm 24:4 Ezekiel 18:4 (?) 1 Thessalonians 5:23 1 Peter 2:11 (?)

Now, having looked up the verses, and having put them in simple categories, write a simple answer to the question: "What's a person's soul?" Go ahead, give it a try!

"It seems to me the most commonly implied definitions of *soul* in the Bible are . . ."

_____

_____

_____

_____

Example B: Topical Bible Study using Cross-referencing

Topic question: "What's the benefit of studying Scripture?"

First, do a quick check of your Bible's Concordance to get a handful of relevant verses. Then pick what seems to be the best or most significant verse from the concordance list, and use it as a starting point for cross-referencing.

Note: the term "cross-referencing" means finding other verses or passages in the Bible which provide more information about the topic you are studying. We can find these other verses using people's suggestions, our own memory, special Bible study "help" books, or the cross-reference aid (the fine print) found in the margins of most Bibles.

Teach your young Christian to pick a starting verse, look in the margin for the number of that verse, then write down the references given for that verse. Also teach him or her that the different clauses or phrases in a verse are lettered (with lower case letters), and that the cross-reference verses correspond to those letters.

Example: John 3:16 "For God so (a) loved the world that (b). He gave His (c) only begotten Son . . ." The cross-references shown in the margin after (a) will pertain to the phrase, . . . *loved the world* . . . the cross-references shown for (b) will pertain to the clause . . . *He gave* . . . etc.

Do three "Rounds" of cross-referencing. That is, for the first "round," write down all the fine print Bible references shown in the margin for 2 Timothy 3: 16, 17. Find the verses in the Bible, read them to see if they are meaningful for your question of "What are the benefits of studying Scripture?" Put OK next to those you think are relevant, and NO next to the ones which are not.

What do I mean by relevant or not relevant? Let's say you're trying to find out from the Bible about the nature of angels, and you start with a verse which has the phrase ". . . a multitude of angels . . ." You may find a cross-reference verse that contains the phrase ". . . a multitude of sheep were there." Obviously, the concept being cross-referenced is "multitude," and that verse doesn't help your study on angels. That would be an irrelevant cross-reference, against which you put down a NO.

Jot down a brief note on each verse you think is helpful. Now find the cross-references for each of the "new" verses you got in the first round. In other words, locate each relevant verse in your Bible and look at the cross-references listed in the margin for each of these verses. This is Round two.

Do the same a third time. By this third round of cross-referencing, you'll notice the verses are either mostly irrelevant or the same ones you've already got.

Here's an example of a topical Bible study using cross-referencing. The topical question, from above: "What's the benefit of studying Scripture?" The starting passage is 2 Timothy 3:16, 17 (using the Ryrie, Moody Press, NASB Bible).

"All Scripture is inspired by God and profitable for teaching, for reproof, for correction, for training in righteousness; that the man of God may be adequate, equipped for every good work."

Round one of cross-referencing, using
2 Timothy 3: 16, 17 as a starting point:

—Romans 4:23, 24 (jotted note) = not only for Abraham's sake was the Bible written, but for ours, in regards to salvation through faith. OK

—Romans 15:4 = what was written in earlier times was written for our instruction, that through "perseverance and the encouragement of Scripture" we might have hope. OK

—2 Peter 1:20 and following verses = refers to the Bible inspiration (doesn't apply to the specific question, even though it's a great verse!). NO

—1 Timothy 6:11 = talks about fleeing from unrighteousness. NO, not really.

—2 Timothy 2: 21 = "... if a man cleanses himself from these things ... prepared for every good work..." = refers to one's preparation for ministry. OK

—Hebrews 13:21 = equip you in every good thing to do His will ... OK (we saw from 2 Tim. 3:17 that Bible study will equip the person of God for good works, so this is relevant as it pertains to good works)

Round two of cross-referencing, using the OK verses from Round one:

Verses in the margin for Romans 4:23, 24

—Romans 15:4 = NO—already have this one

—2 Corinthians 9:9 = NO

—1 Corinthians 10: 1 = "these things" refers to verses 1 through 10, things that happened to them as an example, and they were written for our instruction. OK (great passage!)

—2 Timothy 3:16 = NO—already have this one

Verses for Romans 15:4

—Romans 4:23 = NO already have

—2 Timothy 3:16 = NO already have verses for 2 Timothy 2:21

—1 Timothy 6:11 = NO

—2 Timothy 2:15 = "... workmen not ashamed, rightly handling the Word of truth ... OK

—2 Corinthians 9:8 = God provides all we need for good works ...OK?

—Ephesians 2:10 = good works which God prepared us to walk in ... NO

—2 Timothy 3:17 = NO already have

Verses for Hebrews 13:21 (first part of the verse only)

—1 Peter 5:10 = refers to the fact that those who minister will suffer ... NO

Round three of cross-referencing, using OK verses from Round two:

Verses for I Corinthians 10:11

—1 Corinthians 10:6 = NO same as 10: 11

—Romans 4:23 = NO already have this one

Verses for 1 Timothy 6:11

—2 Timothy 2: 22 = NO already have this one

—2 Timothy 3:17 = NO already have this one

Verses for 2 Timothy 2:15

—Romans 6:13 = don't present your bodies as instruments of sin = NO

—James 1:2 = after suffering comes crown of glory = NO

—Ephesians 1:13 = after listening to the gospel, the message of truth, you were saved and sealed into the Holy Spirit = OK

—James 1:18 = He chose to give us birth through the word of truth, that we might be a kind of firstfruits of all he created. = OK

What do we have? Even though it took some effort, we've gotten some good information about the rewards of knowing the Bible. Here's a quick summary:

- 2 Timothy 3:16, 17 = Bible study is profitable for teaching us truth, it "reproves us" if our thinking is wrong in some way, it corrects us, and then it trains us to live in a right way.

- Romans 15:4 = study the Bible for encouragement and to give us hope.

- 1 Corinthians 10:11 = (referring to verses 1 through 10) for our instruction, to avoid the disqualifying sins of people in the past ... this passage is a gold mine!

- 2 Corinthians 9:8 = to know that God will give us what we need to serve Him in doing good works.

- Ephesians 1:13 = knowledge of the Word brings people to salvation and "seals" them into the safety and protection of the Holy Spirit. Good in two ways: we're "sealed and safe" in the Holy Spirit, and we can use the Word to lead people to salvation.

- 2 Timothy 2: 21, 22 = this is a bit of a stretch, but it has to do with a person fleeing from things which would prevent him from being prepared and doing good works ... we know what these contaminates are and how to flee from them by study of the Word (John 8: 31, 32 "... know the truth and it shall make you free.")

- 2 Timothy 2:15 = Great verse on doing Bible study! Knowing the Bible allows us to "... rightly handle the word of truth." that is, to be able to use the Scripture to help other people with their life issues.

- Hebrews 13:21 = when we're equipped to do good works, what it really means is that we're equipped to do God's will ... and that makes us His close family "Who are My brothers or mother but those who do the will of God. Also, Romans 12:2 = don't be conformed, but be transformed by the renewal of your mind, that you may know the will of God, what is good and acceptable and perfect.

- James 1:18 = God "brings us forth by the Word of truth, that we may be the first fruits ...

Now the young Christian can write a summary of his/her Bible study in a simple format. She/he doesn't need to cite the references again; those are available above.

Summary: "The five (seven . . . nine . . . etc.) greatest benefits of doing Bible study are as follows:

—It teaches me truth, gets my attention when I'm wrong, corrects me, and gives me training in right living.

—It gives me the tools and ability to help others spiritually

—It gives me encouragement and hope

—Etc.

And this is just a start; once we're in the Scripture and get our brains thinking about benefits of Bible study, we'll pick up on lots of others as we read Scripture, e.g., during our quiet times.

Example C: Passage Analysis Bible Study

All Bible study is based upon 3 practices:
What does it say?   Observation
What does it mean?   Interpretation
What can I apply to my own life?   Application
The procedure is simple.

First, read the whole passage (e.g., John, chapter 4) to get an overall idea.

Write what you think the main idea of the passage is in one sentence.

Secondly, read each verse slowly and determine if it has interest or poses any questions or puzzles. (Observation). Jot down any thoughts or questions. *You do not need to consider every verse.* Hold off on trying to interpret at this time.

Thirdly, do some quick cross-referencing on the verse, using the cross reference aid in the margin of your Bible (see Example B) or any other helpful aid in the back of your Bible, such as an Index of Topics, maps, etc. In a very real sense, passage analysis Bible study is doing a series of mini-topical studies. Each question, or interesting point about which you'd like to know more, becomes a little topical study. The same tools and techniques apply that we used for doing a topical study: i.e., the concordance and marginal cross-reference aid.

Fourth, answer your questions. Go ahead and interpret the verses. (Interpretation). Again, don't be afraid say what you think the passage means. Your goal is to find out what the writer of Scripture, "carried along" by the Holy Spirit (2 Peter 1:21), meant when he wrote the passage. It is true that there is only one meaning intended by God in Scripture, and our job is to find that meaning; but there can be numerous applications.

Fifth, see if there is any practical application to your own life, either immediate or long-term. (Application). Be realistic . . . you can't find applications for every verse in the Bible. Determine if there is any larger application you can derive from the entire passage, e.g., "Is the application something I should act upon? Is it something I should learn? It is a reaffirmation of a truth I already knew? Is it one part of a greater understanding or action?

Do a study of Chapter 4, verses 1–42, of the Gospel of John: "Jesus and the woman at the well"

Verse:	Observation / Questions:	Interpretations:	Applications:
4	Question: "Where is Samaria?"	Look at map: area between Jerusalem and Galilee	None
6	Observastion: Jesus gets tired!	He really is human!	Do a quick study on Jesus' human / God nature
9	Question: "Why does the woman say Jews have nothing to do with Samaritans?"	See Ezra 4:1-6 (from the marginal cross-reference aid)	Be aware of cultural and religious differences when talking with people
10–13	Observation: Jesus makes a transition from H2O to "living water."	Jesus ties real life issues to eternal life; He's evangelizing.	How can I do this when I am sharing?
etc., etc.			

DISCIPLESHIP PLANS
PLAN SIX: WITNESSING

Goal:

That the young Christian would come to understand that sharing the gospel of Jesus Christ with non-Christians is a commandment, not just a gift exercised by a few. That she or he would learn to share a gospel illustration effectively and confidently. That he would come to a point in his Christian life in which witnessing for Christ is a life-time commitment.

Message to Motivate:

"Courtroom Trial" illustration—Just as in a courtroom, witnesses simply say what they have seen and heard. They are not the lawyer, nor the judge. Witnesses don't try to persuade; they just state the truth.

Three facts & one conclusion -

Fact one: people without Christ will spend an eternity in torment. (Revelation 20:10, 15).

Fact two: people cannot believe in Christ unless they hear about him. (Romans 10:14).

Fact three: people will not hear about Christ unless a human being tells them. (Romans 10:14).

Conclusion: *You* are a human being who can tell people about Christ.

"Logic Loop" about witnessing for Christ:

The start of the "loop." The early disciples, though they had been ordered by the religious authorities to not witness for Christ, made the statement that they could *not not* speak about Christ.

". . . we cannot stop speaking what we have seen and heard." (Acts 4:20 NASB)

While many Christians' "discomfort zone" involves speaking about Christ, these men were uncomfortable about *not* speaking. This verse was a great challenge to me personally as a young Christian. I told God that I wanted to be such a disciple, a man incapable of *not* telling others about Christ.

How did the early disciples come to this point?

"But Peter and the apostles answered and said, 'We must obey God rather than men.'" (Acts 5:29)

This gives us an insight into the hearts of the disciples. Their basic motivation was one of obedience. What were they obeying? Has God commanded believers to tell others about Christ?

"I solemnly charge you in the presence of God and Christ Jesus, who is to judge the living and the dead, and by His appearing and His kingdom: preach the word; be ready in season and out of season . . . be sober in all things, endure hardship, do the work of an evangelist, fulfill your ministry." (2 Timothy 4:1, 2, 5).

This Scripture states very strongly that we are to be bold in proclaiming God's Word whether is seems "convenient" or not (". . . in season and out of season . . ."). Verse 5 implies that even if we might feel "I'm just not an evangelist!" we are never-the-less to *do the work* of an evangelist. What's the result, for us, when we obey God in this regard?

" He who has My commandments and keeps them, he it is who loves Me; and he who loves Me shall be loved by My Father, and I will love him, and will disclose Myself to him. (John 14:21)

This verse says that Christ loves those who obey his commandments and that he will "show Myself to him." This is a great truth: Jesus reveals himself in a real, exciting way to those who obey him Maybe this is why so many Christians seem to find their faith so boring, they don't obey—or "selectively" obey—and do not see Christ in their lives. The early disciples in Acts 4:20 said they couldn't stop speaking of what they had seen and heard; today we can be excited and motivated just as they were, by Christ revealing himself to us in his Word and through the Holy Spirit as we obey him.

What keeps Christians from boldly sharing their faith in Christ?

(Paul says) "For I am not *ashamed* of the Gospel . . ." (Romans 1:16)

The witnesses in Jerusalem were hauled before the religious leaders and flogged because they had been witnessing. As they left the place of their beating, they were . . . ". . . rejoicing because they had been considered worthy to suffer *shame* for His name." (Acts 5:41).

"And so Jesus also suffered outside the city gate to make the people holy through his own blood. Let us, then, go to him outside the camp, bearing the *disgrace* that he bore." (Hebrews 13:12, 13 NIV).

So, the issue is shame, or embarrassment. Christians may be bold about Christ inside their church communities, but embarrassed about him out in the world. But Jesus did not die in the Temple or any religious place; he died in public, naked and (supposedly) in disgrace. We as Christians today are also to "go outside the camp"—take the gospel *out* of the walls of the church—being willing to be embarrassed about identifying with Jesus Christ and boldly telling the lost about salvation through Christ.

As we do so, we have the assurance of Isaiah 55:11, God's word will not go out into the world and return empty; it will accomplish what he wants it to do in peoples' lives. Our job in witnessing is to simply tell people about Christ . . . it's up to the Holy Spirit and the power of the Word to do the persuading. This takes the burden of us to "convert" people, and puts it on God where it belongs.

Three stages in the growth of a witness for Christ:

Ability . . . simply knowing how to share the Gospel, using an illustration, tract, or testimony.

Availability . . . the attitude that "God, I'll tell someone about Christ if you bring him or her to me." This is the stage which defines most Christian leaders, pastors, full-time workers.

Accountability . . . the conviction that God wants us to take the responsibility to go out and try to reach people—not merely wait for them to come to us—and the commitment to do it.

Get Him/Her Started:

Realize that for the great majority of young believers, this is the most challenging part of being a Christian. They may have more anxiety and nervousness about witnessing than any other activity.

The very best motivator to help someone get started in witnessing is to take them along with you as you share the gospel, either in a "bold turkey" situation or with someone you're already talked with who's indicated interest. It's good to start with door-to-door witnessing using the 5 Question Survey (see below) as it's easy to teach, usually results in a quick opportunity to share the gospel, and (though scary at first) is less emotionally risky, since rejection by a total stranger is not nearly as upsetting as a family member, e.g., saying "No, thanks!"

Here are the two irreducible elements in personal witnessing: (1) I cannot lead someone to Christ whom I have not met, and (2) I cannot lead that person to Christ unless I actually tell him about Christ. "Hinting" at the gospel, or trying to maneuver into the perfect sharing situation, just doesn't work. When we go door-to-door at apartment complexes, it may seem daring, but it is actually often easier than trying to share with a family member or friend where the relationships are more complex. "Cold turkey" witnessing can be viewed as simply a way of meeting people and immediately determining if they are interested in hearing the gospel . . . by asking them.

All witnessing, whether door-to-door or relational, is essentially coming to a point in a relationship in which you ask the person if they would like to see a brief illustration that explains what the Bible says a Christian is. This point may be five minutes (e.g., in door-to-door witnessing) or five months into the relationship. This is an easy question to ask of a stranger when doing a religious survey door-to-door; but it may seem quite difficult with family members or long-time friends. Asking the question, "What do you think a Christian really is?" then asking, "Would you like to see a quick illustration that gives a pretty good answer? I'd like to see what you think of it" basically paves the way for sharing the gospel. If a person says, "no," there's really no big emotional cost.

We may fear that if we don't do this just right that we've hurt the person's chance at salvation. This is simply not true, but Satan would love to de-motivate us by making us think that witnessing has to be done perfectly or not at all.

Teach her/him the 5 Question Survey form and the "SDSD, All 3" illustration. (See below).

Take her/him out to some apartments near a college campus and do some door-to-door surveying. Don't spend more than 40 minutes with a person new to this activity, no matter how well it goes. Tell him/her that she/he doesn't need to say anything at all until he/she wants to, that you'll do all the talking. Do everything the first few times you go out . . . knock on the door, explain you're doing a survey, ask the survey questions, ask if they'd like to see the illustration (either then or later), and either do the "SDSD, all 3" illustration, or say "so long." Then each time you go out, transfer a bit of it to the young Christian, if she or he wants to. He knocks and does the little opening statement, then you do the survey etc. Next time, she knocks, does the opening and the survey, etc. Eventually your young Christian will be doing it all, and can even practice transferring it back to you, good practice for when he/she takes someone else out!

Keep him/her going:

Have him or her read one of the many good books found in Christian bookstores on witnessing.

Help her/him write a three-minute testimony, with two good verses.

Arrange to have her or him talk with someone who is not necessarily gifted in the area of witnessing, but who is faithful and excited about sharing Christ with others. This is *very* motivating.

Continue to go out witnessing with him door-to-door and pray he'd be able to share the gospel several times and see the powerful effect the Word has on people.

Have her join you as you meet with one of your friends with whom you are going to share the gospel illustration in a more relational setting, i.e., fast food restaurant.

Develop a "5 Most Wanted" prayer list, non-Christian friends she can pray that she'd have a chance to share with. Or use the "5 steps" tool for relationship evangelism.

Give him/her lots of praise for her obedience in witnessing. When you critique his gospel presentation, or the way he's building evangelistic relationships, always be sure to stress three good things she/he does for every one thing to work on. Let her know that what she is doing is well pleasing to God.

Evaluation:

How did he/she respond to the message to motivate?

Did he say he'd go out witnessing with you, at least to go with you as you do it, and thus identify himself with Christ?

Was she diligent in learning the gospel illustration and writing a testimony?

Is he at ease, or at least bold, in talking to people his own age?

Does she share on her own, or only during the "official" witnessing times?

Does he/she seem to look for opportunities to share, or does he seem to avoid them?

Remember, this is the major turning point for many Christians in their lives as believers. Pray for them, encourage them, and praise them when they make a good effort in this regard. Then they can claim two great verses: Acts 4:13 and Acts 4:20!

Quick Summary:
Three facts and one conclusion
Logic Loop
    Acts 4:20
    Acts 5:29
    II Timothy 4:1, 2 & 5
    John 14:21
What hinders us from witnessing? Shame
    Romans 1:16
    Acts 5:41
    Hebrews 13: 12, 13
Three Stages of growth in witnessing
    Ability
    Availability
    Accountability
Get him started by taking him out with you as you survey
Teach her the three tools
    Survey
    SDSD, all 3 Gospel illustration
    Five steps of relationship sharing

Five Question Survey

Questions:

1. Do you have any religious affiliation or background?

2. On a scale from 1 to 10, what number would you give to your own personal interest in spiritual issues . . . ? (1 being very little & 10 being very high interest)

3. Would you say that interest has increased, decreased, or stayed the same during the past two years?

4. What one thing would you change (if you were able) about orga-

nized religion? (or what bothers you about religion?)

5. If a person from another country or culture were to ask you to define what a Christian is, what would you say to them?

6. *** Would you be interested in taking a few more minutes to see an illustration from the Bible that answers than last question?

A few more thoughts on sharing the gospel at apartments:

Student apartments near a university are best. Most college students will be interested in responding to the survey.

Dress casually (jeans: yes; ties: no). Be friendly and low-key. "Hi, we're with a Christian group and doing a little survey . . . 5 questions . . . takes 3 minutes. What'd you say?" No long pauses, solemn looks, etc. Don't introduce yourselves; they don't care and it's awkward. Jot down their first name later if they say you can come back. Don't write their phone number . . . that'll make them nervous. You already know where they live.

Do not be defensive, or judgmental of them, no matter what they say about God or religion. The lost are not the enemy; they're the victims of the enemy. Give some praise to the people you're talking to, even if they are negative about their experiences/opinions about religion. e.g., "I appreciate your saying that. It shows you've really done some thinking about these things." Do not argue!

Some people will be agreeable to seeing the gospel illustration then and there, but even more will agree if you ask if you can come back another time. This way they don't feel trapped, and it lets you keep your word about how much of their time you said you'd take.

Remember, our job is to present truth to people, not to try to *persuade* them to become Christians. (". . . not by the will of man . . ." John 1:13). If you get intense in a way they perceive as pressuring them, they will quite understandably become defensive. The goal of surveying is to share the gospel with those who might not have heard. It is between them and God, under the conviction of the Holy Spirit, whether they make a decision for Christ. And that decision may well come at a later time which means we may not ever know about it. That's okay. Some sow; some water; some reap. But it's all valuable for the God's kingdom.

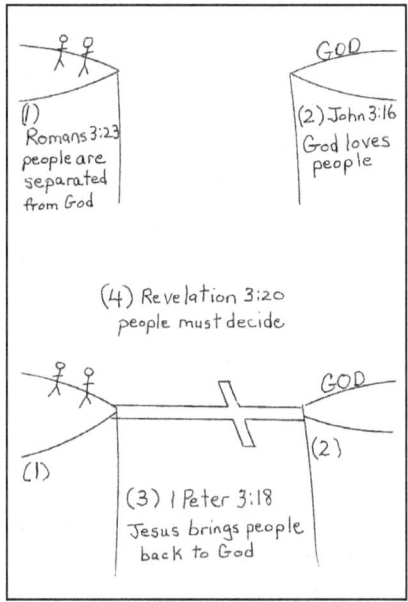

The Gospel illustration: "SDSD, all 3"

This is a simplified "Bridge to Life" illustration, originally designed by the *Navigators* ©. Used by permission. The SDSD refers to the first letters of the four points of the illustration; the "all 3" refers to each verse being from a chapter three:

S = Peoples' Situation—Romans 3:23 (NIV) "... for all have sinned and fall short of the glory of God."

D = God's Desire—John 3:16 (NIV) "For God so loved the world that He gave His one and only Son that whoever believes in Him shall not perish but have eternal life."

S = God's Solution—1 Peter 3:18 "For Christ died for sins once for all, the righteous for the unrighteous, to bring you to God. He was put to death in the flesh, but made alive by the Spirit." (NIV).

D = Peoples' Decision—Revelation 3:20 "Behold, I stand at the door and knock. If anyone hears My voice and opens the door, I will come in and dine with him and he with Me." (NASB).

This is a pretty simple illustration to remember. Each of the four verses is from a chapter three, and once you get past the first one, Romans 3:23, the verse numbers go 16, 18, 20.

Begin the illustration by having the person read Romans 3:23, using his or her own Bible if possible (if she/he has one). People will trust their own Bible more than yours. When the person reads the verse aloud, he sees the verse, and hears the words in his own voice in his own ears. This seems to give added credence to what he is reading.

Ask "What do you think that means?" for each of the four verses, and a few more detail questions about each verse. Let most of the statements about what the verses mean come from the person to whom you are witnessing. Your part is asking questions. "SDSD, all 3" is mostly presented by asking questions and listening carefully to the answers of the person considering the gospel. That way she/he cannot really dismiss the conclusions as being your opinions or interpretation. Trust me, the Word has great power and people of sincerity arrive at accurate understanding.

After the person has read the first verse, draw the two cliffs with people on one side and God on the other. Draw in the bridge itself after you've discussed 1 Peter 3:18. After completing the illustration, simply ask, "Where would you say you are on this illustration . . . with people (apart from God), with God, or somewhere in the middle?" Most will say, "Somewhere in the middle." This is good! It means they have some interest, and you can say, "Yeah, I know what you mean. Hey, I'll be over here next week. Maybe we can talk about this some more then."

The basic Biblical concepts are quite clear:

—Romans 3:23 . . . people do wrong things and it separates them from a holy God.

—John 3:16 . . . God loves people, but they can't get back to him on their own, so he sends an "agent", his Son, Jesus, to be the bridge.

—1 Peter 3:18 . . . (best verse in the Bible about what Jesus did specifically!). Jesus dies for all sin, for all people, for all time to bring us back to God. This verse mentions the resurrection, God's proof of His power over death.

—Revelation 3:20 . . . each person must make a personal decision whether to open the door of his or her life and ask Jesus to forgive his sin and come into his life.

The key thing to remember is this: do not preach at people. As my shop teacher used to say, "Let the tool do the work." In this case, let God's Word and the conviction of the Holy Spirit do the work of persuading. You simply, graciously, and kindly, present the truths to the person.

How To Share The Gospel Relationally

Here's a simple 5-step plan to help you think about how share with family, co-workers, and friends. How to Share the Gospel Relationally—Five Steps to Get There . . .

1. Friendly talk—"I have become all things to all men . . ." (1 Corinthians 9: 22)
2. Identify with Christ—"I'm not ashamed . . ." (Romans 1:16)
3. Serious talk—". . . I observe that you are very religious . . ." (Acts 17:22ff.)
4. Share *your* story—Paul tells his story of how he became a Christian. (Acts 26: 4–23)
5. Share the gospel (SDSD, all 3)—"There is salvation in no one else . . ." (Acts 4:12)

The idea of these five steps is that it allows us to think about where we are in our relationships with people, and how we could get to share Christ with them in a clear, inoffensive way. It's a great prayer stimulus. We can pray briefly each day for a couple of people, asking God to help us get to the "next step" in our relationship so that we might share the gospel with them. For example, if I can talk about everyday topics in a friendly way with "Kyle," I can pray I'd be able to let Kyle know that I'm a Christian, or at least, that I'm religious. When that happens, then I can pray that Kyle and I could get to talk about more serious life issues. Then, on to the next step! I don't want to make this sound like a devious scheme, but it's good to be intentional about trying to share the gospel with people. Teach your young disciple how to do this.

When the young Christian you are discipling has shared the gospel message relationally with a friend, neighbor, or co-worker, it's a tremendous victory. It gives her or him confidence to look for other opportunities to share.

One question, however, that will probably come up is this: "Okay, I've shared the gospel with my friend. Now what do I do?"

We want our young disciple to recognize that peoples' coming to Christ is usually a process, rather than an event . . . i.e., making a decision the first time she or he hears the gospel. Most often the process is one of hearing the gospel (planting seed), considering it (cultivation), and finally making a decision (reaping). It often looks like this:

- We build a relationship with a person and have the privilege of sharing the gospel of Jesus Christ. It's not phony or bogus because we *do* care about them, as people on earth with all of life's issues, and also as eternal beings who need salvation. Paul's statement, ". . . that I might save some . . ." (1 Corinthians 9:22) does not indicate a heartless, project-oriented perspective, but rather a grasp of the importance of peoples' eternal destinies.

- After we have shared the gospel, it's usually pretty easy to know if the person is interested or not. An amazingly accurate verse of Scripture in Acts says this, "When they heard about the resurrection of the dead, some of them sneered, but others said, 'We want to hear you again on this subject." (Acts 17:32 NIV)

Isn't that the truth! In the margin of my Bible next to that verse, I've written, "It's always this way . . . some laugh at it; others want to hear more." In the days following your sharing of the gospel, as you talk with the person, see if you can determine which the person is, one who finds the gospel ridiculous, or one who has a growing interest in hearing more about this.

- Another thing to keep in mind is that at some point in our relationship with people we realize that they are knowledgeable enough about the facts of the gospel, and have considered it enough, to make a decision either to receive Christ, or to turn away. In the book of Mark, there is this illustration of the kingdom of God:

"The kingdom of God is like a man who casts seed upon the soil; and goes to bed at night and gets up by day, and the seed sprouts up and grows—how, he himself does not know . . . But when the crop permits, he immediately puts in the sickle because the harvest has come." (Mark 4: 26, 27, 29).

The farmer plants the crop, tends it, sleeps at night not really understanding how the plant grows, but he *does* know when to harvest it!

Just a gentle question to a friend like, "Wouldn't you like to ask Christ in now?" can be the point of decision for some.

For those who decide to ask Christ into their lives, asking for and receiving forgiveness, they are new creations in Christ! (2 Corinthians 5:17), and we can then pray about helping them to grow.

- Those who seem to be not interested does not mean that either we or the Word of God has failed. They may become interested in hearing more at a later time, or they may simply find the whole issue boring. Our role is to witness to what we know to be true. We are not the advocate who persuades; that's the Holy Spirit. We are not the judge; that's God. Being a witness may seem scary, but it is one of the most exciting things a Christian can do, and one of the most convicting as we see the power of the Word of God at work in hearers hearts.

DISCIPLESHIP PLANS

PLAN SEVEN0: SCRIPTURE MEMORY

Goal:

That the young Christian would become convinced of the value of memorizing Scripture as an important aspect of his Christian life, both to guard his/her own walk with God and to minister to others.

Message to Motivate:

There are two major benefits of Scripture Memory:

It helps us.

"How can a young man keep his way pure? By guarding it according to Thy Word... Thy Word I have laid up in my heart that I might not sin against you." (Psalm 119:9, 11 RSV).

The passage in Matthew 4:1–11 recounts the temptation of Christ by Satan in the wilderness. In each temptation, Jesus answered by quoting an appropriate Scripture. If we have the truths of Scripture "laid up" in our hearts, we have an instant response to the temptations in our lives too.

"This book of the law shall not depart out of your mouth, but you shall meditate on it day and night that you may be careful to do according to all that is written in it. Then you shall make your way prosperous and then you shall have good success." (Joshua 1:8 RSV)

Here explain to the young Christian what it means to meditate. Our culture and fast-paced lives do not promote deep thinking, mentally dwelling on issues or ideas for an extended period of time in order to get beneath the surface level of understanding, i.e., the obvious. Reflecting at length on a passage of Scripture is greatly helped by memorization, for it allows the person to think deeply while doing other mundane things, daily chores that require little thought. (This is probably okay if you're driving on the Interstate, but probably not good in downtown traffic.).

We can use the memorized Word to help others.

"For the Word of God is living and active. Sharper than any double-edged sword, it penetrates even to dividing soul and spirit, joints and marrow; it judges the thoughts and attitudes of the heart." (Hebrews 4:12 NIV)

Simply having an appropriate verse of Scripture to share with another person in a time of need is often the best help we can give. It is the nature of the Word of God, as Hebrews 4:12 points out, to clarify an issue and even reveal if a person has a wrong heart attitude about the issue. And we don't have to mention chapter and verse, or quote exactly. An accurate paraphrase has power too.

"Be diligent to present yourself approved to God as a workman who does not need to be ashamed, handling accurately the word of truth." (2 Timothy 2:15 NASB).

Get him/her started:

1. This is simple. Give him a Navigators' *Topical Memory System*. Or rather, have him or her buy one. Sometimes if something is free or cheap, it may not be valued but rather treated cheaply.

2. Don't over-challenge. One verse per week, with review, is probably about right for most people. Scripture memory can be one of the areas of great encouragement and success if the expectations are realistic.

3. Stress the need for memorizing "word perfect." Idea here is that you can't review a verse if it's paraphrased or quoted slightly differently every time.

4. Tell him/her that checking verses will be part of your time together. The vast majority of young Christians really like checking verses. It gives them a sense of victory and progress in their Christian lives, something that many young believers seldom feel.

5. Talk to her about *how* to memorize. It may seem unusual to discuss the "mechanics" of memorizing, but today's culture—with electronic spell check, phone number auto-dialing, etc.—is one in which a surprisingly large number of people are not used to memorizing words or numbers. The booklet included with the *Topical Memory System* is quite good in presenting ways to memorize and review verses. Mention that different people memorize in different ways.

   . . . some actually visualize the verse card itself.

   . . . some learn by rote . . . saying the verse over and over again until it *sounds right* when they quote it.

   . . . some memorize by first grasping the concept of what the verse means, then "hanging" the actual words on the framework of the meaning.

   . . . some join the reference to the verse by use of a mental picture—this is helpful for verses which seem unusually difficult to remember. I did this for Hebrews 10:31, a verse that just seemed to elude me. I pictured a tent pitched near a cliff; a Hebrew (robes, etc.) walks out of the tent to get a drink because he is a "thirsty one." He falls over the cliff into a giant hand. Get the picture? Hebrew-tent-thirsty-one (Hebrews ten, thirty-one) "It is a terrifying thing to fall into the hands of the living God."

6. Memorize the first verse of the TMS with her/him. This will give you both a good idea of what to expect, and jump-starts the whole process.

Keep her/him going:

Occasionally call on him/her in Bible study, or Sunday School class and ask her to quote a verse you know she's learned well. Do this as part of your lesson or message so that it fits in and shows others that this guy or woman is committing the Word to memory. I know this sounds really politically incorrect and competitive, but a couple of things we want our young Christian to have are a sense of progress and achievement, and a sense of confidence with the Word. While there may be the rare person who would become boastful about Scripture memory, many young believers today seem to fall into the other class of person: those for whom a shot of self-confidence is healthy.

Discuss the meaning of the verses he's memorizing. Ask him if he finds himself thinking about the verses. Ask what he's learned as he dwells on them a bit.

Ask if he's had any situation in which he got to use any of the verses to help someone else.

Talk about any problems she's encountered in doing Scripture memory.

Talk about how to set up a good review system when he's memorized about 12–15 verses. The TMS instruction book has a good plan.

Encourage her to carry the verse pack around with her, and get in some memory work during the odd free moments of the day . . . traffic jams, standing in lines, etc. "Redeem the time!"

Evaluation:

How did he do on the first few verses? What patterns or potential problems do you note, e.g., forgetting the reference, skipping transitional phrases, being satisfied with less than word-perfect recall, etc.

Was she excited about learning verses? Most young Christians *are* excited about Scripture memory because they equate "knowing verses" as a sign of a mature Christian.

Does he seem to be trying to memorize the verse only moments before meeting with you? This practice will more obviously reveal itself when review of old verses comes up. But getting a good review system going also helps eliminate this last-minute cramming.

Has she shared any verses with her friends, either Christian or non-Christian?

Quick Summary

Two major benefits of Scripture Memory:

—It helps us.

> Psalm 119:9, 11

> Matthew 4:1–11

Joshua 1:8

—We can use the memorized Word to help others.

Hebrews 4:12

2 Timothy 2:15

DISCIPLESHIP PLANS

CHARACTER BIBLE STUDY: PURITY / HOLINESS

Basis assumptions:
- Bible is our ultimate guide: 2 Timothy 3:16, 17
- Bible does speak to the issue: 2 Peter 1:3, 4
- What God commands is for our good: Deuteronomy 10:12, 13

1. Read 1 Corinthians 10:13.

    What does it say is common to all people?

    What control over times of temptation does God exert?

    What does God always provide?

    How do these promises help us to actually achieve the goals asked of us in 1 Peter 1:14, 15?

2. Areas of temptation that involve purity and holiness:

    - M & M's (money and materialism—covered in separate study)

    - Pride and self-esteem issues (covered in separate study)

    - Physical appetites:

        Food issues (1 Corinthians 6:19, 20 & 1 Corinthians 9:27)

        Sexual appetite . . . an area most find to be the key to purity.

3. Sexual purity:

    Discuss . . . how would you describe the way the world thinks about sex?

What is the world's "recommendation" to people concerning how they should handle sex? What effect do you believe the worldly philosophy about sex has on Christians' thinking about sex?

—no effect at all

—a helpful effect..."balances" the Bible out

—a damaging effect

What is the Bible's general teaching about our bodies and sex?

Romans 12:1
Romans 6:12–14

1 Corinthians 6:15–18 (especially as it pertains to sex outside of marriage)

1 Thessalonians 4:3–6 Why is it important that we "control" our sexuality, rather than be controlled by it?

Keeping our thought life pure:
Read James 1:13–15 What is the process that begins with temptation (which is *not* sin in itself) and ends with an "accomplished sin"?

Temptation		Sin accomplished

Here are some other verses on having a pure thought life. What is the key truth of each?

Colossians 3:2
Romans 8:6
Philippians 4:8
2 Corinthians 10:5
Romans 12:2

Some thoughts on dating.

The Bible doesn't say much specifically about the relatively modern practice of dating, but there are valuable principles of mutual respect, trusting God for a mate, and holiness in relationships. Probably the worst example of dating in the Bible is found in Judges 14:1–3. Samson's relationships with women are definitely not an example to follow. If you are married, teach these principles to a young man or woman. If you are not married, but believe that God may have you to be married sometime, do a good Bible study on *marriage*, and how to find that godly mate.

Three guidelines for Christian dating
1 Timothy 5:2 (Key principle)
1 Corinthians 6: 19, 20
2 Corinthians 6:14

Some practical steps in building a life of purity:

- Of first importance! There is always God's forgiveness for when we fail. "If we confess our sins, He is faithful and righteous to forgive us our sins and to cleanse us from all unrighteousness." (1 John 1:9)

- Don't take that second look! 2 Samuel 11: 2–4 David was tempted when he saw Bathsheba, but he could have had victory over the temptation. Instead, he sent for the woman he saw taking a bath, and adultery and murder followed.

- Determine in your heart that you really want to be a pure man or woman of God.

Read James 4:4. Can a person really love and follow the Lord and be "friends with the world" as well? What does it mean to be friends with the world?

- Read 2 Timothy 2: 21, 22 ("the key is to flee..."). Often the best and simplest way to victory is *get away* from the temptation. We each know very well the things and situations which tempt us to sin.

  Suggestive pictures in magazines

  Romance novels... as distorted image of real love as pornography is of true sex

  Certain TV and movies... don't be deceived; they do have an effect

  The internet

  What are your most vulnerable areas?

- Read Luke 16:10 Begin where you are, and be faithful in the little things.

- Get in a good accountability relationship with another serious Christian, and *do* look out for each other! Read Hebrews 3:13 & Ecclesiastes 4:9, 10.

- Starting right now:

    Who is the person I can ask to have an accountable relationship with me concerning purity?

    What key areas will we agree to check each other on?

    What are two key issues of purity in my own life I want to ask God to help me have victory in right now?

DISCIPLESHIP PLANS

CHARACTER BIBLE STUDY: GOD'S PERSPECTIVE ON MONEY & STUFF

Preface: This study is one of three based on overcoming the three areas of sin listed in 1 John 2:15, 16 "... lust of the flesh, lust of the eyes, and the boastful pride of life..." This study concerns the "lust of the eyes" aspect. Learning to be content with what we have is part of it; the larger view is learning to have God's perspective on money and material goods.

Money and stuff

1. Read Luke 12:15 What is the foundational truth Jesus was teaching here?

2. Look at Matthew 6:31–33 What is the great promise of God concerning our physical needs in verse 33?

    What are the conditions of the promise?

    What would it mean in your own life to seek first his kingdom and (seek first) his righteousness?

    Though desire for material goods (cars, clothes, houses, etc.) can be a strong force, the Bible implies that desire for money is an even more powerful force. Why do you think this is so?

What insight does Ecclesiastes 5:10 give?

3. Look at Ephesians 5:3 and Colossians 3:5 Why do you think the Apostle Paul (in Colossians) says greed actually *amounts to idolatry*?

4. Read Matthew 19:21–26 What is the result of love of money upon non-Christians in terms of their spiritual position?

5. What do the following Scriptures say about the effect of love of money, or worrying about money, on Christians?

   Matthew 13:22
   I Timothy 6:6–11

6. What do you think is the difference between "love of money" and "anxiety about money"? See Philippians 4:6 & 11–13.

7. Look at Luke 16: 11–15 What truth does Jesus give about a person's relationship with money, and his qualification to be a spiritual leader or minister?

8. Read Hebrews 13:5–6 (one of the best passages in the Bible about this topic). What does verse 5 say is the opposite of love of money?

   What is the wonderful commitment God makes to us that allows us to be content?

   What is one key financial issue, or desire for something, that I can trust God with right now?

9. James 4:4 makes a powerful statement. It says

   "... do you not know that friendship with the world is hostility toward God? Therefore whoever wishes to be a friend of the world makes himself an enemy of God."

   The decision whether to follow the world's value system concerning money and stuff is ours. We decide whether we want victory in this area or not.

   How could a person know if he or she had a love of money, or unrighteous concern about material things?

What's the first step in getting victory in this important issue?

Giving

The following questions focus mainly on two passages of Scripture: 2 Corinthians 8:1-15 and 2 Corinthians 9:6-15. Quickly read through these verses to get a general grasp of the New Testament principles on giving.

1. Jot down three major principles you see in these passages about financial giving . . . any three:

2. Is giving money to God's work something only those with lots of money can do effectively? Read 2 Corinthians 8:1-4 Why or why not?

    Did the churches in Macedonia consider it a burden to give? What was their attitude about it?

3. What is the "leveling out" principle discussed in 2 Corinthians 8:13-15?

    How does this concept work? Read 1 John 3:17

4. What is the effect on the giver of generous giving as opposed to meager giving, according to 2 Corinthians 9:6? (See also Luke 6:38 for another way of putting it.)

    Do you think this concept would cause someone to give generously for the wrong reason? Why or why not?

5. Read 2 Corinthians 9:7 What does the Bible say about the *attitude* a person should have when she/he gives? What is pleasing to God and what is not?

    What is the promise God makes to glad givers? See 2 Corinthians 9:8

6. Your own thoughts on giving:

    Do you feel that financial giving is a reluctant duty . . . or a privilege? Explain your answer.

    What are the benefits of giving—for the giver?

Appendix 267

To whom should you give, to most effectively invest in God's work?

7. Read 2 Corinthians 9:7 again. How does a person determine how much to give? (Was the widow in Mark 12:42–44 stupid or righteous?)

8. Read Proverbs 3:9, 10 Why do you think it says "... from the first of all your produce ..." (profit)? What's the difference between making giving a top priority and a low priority?

What might happen if we leave giving to the end of the month?

How does consistency in giving relate to other areas of the Christian walk, e.g., QT, Bible study, Scripture memory?

DISCIPLESHIP PLANS

CHARACTER BIBLE STUDY: HUMILITY..."SEEING OURSELVES AS GOD SEES US."

Pride

1. What truth does 1 Peter 5:5, 6 teach us about God's attitude toward pride?

    What do you think "He gives *grace* to the humble" means?

2. What can cause a person to become prideful or arrogant?

    Luke 18:9–14

    1 Corinthians 4:6

    James 4:13–16

    Can you think of an event or occurrence which caused you to have an inflated view of yourself?

3. Look at Hebrews 13:17 & Matthew 11:29. What problem can result if a person is too prideful to submit himself or herself to spiritual leadership?

    What can a person do to be more humble if he feels he tends to be prideful or arrogant?

> 2 Corinthians 12:9, 10 "Realize that . . ."
>
> Philippians 3:7–9
>
> Philippians 2:3, 4

4. Perhaps the two most important verses on overcoming pride are these:

> 1 Corinthians 4:7 What is the truth expressed here?
>
> Romans 12:3 How can this be done? (John 8:32)

5. Read Luke 16:10. What is the first "little step" toward increased humility I can take right now?

Insecurity

1. Though it may seem self-contradictory, another aspect of human pride is insecurity:

> Poor self-image or being self-deprecating (putting one's self down). Look at the following verses; what are some things that can cause a poor self image?
>
> > 2 Corinthians 10:12
> >
> > I Samuel 16:7
> >
> > Luke 17:12, 13 (what would be *social* leprosy?)
> >
> > John 9:1
>
> Can you think of an event or occurrence that caused you to have negative self-image?

2. What assurance do the following truths give us about our self worth?

> Psalm 139:14
>
> Matthew 6:26

2 Corinthians 5:21

Romans 12:6

3. What about a poor self-image that comes from sin in our lives?

   What does Hebrews 10:17 say about past sins?

   How about present sins? 1 John 1:9

4. Some people feel defeated because of hurt that they have suffered from other people (young people feel this); some feel guilt-ridden because they have caused hurt to others (older people may feel this). The Apostle Paul is an example of a person to whom both of these situations apply.

   - Read Acts 8:3 & 26:10, 11 How do you think Paul could overcome the guilt of what he had done to innocent people?

     1 Corinthians 15:9, 10

     2 Corinthians 5:17

   - Look at Acts 24:27 & 2 Corinthians 11:24, 25 How could Paul overcome the bitterness of this kind of mistreatment from people? Colossians 3:13

5. How does Romans 8:28 help us know how to accept the hurt and pain of life without guilt or bitterness?

6. Is there one area in my life right now where I have an incorrect negative self-image? What could I do to give this to God?

Bibliography

Centering Prayer. Leaflet, The Youth Ministry & Spirituality Project, 2004.
Grolier Encyclopedia, Volume 13. Danbury, CT: Grolier Inc.,1990.
Lewis, Clive Staples, *The Last Battle.* New York: Harper Trophy Publishing, 1994.
The Ryrie Study Bible. NASB. Chicago: Moody Press, 1986.
The Topical Memory System. Colorado Springs: NavPress, 1969.

If you, the reader, have any questions about ministry raised by this book, please e-mail the author at this e-mail address: LTLcunneen@gmail.com

www.ingramcontent.com/pod-product-compliance
Lightning Source LLC
Chambersburg PA
CBHW050339230426
43663CB00010B/1925